P44165 B2(C)

PORTRAIT OF COVENTRY

Portrait of
COVENTRY

E. B. NEWBOLD

ROBERT HALE · LONDON

© E. B. Newbold *1972 and 1982*
First published in Great Britain 1972
Second edition 1982

ISBN 0 7091 9751 9

Robert Hale Limited
Clerkenwell House
Clerkenwell Green
London, EC1R 0HT

ι

PRINTED IN GREAT BRITAIN BY
ST. EDMUNDSBURY PRESS, BURY ST. EDMUNDS, SUFFOLK
BOUND BY HUNTER AND FOULIS

CONTENTS

	Preface	9
I	Setting the Scene	11
II	Coventrated	24
III	Rebuilding a City	37
IV	Cathedral of our Time	62
V	Keeping the Past	77
VI	Coventry is a Community	87
VII	Friends Everywhere	104
VIII	The City Council	113
IX	Pioneers of Industry	123
X	Coventry Personalities	141
XI	Then—and Now	157
XII	Highlights of History	176
XIII	Ten Years On	196
	Index	203

ILLUSTRATIONS

between pages

1 Coventry Cathedral ruins, the spire of Holy Trinity on the right (courtesy of Coventry Cathedral Provost and Chapter)   24 and 25

2 Coventry's inner ring road and precinct area   ,, ,, ,,

3 Looking down the Burges toward Bishop Street after bombing   ,, ,, ,,

4 Smithford Street after the bombing   ,, ,, ,,

5 The Lady Godiva statue in Broadgate (courtesy of Coventry Corporation)   40 and 41

6 Broadgate in 1939   ,, ,, ,,

7 The Lower Precinct (courtesy of Coventry Corporation)   ,, ,, ,,

8 Rooftop parking in the central area (courtesy of Coventry Corporation)   ,, ,, ,,

facing page

9 The Belgrade Theatre   48

10 An engineers' strike meeting in the Precinct   48

11 Inside Coventry Baths (courtesy of Coventry Corporation)   49

12 The University of Warwick   64

13 Whitley Abbey comprehensive school   64

14 Award-winning housing estate at Henley Road (courtesy of Coventry Corporation)   65

between pages

15 The cathedral from Priory Street (courtesy of Coventry Corporation)   72 and 73

16 The cathedral and Holy Trinity   ,, ,, ,,

17 Graham Sutherland's cathedral tapestry (courtesy of Coventry Cathedral Provost and Chapter)   ,, ,, ,,

ILLUSTRATIONS

between pages

18 Epstein's St Michael and the Devil on the wall of Coventry Cathedral (courtesy of Coventry Cathedral Provost and Chapter)   72 and 73

19 Ford's Hospital and the new Eventide Homes   ,, ,, ,,

20 The canal basin during the annual rally in 1971   ,, ,, ,,

facing page

21 Coventry canal basin awaiting redevelopment   112

22 Bayley Lane and St. Mary's Hall, a conservation area   112

23 The Coventry Boy statue, Priory Street   113

24 The velocipede of 1861   128

25 The early Daimler Wagonette with steering handle   128

26 The Daimler Sovereign (courtesy of Jaguar Cars Ltd.)   129

27 One of the three assembly lines at the former Triumph factory (courtesy of the Triumph Motor Company)   129

28 Cheylesmore Manor House Gateway restoration (courtesy of Coventry Corporation)   160

29 The abbey and moat in Coombe Countryside Park   160

30 Butcher Row, cleared away for the Trinity Street scheme   161

31 Lady Godiva statue, Broadgate garden island   176

32 The Godiva clock   177

33 Peeping Tom, as he appeared in Bull Yard   177

Map of Coventry   *pages* 12 and 13

PICTURE CREDITS

Richard Sadler: 1, 9, 16, 17, 18, 24, 25, 30; Aerofilms: 2; Coventry Evening Telegraph: 3, 4, 6, 10, 13, 19, 20, 21, 22, 23, 29, 31, 32, 33; Vivian Levett: 7, 8, 15, 28; Thomas-Photos: 12.

PREFACE

WHAT a difference a decade can make! When *Portrait of Coventry* was published in 1972 it mirrored a busy city. There had been some hiccups but in general things were going well, as they had been in fact since the war. Ten years later the image is very different. Factories have slimmed down their work forces; some have closed. About 26,000 people are unemployed; 15 per cent of the work force. Other towns have been hit by the trade recession, but on top of it Coventry has been affected by the policy of British Leyland—B.L. as they are known—to concentrate production at other places. So car production has ended at the important Canley factory of Standard-Triumph, and thousands have been made redundant. Coventry's big Alfred Herbert machine-tool works also came to its knees with thousands of redundancies. All those union wage demands and strikes of the days of plenty did not help matters, but workers will tell you that management was also to blame for the fall. They did not invest sufficiently in new tools and equipment to enable them to compete with the Japanese and other car makers who invaded the British market.

But Coventry has weathered other depressions in the past and already the news is good from Talbot, the former Rootes Group, who have announced that they have improved their rate of production to the point where they are matching Continental output—and the French parent company is investing more money in the Coventry plant. B.L. have announced that the Canley plant will become their main design and engineering centre, although it will employ only a small work force. And a new thrusting firm, using the Alfred Herbert name, are employing 800, and are optimistic.

So we may not have the swinging image of a decade ago, but we are fighting back. We always do.

To Marie, my dear wife

I

SETTING THE SCENE

THE physical scars have nearly gone, hidden under some £60 million worth of brickwork and sandstone, concrete and glass, in the bright city centre face of Coventry. The deeper scars of wartime enmity went long ago, when Provost Howard put up his cross of charred timber in the cathedral ruins with the words "Father Forgive", and the city council opened their unofficial foreign office to form links of friendship with places overseas and to pay goodwill visits to them. Reconstruction and reconciliation have gone hand in hand in post-war Coventry and in its rebuilding the people of many lands have played their part with encouragement, gifts, and practical assistance.

A new city centre has been built on the bombed sites and a new cathedral. For an exciting quarter of a century after the Second World War, cranes were part of the Coventry skyline, there were traffic diversions and temporary footpaths, and buildings were being constructed non-stop. The centre, unfinished yet, with almost all its stores, shops, office blocks, college buildings, swimming baths, its art gallery and museum, and its theatres, built since the war, spreads over about 450 acres. They are neatly enclosed by the new ring road, which collects incoming traffic and if it has no business in the centre, diverts it round. Beyond the ring road, outward to the city boundary, the new railway station, more colleges, large housing estates, a university, a fine new hospital, a whole chain of comprehensive schools, and the continuous drive of redevelopment, replacing old with new, making new roads, housing layouts, shopping centres, and schools, in those hectic post-war years.

Coventry after the 1939–45 war was a vibrant, forward-looking place, its factories busy, its industry expanding, wage levels above the average. Observing it today it seems incredible that there was a time when it was battered to its knees in the wartime air raids,

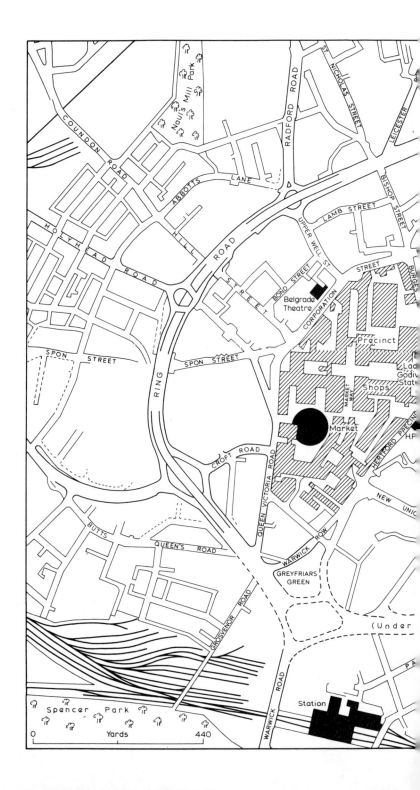

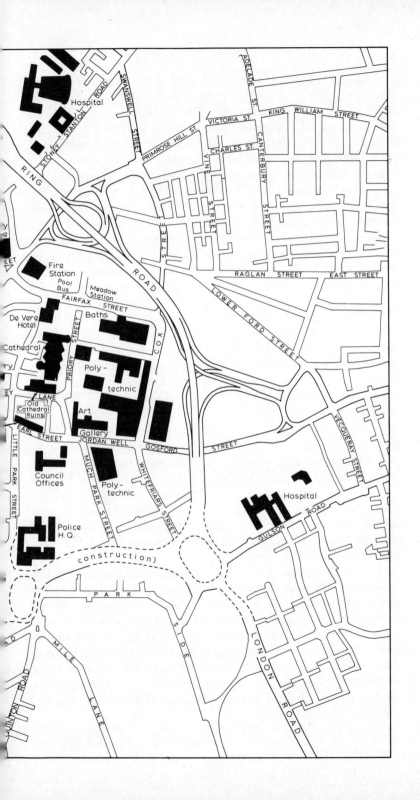

so massively bombed in November 1940, in the most concentrated raid on any British provincial town, that the Germans coined the word 'Coventrated'—destroyed. The damage was devastating, but, apart from the cathedral ruins, there is little sign of it. The city has bounced back and not as just another town. It is an unusual place that has aroused national and world interest.

In planning it was a pioneer, first in many of its policy decisions. Its central layout, on the shopping precinct principle, separating cars from pedestrians, led the way in this country. The new cathedral broke away from traditional architecture and was built in the twentieth-century mould. Coventry led the provinces in deciding to build comprehensive schools. It was a pioneer of smoke control of premises. For these, and other reasons, it has been a magnet, drawing civic parties and bodies of professional people, of this country and from overseas, eager to see what Coventry has done, before going ahead with their own schemes.

Coventry's centre is unique not only in being so comprehensively precincted but in the extent of the corporation's ownership in it. An area of 274 acres was designated by the Government as a declaratory area of extensive war damage in which the city council had the right to make compulsory purchase. They own, as a result, most of the freehold. On a large part they have built their own commercial properties—shops, offices, theatre, flats—and in most of the other part privately-built premises are on a leasehold basis, the corporation holding the leases. This was the policy of the Labour-controlled council which was in office from 1937 to 1967. Corporation real estate yields a yearly income of £1 million (1981) and it will grow with revisions of rent, and with the paying off of building debt charges. Ratepayers, shopping in the precincts, can reflect that much of it belongs to them.

But it is not all concrete and glass. No industrial city can possibly have done more to fashion a pleasing environment. There are green spaces, flower beds, shrubs and trees. The precinct layout provides vistas from its central point up to the spire of the cathedral, or along the precinct avenues to the outline of the tower blocks, Hillman House and Mercia House, which stand at the entrances. The green slate frontages, the tan-coloured brick walls freely broken up by generous expanses of windows, the slim footbridges, the long colonnades in front of the shops, and the sculpture, gladden the eye.

On busy days the scene is animated and cheerful. Crowds of people spread over the paved areas talking and laughing, busily going around shops, or chatting in groups, some resting on the public seats to look at flower bowls, water features or sculpture. In the circular café the customers have a view of all this below them, and it seems on a bright day as if there is a general holiday. In the boom years, this scene was limited to Saturdays when people were free from work. Now, in the depressed 1980s, it is daily. The central area draws them in, to talk, shop, have a cup of tea, and transact business. Bands play; there are dancing displays. There are snatches of music from the television and music shops. And the casual, gay way that young people dress adds to the attractive scene. The precincts have an atmosphere, coming to life as the people flock into them. And a pleasant atmosphere it is, without the noise and smell of motor traffic.

Local people who have watched it grow bit by bit, and seen the paving laid and the saplings planted, have a feeling of pride and pleasure in it. They dodged about the building sites for years. It all resulted in this splendid layout where the trees have matured and look lovely in blossom time.

There has been change and great interest all around. The centre, a planner's dream come true, with forethought for the traffic and for the pedestrian, office and shop blocks and public buildings conforming to a single plan, all laid out with loving care according to the master model in the city architect's department. Precincts, functional and decorative, with water features, plantings, seats, litter baskets, and team of Mrs. Mopps constantly cleaning up. Onlookers have found it stimulating to be caught up in it all! Critics, who did not know what lay here before, complain of a uniformity of buildings, of modern 'square boxes', and they compare these with the beauty of individual buildings of the past. It is realized that there is need for the more specialist and exclusive shops, which Coventry has not been able to attract. These are found in smaller towns close to Coventry, and are within easy reach.

There is little in the city centre that is not new. The city has not had much luck with its old buildings. Centuries ago beautiful buildings like the first cathedral, Greyfriars Church, Whitefriars Church, and Charterhouse, were destroyed when Henry VIII ordered the dissolution of monasteries. Then Charles II had the great city wall demolished. Coming to our own time the pre-war

Coventry Cathedral, St. Michael's, was blitzed, also Christ Church; only its steeple remains. A few years before the war, old Coventry properties were cleared to make Trinity Street, and, since the war, more have gone in the path of redevelopment. What we have today, however, is enough to show that it is a historic and mellowed city. Holy Trinity has a notice board which says it dates from 1043, and a flight of ancient stone steps opposite the entrance of Gulson Library has been worn into deep hollows by countless footsteps. The cathedral ruins have dignity and grace; St. Mary's Hall is a jewel among guildhalls. There are the restored remains of the Whitefriars Monastery, now a museum; and the remains of the Charterhouse.

A short walk from Broadgate, St. John's Church, and behind it the half-timbered charm of Old Bablake and Bond's Hospital. In the opposite direction, Ford's Hospital, a sixteenth-century alms-house. Nearby, the restored Cheylesmore Manor Gatehouse and spire of Christ Church. It is one of three slim spires giving Coventry a landmark—the others are the cathedral and Holy Trinity. To see them fresh every day on the skyline is a pleasure. The poet Michael Drayton, in the seventeenth century, wrote

> Coventry, that do'st adorne,
> The countrey wherein I was borne . . .

and the spires, poised lightly in the air, probably gave him some of his inspiration—although, to be honest, he was writing the poem to his love who lived here.

The spires caught the eye of Lord Tennyson, who began his poem on Lady Godiva with these lines:

> I waited for the train at Coventry;
> I hung with grooms and porters on the bridge,
> To watch the three tall spires . . .

Seen from various angles, perhaps as the bus swings round the centre, the spire of the old cathedral is not only the tallest but the most handsome. Its battlemented tower and flying buttresses give it individuality. And from the distance, the trio of spires look like three friendly beacons, a sign of home that is etched in the memories of Coventry people now living far away. More than anything else of old Coventry, they give a feeling of continuity and are a tangible link with the past, standing sentry as the city below has changed and grown; while straw thatch has been replaced by slate and tile, and timbered houses of wealthy merchants have been replaced by concrete blocks; through trade booms and slumps, and through wars, up to the last, which for Coventry was much the worst. Coventry was the fourth largest city in the country, outside London, during the Wars of the Roses. Now it is eighth. It is a city that has had a colourful, rich past. England's kings and queens and nobility often visited it, a fair place of pleasing buildings inside a stout-gated wall, where large crowds watched craft guilds perform the famous miracle plays. From one moment in history—the legend of Lady Godiva. From another—the saying, "sent to Coventry".

There are frequent reminders of the past, although not so many as when reconstruction was at its height, when that genial soul the late Mr. J. B. Shelton was haunting the excavations and persuading and tipping workmen to save any relics they found. Mr. Shelton, collecting the fragments of tile and leather, would lovingly clean them and label them, and preserve them in his Benedictine Museum in Little Park Street, against the time when he could give them to a Coventry museum. Every fragment had a story for this kindly old man who, when his house was destroyed, lived on in its kitchen, with a caravan adjoining for his bedroom. Today, when all trace of his home has disappeared and city police headquarters cover the spot, archaeologists on Coventry sites still excavate remains of long ago—traces of monastic foundations, perhaps, or of one of the crypts to be found in the centre.

These crypts, the work of craftsmen, are solid sandstone, with thick supporting columns and archways, and are said to have been storeplaces below the large houses of wealthy merchants. One is still a storeplace, under offices in High Street. Another, under the Council Offices in Earl Street, was used as a staff club. How the city prizes its past is illustrated by the full-scale but unsuccessful dig that was made after the war in Priory Row to find the tombs of Earl Leofric and Lady Godiva. The dig took place on the land alongside Holy Trinity, where the wooden belfry tower, an unusual sight, stood. This housed Trinity's bells when it was found that the church tower was not structurally strong enough for them.

Nor can we get away from the past when we look at Coventry's industries. From wool and cloth, through weaving and watchmaking, to the modern trades—bicycles, motor-cycles, cars, aircraft, general engineering, electrical, textiles—there has been a craft tradition, and Coventry has an apprentice-to-freeman system of training that spans them all. Coventry has been an industrial pioneer. The first bicycle, and the first car made on a commercial basis, came from Coventry; it was the first English city to make Dunlop pneumatic tyres. They brought an era of prosperity in Coventry, and for England. In the modern central area you will hardly be reminded of industrial activity, but until the bombing there were workshops almost up to High Street— and one or two survived for a time after the war. One large bombed factory, Triumph, in Priory Street, once stood on the site of what is now Cathedral Square.

The industrial pattern is very different today. Much of the central area industry was bombed out, and what was not has been planned out to make way for redevelopment. The shadow factories that sprang up on the city outskirts for war production have established on the perimeter a ring of industry sited away from housing. Where there are factories long established in residential districts, there is tight planning control with a view to holding, if not improving, the position. Large firms include Rolls Royce, Dunlop, Courtaulds, Talbot, Jaguar, B.L., British Celanese, G.E.C., Massey Ferguson, and Wickman—to name just a few. Some began on what were the outskirts years ago, and have since had housing estates built around them. But there is a watch on such drawbacks as emission of grit and too much noise, and for a city of large industrial premises Coventry is remarkably clean. It is as good a city to work in as any in the country.

Its population has grown at a faster rate this century than any other city in the country, from just under 70,000 to 340,500, or five-fold in seventy or so years. The pace accelerated from 1941, when the population was 190,000, to almost double itself in thirty years. Since 1977, however, there has been a slight decline, explained by Coventry newly-weds moving just outside the boundary to find homes, and by unemployed people moving away to find jobs, some going overseas. But Coventry still has a pool of skilled engineering workers and hopes to attract new industries. It has an ideal geographical position right in the middle of the country, within comfortable reach of major ports. The exact centre of the country is marked by a cross on Meriden village green, only a mile or so from the boundary of Coventry.

Standing as it does at the national cross roads, the city has always been on the main stream of traffic, and is conveniently placed for travel to and from all parts of the country—as the organizers of national conferences have begun to discover. It is close to the M1 and M6 motorways, and its inter-city rail expresses fairly fly over the 90 miles to London in a few minutes over the hour.

It is equally convenient for air travel. At Elmdon, which lies between Coventry and Birmingham, there is the major airport handling services across the world. And at Baginton, on the edge of Coventry, is the city's civic airport which handles executive and charter flights, and—useful for an industrial city—freight.

No matter his means of travel, an exile who left Coventry before the war would find on his return a city so greatly changed that he would feel quite lost. Coming by train, he would be impressed by the modern railway station, so light, so clean, and so unlike the tiny station with its one platform up, one platform down, that he last saw. Immediately outside the station, he would expect to be in Eaton Road, with its old residences. Instead, there is an area of modern office blocks stretching towards Greyfriars Green.

And how different the city centre! The old Broadgate, where the trams had their central terminus, has been replaced by a vastly wider central space, and in the middle of it is the Lady Godiva Statue. No Smithford Street, no Market Street, no West Orchard, no Barracks Square. They were all in the area covered today by the shopping precincts. Hertford Street, which was so busy with traffic, can just be identified as a much-altered, partly-arcaded, precinct.

Useless, Mr. Exile, to look for the Market Hall clock, although it is quite near! Its mechanism is in the modern clock in Broadgate where the puppet figures perform.

A visit to old Hillfields, where perhaps he was born, would not make the exile feel any more at home, for here, just a short stroll out of the centre, whole areas of terraced streets have been swept away and have been replaced by blocks of flats, houses, and schools. Even a return visit to some of the well-remembered rural spots on the outskirts where he played as a boy would disappoint him, for most of them have vanished, and housing estates, or shadow factories, or large colleges or university blocks have been built at places like Canley and Gibbet Hill Road, at Bell Green, Tile Hill, Willenhall, Stoke Aldermoor, Wyken and Walsgrave, and Binley.

Much of the old pre-war Coventry has gone, to the regret, understandably, of many of the older generation who had a sentimental feeling about it. Some are not happy at the changes. They recall the days when everything was familiar to them, and when if they went into the town they were sure to meet friends or family because "We all knew each other then". Those among them who feel most at home are the people who live in districts that have seen little change, like Foleshill, Chapelfields, Radford, Stoke, and Earlsdon. Here the roads and streets are familiar. Urban renewal has not made its impact. They still have their familiar pattern of shopping streets, local library, school buildings, and parks.

Elsewhere, what the wartime bombing left standing, schemes like the inner ring road have caused to be demolished. Spon End has lost its old houses and courts, and has become an area of new flats. The Sherbourne, which flowed largely unseen at the rear of the houses and was often littered with domestic junk, now winds pleasantly through a landscaped area until, nearing the centre, it disappears into a culvert. Making walkways and brookstrays is part of council planning policy—just one aspect of a plan that touches on every facet of the life of the city. There are industrial zones, residential zones, club areas, office sites, road schemes, old people's homes, open spaces, all on the town map— the map becomes more of a reality as year follows year.

The whole city has been, and still is, involved in civic planning. There was continuous upheaval in the back streets as urban renewal schemes were carried out, tearing down the old, replacing them with the new, uprooting families who had lived there all their lives, causing alarm, inconvenience and irritation. There were road schemes—would they ever finish?—that carved their way through modern, as well as old property. For several years, helmeted workmen were busy blasting tunnels underground to provide the urgently-needed sewers for the bigger Coventry, and residents above had to bear with noise and traffic diversions. And with housing a dire need, local landscape gave way to new estates.

With so much planning and change, the motorway protestors, the residents' petitions and meetings, the angry shopkeepers, have all been part of the scene. Like it or not, Coventry's progress has held everybody's interest. No one could call it dull. The problem was not simply that of replacing losses of war damage. An unceasing flow of people coming to work in Coventry during and after the war meant that houses, schools, and amenities must be found for them. They came from all parts—home and overseas. People from depressed areas looking for jobs; refugees from occupied countries; immigrants from the Commonwealth.

It is surprising, in view of all this growth, that the city has remained compact, with a 'small town' atmosphere and community feeling about it. This applies although it is a regional centre with people flocking in to work, to shop, and coaches and cars bringing people in to the theatres. With a growing complex of offices—a vast development around Coventry Station—large business houses have set up area headquarters here. It has made a reputation too in sport, with its £1¼ million swimming baths where international matches are held and televised; and its first-division football club, Coventry City, now the Sky Blues, once in less palmy days, the lowly Bantams in division three. Coventry also has a leading rugby football club; a popular speedway team, the Brandon 'Bees'; and its Godiva Harriers. But one aspect of Coventry has changed. Night clubs have opened. No longer can it be said that the city 'dies' at night, when the last bus has run.

And now it has this new image of being a tourist city, a development that surprised locals when it began, but one that was soon accepted as being Coventry's due. With its Godiva statue in the city centre and its puppet clock giving hourly performances in Broadgate, the city has the appearance of being planned with tourism in mind. It was not so when all this began. The aim was: get the city built; give the people homes, shops, restaurants, theatre, and other amenities lacking for a decade or so after the blitz. If it could be made attractive, so much the better. For a long time the only tourists were in fact civic and professional parties, who came to inspect what was being done, and Coventry was a prototype for much planning elsewhere.

Tourism came as a shock when it was seen what vast numbers were involved. After the consecration of the cathedral in 1962, coaches and special trains brought sightseers. In the first two years, 4½ million people saw the cathedral. Coventry now caters for a regular flow of tourists and has joined the regional tourist board; but at that time it was hardly prepared for the enormous queues of visitors waiting to file through the cathedral. There was a shortage of restaurants and cafés, of toilets, signposts, guidebooks, and seats. There was not enough hotel accommodation for those staying overnight.

Coventry is not a city with great natural features. It does not have a broad river such as some towns enjoy, to capture the eye. No doubt many of its residents, when they rush from the Midlands to the sea edge for their holidays, would like to stay where the scene is so attractive. Coventry, with its modest slopes, cannot compete on those terms, but it is a pleasant place and prizes its green spaces and trees. When there were plans to widen Warwick Road, which would have meant the removal of a line of mature trees, Coventry rose almost to a man against this, even though young replacement trees would have been planted. There was a 'giant' petition of 47,000 signatures, and after a lively controversy, the scheme was dropped. The city council are worthy guardians of trees and spaces, but in this case they found that the public disagreed with the priority given to traffic.

And 'hats off' to the council of fifty years ago for their fore-sight, when, in 1926, they acquired from Lord Leigh of Stoneleigh Abbey over 2,200 acres of land to the south and west of Coventry, mainly to preserve some of the countryside. One result of this is the beautiful approach to the city along Kenilworth Road with its continuous spinneys. Another part preserved is Tile Hill Nature Reserve. The approach into Coventry from Kenilworth Road is regal, through parkland and trees almost into the centre, at Greyfriars Green. The road passes the War Memorial Park, whose 121 acres were bought by public subscription as the city's memorial to the fallen of the 1914–18 war. The monument was unveiled by Earl Haig, in 1927, and was re-dedicated in 1947 to the fallen of the 1939–45 war when Viscount Montgomery of Alamein placed the roll of honour in the chamber of silence. Coventry families have remembered those killed in war in another way. In the park, and in other parks and open spaces, each tree has a plaque, bearing the name of one of the victims, at its foot.

More pre-war foresight, too, enabled Coventry to purchase, by degrees, under an arrangement with the owners, the park, woodland and lake, at Coombe Abbey. This is now a regional countryside park, again ensuring the preservation of some of the countryside around the city.

This is 'our scene', an industrial city that surprises newcomers with its pleasing aspect. Around the city is green belt, and places like Kenilworth Castle, Warwick Castle, and Shakespeare's birthplace at Stratford-upon-Avon; while on the doorstep of Coventry, at Stoneleigh, the Royal Agricultural Show is held. And at Bickenhill, which lies between Coventry and Birmingham, is the National Exhibition Centre, bringing the Motor Show and other national events within the reach of Coventry people. From any part of Coventry, it is a short journey across the boundary to Warwickshire villages, lanes and fields. This is a pretty, well-wooded county. Further afield lie the Malverns and Cotswolds, and other scenery and places that Coventry people visit and enjoy.

"Sent to Coventry" they say when some unlucky soul is shunned by schoolmates, or when a worker steps out of line and is punished by being ignored completely by fellow-workers. It happens occasionally in industrial disputes. If there was ever a case of giving a dog a bad name this is it!

II

COVENTRATED

BEFORE the war Coventry was not well known all over the world as it is today. It was linked by some people with the motor and engineering trades, vaguely by others with the legend of Lady Godiva; and it was not unusual on travels to be asked where it was. But after the blitz on the night of 14th November, 1940, the whole world knew about the city in the industrial Midlands where bombs rained down for eleven hours non-stop. The onslaught was such that the Government departed from the usual procedure of announcing after air raids that there had been a raid "on a West Midland city" or in some other region, and disclosed immediately that the target for the Luftwaffe had been Coventry. Newspapers were permitted to release dramatic pictures, showing the shell of the cathedral, and city-centre devastation.

Estimates of casualties varied, but the final official figures were of five hundred killed and about twice as many injured. News of the blitz produced a sense of shock at home and in the free countries; but this soon turned to admiration at the fortitude and spirit displayed in the bombed city, where people rapidly dusted themselves off and got things moving again, with the immediate declaration that they would rebuild Coventry better than it was before. A pensioner caught the mood of the day when he was talking, long afterwards, about the bombing of his house in a raid before the blitz. As he was groping about for documents in the wreckage, using a small hand torch, a warden shouted to him to "Put that light out—Jerry's about".

Said he, "Jerry be b——d—he's bin!" It was not surprising that, next morning, he was late for work, but he was soundly ticked off all the same! Production was all-important.

Men were soon back at war-damaged factories after the big raid and got on with the job of salvage. The Ministry of Home Security summed up the spirit of the day in the communique:

24

Coventry Cathedral ruins, the spire of Holy Trinity on the right
(overleaf) Coventry's inner ring road and precinct area (right)

"The people of Coventry bore their ordeal with great courage." The Ministry had it on the best authority, for their chief, Herbert Morrison, was in Coventry on the morning after the raid. Another whose testimonial is filed was a Salvation Army chief, General George L. Carpenter. He said, "They do not sit down and whine about their sufferings but have risen up manfully with their faces to the future." The big raid was not the beginning, nor the end, for two hundred had been killed in raids before November. And, after a lull, 'Jerry' came again, at Easter 1941, when there were two severe raids, not so long, but heavy, and three hundred more were killed.

The official total of those killed in raids is 1,200, and 808 of them buried in the mass grave at London Road Cemetery were killed in the 14th November 1940, and 8th and 10th April 1941 raids. Of the 1,200, 115 were Civil Defence members. Coventry people were also among those killed and injured in raids on the nearby towns of Nuneaton and Kenilworth, where they had gone 'for safety'. In one Nuneaton raid 78 people died, and 25 in one at Kenilworth. There had been no thought, no sign, in the early months of the war, that Coventry would be singled out for the special fury of the Luftwaffe.

At first, after the Prime Minister's grave radio announcement that we were at war, we had half-expected to see enemy bombers overhead at any minute. But nothing happened. Soon people were assuring one another that Coventry would be a difficult place for them to find, "in a hollow, and in the middle of the country". Meanwhile we were busy fixing the black-out, getting our national registration cards, ration books and petrol coupons, putting up the Anderson shelters in the back gardens, enrolling as blood donors, joining the Home Guard, going into the Forces, and persuading ourselves that the war would soon be over. The action was all happening elsewhere. There were Whitley bombers —Coventry-made—in air-raids over German docks and oil depots. There were Coventry men in a headlines action between the three British cruisers, *Ajax*, *Achilles* and *Exeter*, and the *Graf Spee* pocket battleship, at the end of 1939. Time, in those static days on the home front, for the mayor to give seven Coventry heroes from the cruisers a civic reception.

The first freezing winter of the war, with its nightly frosts and heavy snow, passed without any need to use the air-raid shelters erected in such a hurry, and the only incidents overhead were

Looking down the Burges toward Bishop Street after bombing
Smithford Street after the bombing

when an occasional escaped barrage balloon floated away, trailing its cables and riping tiles off roof tops. Five bombs fell on Ansty Aerodrome outside the city in June 1940, and the first raid on Coventry itself was in August when bombs were dropped in Canley Road and Cannon Hill Road, damaging houses but not causing casualties. The first heavy raid was on Sunday 25th August and in the course of it, the new Rex Cinema in Corporation Street was hit. The first Coventry raid casualties came a few nights later when sixteen people died in Hillfields.

Birmingham was a frequent target for enemy bombers, Coventry had occasional raids, and, much more frequently, had the warning sirens. They sounded during a Coventry City versus Reading afternoon match at Highfield Road, and spectators demonstrated when they thought the referee intended to stop it. He had a few words with the captains and allowed play to go on! A daylight raider avoided the balloon barrage and the gunfire on 26th September, hit the Standard Motors factory at Canley and caused a fire. In October the raids began in earnest, almost every night. About one hundred people died, factories were damaged, and among places hit were the City Arcade, the Owen Owen store, the Opera House, and Ford's Hospital, where the matron and seven of the old ladies who were its residents were killed. People who did not have to stay in the city to work now made for the countryside, slept in village halls and farm barns, wherever there was shelter.

Workers drove out in their cars and slept in them in quiet country areas. If they did so on the night of 14th November, they were lucky. At 7.10 the sirens wailed and people went into their shelters, in the streets, in their back gardens; Civil Defence workers—the old ARP—were at their posts. In the cathedral the provost and three fellow fire guards were at the ready. But it was to be a night unlike any other, when an aerial bombardment of death and destruction was to batter Coventry non-stop throughout that clear moonlight night. Those who went into the shelters at dusk were not to emerge from them until morning—and some not at all. "Raiders passed" was at 6.16 a.m. Nobody heard it, for there was no electricity. Waves of bombers—about four-hundred were thought to have been in action—operated a shuttle service over the city, flying over in varying strengths. They dropped 30,000 incendiaries, setting the target ablaze. They poured in 1,000 high-explosive bombs. They dropped parachute mines. It was thought that two aircraft were brought crashing down some miles away from Coventry.

In the first hour alone incendiaries caused some 240 fires, and so many bombs fell that a count could not be made of them. The control system was wrecked early in the raid, and young heroes ran or cycled with messages—and had their casualties. A system for calling in support of fire units and ambulances was operated and many came from a wide area, but there were all sorts of difficulties. Due to craters and debris, streets were impassable. Due to the shattering of water mains, water supplies from this source were not available, and only limited use could be made of the canal and River Sherbourne. There was even, for a time, no ammunition, until supplies came to the weary gunners. After the November raid static water tanks were provided—but that night, the fires burnt on.

Of hundreds of fires, the biggest was at the cathedral. It was reduced to a shell. Only the steeple, smoke-blackened, was standing. Provost Howard and the three other fire guards tackled incendiaries with their stirrup pumps and sand. But many fell, and those that lodged into the space between the outer roof, and the inner, could not be reached. The fire brigade could not help, with the whole city on fire and not a man or machine available. When a relief crew, from Solihull, turned up, they directed a jet on to the burning cathedral, but the water supply gave out because the main was smashed. When they found another main, it yielded only a trickle before this, too, stopped. Coventry Cathedral burnt to the ground while the provost and the firemen from Solihull looked helplessly on.

When people left their shelters in the morning, dazed after the hours of bombing and gunfire, thousands found their homes destroyed or damaged, fires still burning, and a pall of smoke over the city. There was no water, gas, or electricity. Sewers were damaged and exposed. There was no transport. There were over three hundred bomb craters, some so large they would hold a bus. There was rubble everywhere, buildings collapsing, weary fire-fighters and rescue workers with blackened faces and soiled clothing.

It must have seemed an unreal theatrical scene: buildings in the central area were being blown up to isolate fires still being fought all that day; lorries were taking bomb-disposal parties round to tackle unexploded bombs, their vehicles bearing scrawled insults to Hitler, and the cheerful message: "Bring out your bombs". Lorries were carrying soldiers into the city to help with rescue work and removal of debris; coaches and buses were taking children to evacuation centres; some people with what possessions they could carry, were making their way through it all to get away into the countryside, hoping to find a temporary home in a safe place. Others, in a state of anxiety, were waiting at the Council House for news about relatives.

Over 50,000 houses had been damaged and of nearly 1,000 city-centre properties only a few were intact. Many of the houses had no occupiers—they were either away in the Forces or evacuated, or killed or injured—and due to damage or the effect of bomb blast properties were 'open house' to anyone. "My wife was evacuated and I was in the army," one Coventry resident told me, "and it was several weeks after the blitz that a message reached her that the house was wide open. Yet when we arranged for the doors to be nailed up—they had been blown open by blast—it was found that the contents of the house were untouched." Few householders in peacetime would leave their house open at any time, but this was a matter of several weeks!

Life returned to the stricken city by a combination of voluntary aid and official action. Quickly on the scene were the Women's Voluntary Service (the 'Royal' in their title was to come later). Even as the German communiqués were referring to the destruction of Coventry—"The batteries of Coventry are now silenced"—and as their pilots were reporting that it was "a dead town", WVS, and other organizations had mobile canteens from all over the Midlands there, handing out cups of tea and refreshments by the thousand, and postmen somehow struggled round with a salvaged delivery of mail that did wonders for public morale. The Home Secretary soon had 1,500 men from the Forces at work helping to remove debris, demolish dangerous structures and make repairs to services. Men were released from the army if they were tilers and slaters, and builders' workmen from other towns were directed to Coventry. The country was scoured for thousands of tarpaulins to be placed over roofs until repairs could be made. There were no bakeries functioning, so bread supplies were sent in. Thousands of blankets and palliasses were sent to the city.

It was a time when British reserve disappeared. People displayed co-operation and comradeship, sharing what they had in the way of accommodation and food. They cooked meals on coal fires and oil stoves, boiled the water which began to come round in water carts, boiled the milk, and took advice to get inoculated against typhoid. They had lost their ration books, and also many of the shops from which they had bought their food. Food rationing, as a result, was temporarily suspended—but not for long because people from outside the city heard, and moved into Coventry to obtain it! Gradually the situation in Coventry began to improve.

Those directing recovery measures were the seven members of the city council who formed the National Emergency Committee. Alderman W. E. Halliwell was its first chairman, and Alderman G. E. Hodgkinson vice-chairman. The mayor, Alderman J. A. Moseley, and the deputy mayor, Alderman A. R. Grindlay, were *ex officio* members. Others were Aldermen George Briggs and O. M. Flinn, and Councillor G. E. Roberts. Herbert Morrison had suggested that in view of the terrible damage the Government should step in and run the city—a sort of martial law—but he was quickly told that this was unnecessary. So the committee had charge, meeting daily with Ministry representatives, taking decisions on steps to repair the houses, roads and services, and provide food and other supplies. Another committee, with Lord Rootes as chairman, was formed to deal with industrial reconstruction, liaising with the emergency committee. Among measures taken to get things moving again they borrowed buses from other towns, including Blackpool, some of whose buses were still gay in seaside livery! Within four weeks, production was resumed in those factories that could be repaired. Within a few months, aided by the Government shadow factories, production was back to the pre-blitz level.

But long before this improved state of affairs, and when there was still rubble everywhere and some of the dead yet to be extricated from it, the biggest boost to morale had been the visit, within forty-eight hours of the raid, of King George VI, on the 16th. Accompanied by Mr. Morrison, who was again in the city, the King walked for miles seeing the damage. He stood in the cathedral ruins, filled as they then were with debris, and went to St. George's Church, Barkers Butts Lane, where there was a rest centre. Some of the homeless old people had been provided with beds in the church. The King chatted with them, and they insisted on singing the National Anthem. Proof of high morale was evident when the King called at the damaged home of the mayor, Alderman Moseley, in Kensington Road. Someone shouted, "Are we downhearted?" and the crowd shouted, "NO", the King joining in. Mrs. Moseley, the mayoress, in her dust cap, was sweeping fallen plaster and broken glass out of her wrecked dining-room when there was a knock at the street door. "Come round to the back," she called, "that door has been blown off its hinges and is only propped up." The caller, a tall spare figure in a military greatcoat went round to the back. It was the King.

At the Council House there was lunch by candlelight, for the windows were boarded up and there was no electricity. Then the King went to Pool Meadow, where he spoke to AFS and other workers, and the volunteers with the mobile canteens. Many of the workers who were engaged on salvage and repairs had come in from other parts of the country. There was a steady procession of Government ministers to the city, including Lord Beaverbrook, Minister for Aircraft Production; Ernest Bevin, Minister of Labour; Lord Reith, Minister for Public Works and Reconstruction; and Arthur Greenwood, Minister without Portfolio.

The massive bombing of Coventry played its part in influencing American public opinion about the war, for America was not then involved. The Government at home may well have decided to release the details of the bombing of Coventry next day for this reason. The way the news was received in America was reflected in their newspapers. They came out with comments such as: "Hitler's most ruthless act of indiscriminate bombing since the Battle of Britain began", and "Hitler raises horror to the superlative". The *New York Herald Tribune* said: "The gaunt ruins of St. Michael's Cathedral, Coventry, stare from the photographs, the voiceless symbol of the insane, the unfathomable barbarity, which has been released on Western civilization. No means of defence which the United States can place in British hands should be withheld."

Coventry men and women away in the Forces—as many of the young and the fit were—learned with a good deal of pride after the raid that the people at home, many of them elderly and without their sons and daughters to give them assistance, had displayed extreme calm and fortitude, so much so that they won admiration for it. Newspapers, official and unofficial records, referred to it. Although "bombs rained in torrents", said one, the wardens were "entirely unperturbed". A first-aid post was demolished at Foleshill Baths by a direct hit and its team, including young girls, carried on with torches tending the injured "without sign of fear or panic". Plans were made to evacuate people, expected to number thousands—and only 300 turned up, with a few children. Commented one report: "The inhabitants preferred to stay where they were." With people of this calibre, the solid and steady people of the Midlands—how could we lose?

The Germans' claim that they had destroyed the city was much exaggerated. Their explanation for the raid was that it was in return for a British raid on Munich, and that they had chosen Coventry as "the centre of the British aircraft industry". Their pilots had said that they could see the glow of the fires in Coventry from the coast. Coventry had no other severe raids for a few months. When they came, it was the double blow, at Easter 1941. The two raids caused further heavy damage and loss of life. In the first, on 8th April, 350 high-explosive bombs were dropped and the 'alert' lasted from 9.50 p.m. to 5 a.m. In the second on the 10th, 450 fell, most of them between 12.30 a.m. and 3 a.m.

In the first of the April raids, the Coventry and Warwickshire Hospital at Stoney Stanton Road, already extensively damaged after the November blitz, was so severely hit that it had to be abandoned. Two doctors, nine nurses, and twenty patients, died in this latest raid. The hospital had acquitted itself nobly. In the November raid, it was hit by fifteen high-explosive bombs yet emergency operations continued under makeshift arrangements, the doctors and nurses diving to the floor each time bombs fell close. It was a time for pluck on the part of the patients. Those who could walk were putting out incendiary bombs and those who had to stay in bed were handed wash bowls to use as shields against falling debris. It was a brilliant moonlight, frosty night, and very cold. Hardly any of the hospital's 1,600 windows had glass in them, but, it is recorded, "nobody grumbled".

In proportion to the size of the population, more people lost their lives in Coventry than in any other city in Britain. For those who died in the big raids there were mass funerals. A cortège of lorries, after the November blitz, carried the coffins, obtained after an appeal throughout the Midlands. Overnight they were lowered into trenches dug by an excavator. The Bishop, Dr. Mervyn Haigh, summed up the feeling of the Coventry people next day when he said at the graveside service: "The Germans can kill our loved ones, but it rests with us whether they break our spirit." On Good Friday 1941, after the two Easter raids, when there were more bombs on the cathedral, there was a service in the ruins. The theme was typical: "It does not matter when you die— it only matters how you die."

The mass grave had to be extended because it was not practicable to allow private burials, and there was another communal funeral. When the war was over, the grave was made into a walled garden, and a memorial, bearing all 808 names, was erected there. The last raid on Coventry was on 3rd August 1942, and was over the Stoke Heath district. The wartime statistics make a formidable list.

The city had a total of 373 air-raid warnings, between June 1940 and August 1942, and there were 41 actual bombing or machine-gunning raids. Of the city's 75,000 properties, 5,566 were a total loss, and 50,479 were damaged. The total losses included 4,330 houses, 624 shops, 73 industrial premises, 84 warehouses, 28 hotels, 14 theatres and cinemas, 4 clubs, 80 garages and filling stations, 4 hospitals and nursing homes, and 5 schools. In the devastated city centre, out of 975 properties 31 stood intact. A grand total of about 2,500 high-explosive bombs dropped on the city.

It was not enough to crush the spirit of Coventry! For those who endured the raids, the rebuilding of the city became a matter of pride, a symbol of their resistance. Even before the heavy Easter raids of 1941, the city council had set up a redevelopment committee, and had begun to plan the city that would arise. They sent a deputation at once to London, to discuss it with Lord Reith at the Ministry of Public Works and Reconstruction, and were told to go ahead, be bold, and work on comprehensive lines for their reconstruction. Afterwards, in his memoirs, Lord Reith was to write that he saw Coventry "as a test case, for the Government and for England". Everyone gave encouragement to Coventry in those dark days. From all parts of the country, and from abroad, letters and cables flowed into the mayor's office, at the rate of 400 a day, offering help, enclosing money, expressing sympathy.

The provost had a huge postbag, about the loss of the cathedral, enclosing money, and offering aid. Letters to the mayor were from rich and poor. A Formby (Liverpool) family went without their 'Christmas money' after the November raid, and sent it,

£2 10s., to be used on relief in Coventry. Customers of a York-shire inn sent £162 10s., from pennies stuck on mirrors and from an auction of customers' ties. There was 5s. from a rummage sale in a Westmorland village, sums from Coventry people and organizations, including £2,500 from Sir Alfred Herbert, head of the Coventry machine-tool firm. There were gifts of clothing and food, and offers of accommodation for those bombed out. There were four lorry loads of boots, shoes, and clothing from the neighbouring town of Leicester, whose Lord Mayor also sent £1,000 that had been collected.

The Canadian Red Cross shipped 1,000 blankets and quilts, America's British War Relief Society sent £5,000, the Lord Mayor of London's fund sent £10,000. Argentine railway workers sent £1,000. Canada sent two ambulances. Wolver-hampton sent £105. The Queen sent £200, and the Mayor of Stafford £250. These are only a random sample of the flow of gifts to Coventry in her plight. The money was used to help those who, at the rate of about twenty a day, knocked at the mayor's door and asked for assistance. One woman had lost her husband and nine children in the raid, and had only her baby left. There had been a direct hit on their house. The Coventry Air-raid Distress Fund reached a total of £67,174 by July 1944, and up to that time 3,576 grants had been made from it, totalling £47,056.

After the war Wellington Gardens old people's homes in Windsor Street were built from another gift of £30,000 from the Lord Mayor of London's Air-raid Distress Fund, specifically made to help old people whose troubles began in the blitz. Sir George Wilkinson, who had been Lord Mayor of London, opened the homes in 1951. They were named Wellington in tribute to the people of Wellington, New Zealand, who gave £60,000 to the London fund when he was Lord Mayor in 1940–41. In 1953, with their own experiences still fresh in mind, Coventry City Council used some of the air-raid fund balance to help others in distress. They sent £3,000 for the flood victims of the eastern counties, and a similar sum for those in Holland. Other gifts followed: £500 each to Greece and Cyprus for earthquake victims; £100 each to Irish and West Country flood funds; £100 to Yugoslavia after an avalanche disaster; £500 for Hungarian relief in 1956, and a further £1,500 to help Hungarian refugees.

When, after the space of several years, it became clear that the fund was no longer necessary to aid people who suffered in the air raids, the city council obtained the approval of the Charity Commissioners, in 1963, to put the balance of £13,906 into a fund called the Coventry Charity for Special Relief. This still operates, and helps needy people.

Many familiar buildings were destroyed and damaged in the raids. Alongside the cathedral ruins is the site, in Bayley Lane, of the former St. Michael's Baptist Church. Its basement became a static water tank. St. Mary's Hall had roof damage, and its Caesar's Tower was demolished. It has since been rebuilt. The King's Head Hotel, at the corner of Hertford Street and Smithford Street, was destroyed—Only its Peeping Tom effigy being saved. The Queen's Hotel, Hertford Street, was destroyed apart from one small part of it which was used for some years after the war. 'The Grapes', Warwick Lane, had only its kitchen left, and this became the bar.

Several public houses were destroyed, and several churches, and some surviving public houses allowed their premises to be used by homeless church congregations. St. Nicholas, Radford Road, and St. Francis, also at Radford, were flattened. St. Luke's, Holbrooks, St. Paul's, Foleshill, and Stoke Methodist, were also destroyed. Christ Church was destroyed in the April raids.

West Orchard Congregational Church was destroyed, and Well Street Congregational was badly damaged. Bombs wiped out ancient Palace Yard in Earl Street. All the hospitals suffered, Gulson extensively, the Whitley Isolation less so. The tram service was knocked out, and many buses were wrecked. Among schools, King Henry VIII was severely damaged, and others that could not be used were All Souls, Edgewick, St. Osburg's, Frederick Bird, Barkers Butts, Spon Street, and Stoke C.E.

One city centre landmark that was practically intact was Holy Trinity Church, where the vicar, Canon G. W. Clitheroe, had felt all along that fire was going to be the real enemy if there was a severe raid. He and members of his family had taken extra precautions to deal with incendiaries. They had stored water and sand in various parts of the church, and had hauled some up by ropes to roof level. They were able to deal with the incendiaries that fell, and luckily there was no direct hit from a high-explosive bomb.

The raids brought Coventry a dazzling array of medals and commendations for bravery. The MBE was awarded to the late

Alderman Mrs. Pearl Hyde, who during the war was head of the
WVS. She was dauntless under fire, always in the thick of it, and
her 'devil's kitchen' in the basement of the damaged Council
House became famous. It was Mrs. Hyde and the WVS who had
the morale-boosting idea of touring public air-raid shelters at
Christmas to give toys to children. They found that people had
decorated the shelters, with streamers and evergreens. There were
heroes and heroines galore.

Two George Crosses were awarded. Thirty-year-old Special
Constable Brandon Moss received one for "superhuman" work
in the rescue of three people trapped in a damaged house. The
other went to Sub-Lieutenant W. G. Taylor, RNVR, for dealing
with unexploded land mines in Coventry, and in Birmingham—
where he was injured by one. There were several George Medals,
including one to Dr. H. N. Gregg who was MO at Barkers
Butts School first-aid post and went out on foot and by bicycle
giving morphine to people trapped under wreckage. A 17-year-
old, Betty Quinn, a volunteer ARP warden, received the medal
for helping to dig out seven people from a demolished shelter,
then tending their wounds. For gallantry at the hospital, the
secretary, Mr. S. C. Hill; Matron, Miss Joyce Burton; Sister
Horne; and Miss Margaret Brown, a volunteer first-aider, each
received a George Medal.

George Medals also went to Mr. Thomas Lee, a civilian who
assisted rescue squads; and to Mr. Frederick Mason, and Mr.
Albert Fearn, leader and deputy leader of an ARP rescue party.
Another to Chief Officer G. Collier, of the Humber Fire Brigade,
and a medal to Captain C. J. Kelly, ARP Control Officer and
fire chief at Nuffield Mechanizations. Miss Marjorie Perkins, who
gave first aid to wounded in the Pattison Hoborne works, and
then to those in the streets and in a shelter, also received the
George Medal. Mr. H. L. Brooke, leader of a volunteer rescue
party that saved people from a demolished house, also received
the medal. Two AID men at Armstrong Siddeley, Mr. F. V.
Walker, and Mr. W. H. Yoxall, were similarly honoured, and
another who received the medal was Mr. Gilbert Griffiths, post
office assistant engineer. There were many other awards, such as
the OBE to Miss Joan Westerby, aged 20, who made eleven
journeys in the ambulance she drove, and was on duty continuously for twenty-four hours, during and after the November
raid. And an OBE for Mr. Norman Nowell, for tunnelling flat

on his face for seventy-five minutes to reach people trapped under a dangerous building, with the hazard of escaping gas.

Awards were made to police and fire brigade personnel, and to Forces personnel on duty in the city, such as the two unnamed Staffordshire Regiment soldiers decorated for gallantry. Other civilian heroes included Raymond Corn, one of those who carried messages during heavy enemy action, and Rover Scout Jack Garner, who was in hospital with the injuries he received when he was visited and decorated by Lord Somers, Chief Scout, with the Cornwell Badge, the highest Scout Movement award, for bravery in one of the raids. There were other heroes who dealt with unexploded bombs. The George Cross was awarded posthumously to second Lieutenant A. F. Campbell, of the Royal Engineers, for work in removing an unexploded bomb from the Triumph Works. After this incident he and practically the whole of his squad were killed when a delayed-action bomb suddenly exploded on Whitley Common, where they had taken it to be detonated. The 560-pounder exploded just after it had been unloaded from the lorry that brought it from Chapel Street.

All eyes were on Coventry at this time and its people acquitted themselves well. It was their hour of trial and they passed the test. King George VI, by making three visits, showed his concern for the Midland city. He was accompanied on two of his journeys by the Queen, and on their last wartime visit, in February 1942, the city was as busy as ever with important war production, and its leaders were busy with reconstruction plans which were shown to the royal visitors. They also visited the cathedral ruins, the hospital, the GEC works, and saw a Civil Defence parade. They saw enough to know that Coventry, despite terrible scars, was in good heart. Prime Minister Winston Churchill must have felt a glow of pride in the spirit he found when he visited Coventry in September 1941. Like those of London, Coventry people had shown that they could take it.

For years, after the war, unexploded bombs were being excavated all over Coventry, and German volunteers, over here as prisoners-of-war, were among those who did this dangerous work.

III

REBUILDING A CITY

THE emotions of those days have ebbed away and the city centre is mostly rebuilt. Many other towns have altered their centres to add precincts because of traffic problems. But no place could possibly have known the enthusiasm, the crusading spirit, which Coventry had after the war. Is there another city in Britain that has launched its redevelopment with a public open-air ceremony and service, attended by civics, churchmen, businessmen, and citizens, as Coventry did on Victory Day 1946, when the symbolic act of laying the levelling stone in the bombed centre was accompanied by the singing of "Jerusalem"? They would not cease, they sang, till they had built Jerusalem in England's green and pleasant land.

Nor did they, for in the blitzed area that lay about them they set their garden centrepiece, and from this new Broadgate laid out avenues of shops where no cars are seen and the pedestrian is supreme; avenues in which all the shops are colonnaded and look on to paved and planted areas, from Broadgate to St. John's Church, and across from Corporation Street to Warwick Road. Alongside the cathedral ruins is a wonderful new cathedral, probably the best known in the world today, and there are college and public buildings, greens, courtyards and trees. It is not easy to visualize that this was a blitzed scene. Many of the pioneers who gathered round the levelling stone have died, or retired, but their vision has been turned into reality. Vision was there even as they laid the stone, for it was not just a slab; it was heart-shaped, and engraved on it was a phoenix rising from the flames. Vision, too, in the first actual step in reconstruction. They did not put up a building. They chose to lay out a garden!

The Dutch people had collected money to be used to show their gratitude to the Allied nations for their liberation, and they sent flowers to London, New York, Paris and Moscow, but still had a large sum left. They decided to send shrubs, plants and bulbs to the city of Coventry, which like their own town of Rotterdam had suffered harshly in the war. It was typical of Coventry that it displayed a flash of vision on that occasion. The setting for the Dutch gift might easily have been a park; it would have been the usual thing to do. But a square was planned for Broadgate and what better than this—a central garden island beautified by a gesture of gratitude and friendship from overseas? It would be a vivid splash of colour in the drab Broadgate scene and cheer up citizens whose lives had been grey—war weary, rationed, lacking everyday services like shops, restaurants, housing.

At that time the Government had not issued the order which enabled the city council to make compulsory purchase orders within a specified area of the centre, and the corporation did not own the land. The Dutch offer was a great help. They were able to approach owners of blitzed sites who agreed that the corporation should have immediate access to make the garden island so that the gift would be properly displayed. There was one owner who held back—he wanted to be sure of a corner site in the new centre—but he gave access later when the island was under construction and almost at his door. The Royal Family have taken great interest in the reconstruction of the city, and Princess Elizabeth—now the Queen—opened the new Broadgate with a ceremony on completion of the island in 1948. Now, the public could see for themselves that the new centre was really on the way, and the raids had provided a wide canvas for a sweeping, comprehensive centre that could never have been built in normal times.

There had been intention to redevelop the centre before war broke out, for it was congested by traffic. A city architect, the first that Coventry had, was appointed in 1938. The post went to Donald Gibson, subsequently widely praised for his planning of Coventry and later knighted. On arrival he found what he has described as "a complete lack of civic design". He learned that the city wanted to erect new buildings but could not find sites for them. Among other schemes waiting were an art gallery and museum, for which Sir Alfred Herbert had given the money, and a new police headquarters to replace inadequate premises occupied by the police.

However, he could not replan the centre, much as he felt that this was needed, because the city engineer was the planning officer. So the architect and his deputy and their wives "worked

more or less on the carpet at home in the evenings" on an
unofficial plan. They also made a model, and talked about it
informally with councillors and other people. A clash with the
planning officer seemed inevitable, but war began and all thoughts
about planning went into cold storage for more urgent matters.

If there had not been a war or the urgency and the drive which
were its aftermath, it would have been a slow and difficult task to
redevelop the central area. Traders were established in their
businesses, had the goodwill of their customers to protect, and
would have been reluctant to move out. It would have been
necessary to relocate them before demolishing their properties.
But with war, with raids, a bold and imaginative scheme could
now be carried out, without any of these difficulties.

The council had a free hand, backed by compulsory purchase
powers from the Government; and, with expectant eyes on
Coventry to see how it would cope after the war damage, the
council had a spur to think, and to act, big. They threw out the
idea of orthodox development of roads and shops, however wide
those roads might be to deal with traffic. Instead, they adopted
Donald Gibson's scheme for a comprehensively-planned centre
based on precincted shopping—an idea familiar to everybody
today, repeated large and small and in many congested town
centres, but then untried in this country. The planners were
taking a leap in the dark with it.

Nobody knew what the effect might be on trading. Would
people accept it, or would they prefer the traditional shopping
street with its access by car? The precinct plan required the car to
be left in a park, and from there it was necessary to walk to the
shops in the adjoining precinct, to carry parcels, and finally walk
back with them to the car. It sounded, then, a real nuisance
compared with popping out of a car and into a shop, and off
again. Would it succeed? Timidity was not a Coventry
characteristic, but not everyone was carried away by civic
planning enthusiasm. It was up to the council themselves to show
the way. They did so by building the first block, on their own
land.

This was the £400,000 Broadgate House, comprising shops
and offices, and with it the bridge over Hertford Street. If you
stand in Broadgate today, however, you will look in vain for the
bridge, for there has been a later change. It indicates how successful
precincted shopping has been, in fact, that the council decided in

the late sixties to add Hertford Street, a main shopping street, to it. It was closed to traffic, new shops and offices were built, and some of the old ones retained, the roadway was paved, and the area was partly arcaded. This made the bridge redundant, and the Nat-West Bank built their premises in the gap beneath it, and a pedestrian subway that crossed Hertford Street at this point became the bank basement. Years ago, the idea of closing this busy traffic artery through the centre would have been called ridiculous!

Broadgate House, opened by Lord Silkin in 1953, is on the left at the Broadgate entrance to the upper precinct, looking towards the precinct. There were early qualms by some council members about lack of demand for office accommodation, but the building has been fully let for many years and it runs at a profit. It set the style and the type of finish for the frontages of the central area layout, and Coventry had its first look at canopied shopping, now general. The first piece of private enterprise building was the Owen Owen store (1953-4) which has a frontage to Broadgate too. Designed by Hellberg and Harris, of Coventry, it was the first post-war store and gave the public a wider range of goods to buy on its five sales floors, after the years of 'making do' because of the loss of so many shops. Owen's were making their comeback appearance, for it had been their bad luck, after building and opening the first store shortly before the war, to see it knocked out, in its infancy almost, in the air-raids. The second store uses part of the old site, and the basement of the bombed building has become a tunnel for goods vehicles, from Palmer Lane, under Ironmonger Row, into the basement of the store. With its furnishings the new store cost £1 million. Its 'curtain wall' frontage to Broadgate has been praised, and criticized, by architects.

The lack of shops was matched by lack of hotels. The Hotel Leofric, when it opened in 1955, answered a great need. All sorts of societies, which had been very restricted for venues for social events, applied to hold them at the new hotel—so many, in fact, that Mr. John Wearmouth, the first manager, had to ask some-times for reservation a year ahead! And here was somewhere to stay. The one hundred bedrooms were often insufficient to cope with demands of visitors. As many as fifty people were turned away at week-ends. With smaller hotels also full, they would finish their search for accommodation at Kenilworth. 'The

The Lady Godiva statue in Broadgate
Broadgate in 1939

Leofric' was designed by Coventry architects, Hattrells, and is the twin block, with frontage of shops, of Broadgate House, forming the other corner of the entrance into the precinct. In the lounge is the Peeping Tom who used to be in the 'King's Head'. There are now more hotels in and around Coventry, and they cater more adequately for the flow of visitors and for Coventry's own needs. But the 'Leofric' held the fort!

From Broadgate, the precinct opens out as a wide paved area, spanned by footbridges. They link blocks of shops, on each side, that have two levels of shopping. Somewhere in here was Smithford Street, once a main traffic and shopping street, very narrow, leading to Spon Street. When these shopping blocks— they call them link blocks because they are a link between the corner blocks at the top and the corner blocks at the bottom— were being built, we felt as though we were taking part in an exciting adventure—a renaissance! It was such an animated, complicated, busy scene, with building equipment and materials everywhere, a maze of scaffolding and plank walkways that we had to use. Those not on any pressing duty could gaze and enjoy it all, speculate on what was to come.

When the link blocks did take shape we could appreciate how they were orientated so that the spire of the cathedral, framed exactly between the outlines of the 'Leofric' and Broadgate House blocks, was seen as if along an avenue, a splendid and pleasing vista through the precinct. At the 'cross roads'—if pedestrian ways can have such a term—where the precincts meet, there is still a view of the spire, but from the paved area of the lower precinct the view is obstructed by the circular café in the paved area. In summer, given sunshine, the lower precinct paved area can look Continental, with tables from the café placed outside, and there have been gay moments when the strains of music have been heard, the performers using a temporary band-stand. It must be our uncertain weather that has put a stop to that!

The upper and lower precincts in the centre both have ramps and steps to take people to the first-floor shops, but the upper precinct has had ramp access only since 1981. Until then it was virtually out of bounds for prams and invalid carriages. It has. more than its share of footwear, and clothing, lacking variety. Some shops have ground and first-floor premises above. It was developed by a London company. Coventry Corporation who decided to develop the lower precinct, made a ramp for prams,

(overleaf) *The Lower Precinct*
Rooftop parking in the central area

had a policy of variety of shopping—there is a hairdresser, florist, gift shop, butcher, wallpaper shop—to name a few, and made the upper deck as attractive as the bottom, with different shops on each level.

The architects have sealed off the ends of the precincts in an interesting way. Stand in the centre of the cross roads where Smithford Way and Market Way meet the precincts, upper and lower. Here the views are up to the spire, down to Mercia House, and along to Hillman House, each eye-catching. Mercia House at the bottom of the lower precinct is sparkling in white marble, is nineteen storeys high, and has ninety-six flats. It is owned by the corporation, and on the ground and lower floors is occupied by the C and A store and other businesses; and a night-club, entered on the first floor, is one of its attractions. It cost the sum of £534,225. Hillman House, at the end of Smithford Way, is a privately-developed tower block of forty flats, topped by a 'Taj Mahal' roof dome that gives it individuality. The flats are now owned by Coventry City Council, and its ground and lower floors are occupied by the stores of Boots the chemist, and Allied Carpets. The blocks that form the corners of the precinct cross roads are those of Woolworths, British Home Stores, Marks and Spencer, and Wades. Coventry Corporation own nineteen shops in Smithford Way, seven in Market Way.

In the original plan for the shopping precinct there was no Smithford Way or Market Way—just the upper and lower precincts. The trading interests wanted access for buses and other vehicles to the precincts, and as a concession to them a motor road was added to the layout, coming from Corporation Street, severing the upper and lower precincts, and swinging right to terminate in Queen Victoria Road. Mr. Donald Gibson left Coventry in 1955 to take another post, and was succeeded by Mr. Arthur Ling, and he as a newcomer was able to persuade the council that to construct this road would be what he called a "ghastly compromise". The roadworks had begun and you can see traces of them between Woolworths and British Home Stores. It was an eleventh-hour reprieve for Smithford Way and Market Way, and for pedestrians, who would have had to go from one precinct to the other by subway under this motor road.

Mr. Gibson had pioneered, and Mr. Ling followed, on the bombed sites; they had given us the feeling of exciting developments, as we watched the lines of old streets disappear, and landmarks get fewer. The ruins, where willow herb grew in masses and sent clouds of 'angel' seeds floating over the centre, gradually vanished. Coventry became a vast construction site full of deep excavations, dominated by tower cranes and conjured up from the 'nerve centre', the first offices of the city architect's department, at Bull Yard, in the adapted workshops of what had been, long ago, the Rover Company, and with a front office in Warwick Road that had been the wartime Food Office for Coventry.

Mr. Ling (he was later succeeded by Mr. Terence Gregory) took over the grand design and stamped his mark on it, and the emphasis on shops which had the effect of giving the central area a 'ghost town' appearance at night, after they had closed, switched to projects that would breathe life into it. The Locarno dance hall in Smithford Way, later re-named Tiffany's, was one of the first of these, but Mecca, the organisation who owned it, closed it in 1981. It had lacked support and was not a success. The Belgrade Theatre, several public houses—there is to be a limit of forty-six of them in the central area—restaurants, and blocks of flats, have given an injection of movement of people in the area—but in no great number today with hooligans abroad and muggings taking place.

Precinct shopping has been gradually extended, adding the City Arcade, Shelton Square, and Hertford Street. In the central area precincts and shopping thoroughfares, there are over 250 shops and several large stores. Off Market Way there are two features of special interest: the arcade, and the retail market. The arcade is in direct contrast to the wide main precincts. It is cosy and intimate. The shopkeepers can almost lean across and shake hands with their opposite numbers. It has thirty-six shops, including restaurants, and two public houses. The enclosed circular market is a surprise, and seems like a maze at first. If you enter at one point, you are unlikely to leave by it. You cannot find it! The stalls are in rings, each ring for its particular line of trade, a layout that encourages shoppers to circulate rather than make direct for an objective, and it also means that no stallholder has a better site than his neighbour. Princess Alexandra opened it in 1958. A colourful and attractive place, it even has a wall mural designed and carried out by students of Dresden, East Germany. Goods access is to a basement, where there is storage and rubbish disposal.

The market was the only one of its kind in this country, and has brought many civic parties to Coventry because of its unusual design. It is 276 feet in diameter, 15 feet high internally, and has 160 island stalls; 44 shop stalls are set into the perimeter wall, 16 of them facing outwards so that the open-air market touch is given to an indoor one. One departure from open-air market tradition is that the 'barking' of wares is not allowed, so there are none of the scenes at some markets, where all the shoppers seem to be gathered round one particularly vocal salesman and the others are doing correspondingly less business. Stallholders are happy with their market in Coventry and there has always been competition for vacant stalls. Its roof was specially strengthened when it was constructed to serve as a park for 200 cars, and there is more car parking, joined with it, above the arcade (140 spaces) and over the twenty-six Shelton Square shops.

The market is linked to Victoria Buildings, which has the fish market with fourteen stands in it, where the pillars are adorned with mermaids and other appropriate figures. Victoria Buildings, unlike other buildings in the centre, were a conversion from factories, which explains their rather solid bulk. It is an excellent conversion, with frontages of canopied shops, a supermarket, a small arcade, and a billiards room, and some offices and light industry on the upper levels. Buses drop passengers close to precinct entrances and the shoppers rapidly disappear into them, exchanging the traffic noises for the sounds of pattering shoes and of conversation.

In addition to local people doing their shopping, there are always visitors, in small groups or large organized parties, looking round. Nothing has been allowed that might spoil the look of the precincts. The absence of advertising—some think it dull without it—is due to planning control, even over modest shop signs, to the annoyance at times of traders who have wanted to draw more attention to their shops. Where there might be hoardings, there are instead illuminated panels depicting crafts, or murals, touching on the city's history. Here and there are ornamental touches, like the martyrs' memorial mosaic in the entrance way that leads up to the Bridge Restaurant, Broadgate. There is the pleasant courtyard and pool, and the graceful willow trees behind the council offices in Earl Street.

The 'Coventry Standard', the 56-foot aluminium mast in Broadgate, at the top of the precinct, was given and made by four local firms "as a monument to the skill of Coventry's craftsmen and as a contribution to the rebuilding of the city centre". On top is the elephant and castle from the city coat-of-arms. Another ornamental touch is the sculpture inside the abutments of the precinct footbridge—the one with the water feature. There are two panels by the Kenilworth sculptor Walter Ritchie, depicting man's struggle with himself and with the forces of nature. There is sculpture in the paved area—the 'totem poles' from Coventry College of Art. But is the representation of a bombed house, in Market Way, really necessary?

Another attraction—but only for small children—is the merry-go-round alongside the market. Like many of the Coventry projects, there is a history to it. Jack Statham used to operate it, by hand, on blitzed sites. Families looked forward to it because for years there was not much to see or do in town. But they had to look for it, because the merry-go-round was never at one spot for long. It was 'moved on', not by the law, but by the pace of reconstruction and had to keep one jump ahead. It became so much a part of the city centre reconstruction scene that eventually it was adopted. The architects gave it a design in keeping with the civic layout—it looks gay—and put it on a permanent site, where Princess Alexandra admired it when she opened the market. No more moving on for 'Uncle Jack's' merry-go-round!

One reason why the central area has a clean appearance is the absence of smoke, for before smoke control became national policy Coventry was a pioneer in this respect, and in 1951 30 acres of the centre were designated a smokeless zone. This is more stringent than the smoke-control areas of today, which do permit a slight smoke. In the smokeless centre, roofs are for cars, not chimneys! Buildings are joined at roof level and motorists drive from one roof park to another and link up with multi-storey parks. Roofs were strengthened when properties were built. Motorists familiar with the layout can cross the centre by going over the top, to park and go to a particular shop by means of the stairways that lead to ground level. But they have no chance of doing it at busy times, when cars queue to get in, and out!

There are over 77,000 cars, 8,000 motor-cycles, and 9,000 commercial vehicles registered in Coventry, and car ownership is well above national average. The central area has 4,000 controlled public parking spaces and the capacity of the ring road junctions has set a limit of 10,000 spaces within the central area, based on the discharge rates of car parks, long and short stay. The car-making city planned well for car-owners!

In the precincted area it is a 'safety feather' in the planners' caps that, while cars manœuvre overhead, the pedestrians walk freely and safely on their own particular territory down below. The arrangements have been appreciated by the public, and are not a talking point any more. The walking, car park to shops and back, is taken for granted. Shopkeepers are accustomed to having service roads to their back doors, and reconciled to the idea that never again will shoppers drive up by car to the front door. Nowadays it has in any case become more difficult in general to shop elsewhere by car. The banning of traffic in busy shopping streets makes it necessary to park some distance away from them, too. And the precincts have their own special interest.

There may be Morris dancers, pipers playing, students on rag-week stunts, political or strike meetings, a band, for the wide paved areas offer plenty of scope and are popular for such activities. They lend themselves to exhibitions, especially for the Christmas decorations and lights, switched on during carol singing led by the local choristers. If there is a failure in the Precincts it is not the fault of the planners, but more a matter of supply and demand, for it is generally felt that Coventry lacks high-class shopping. It needs a few specialist and exclusive shops; it needs more book shops. Branches of multiple stores, selling similar ranges of shoes and clothes, predominate. Coventry has not been able to attract the 'upper bracket' shops.

Perhaps precinct trading put them off in the early days of development, for it had yet to prove itself. Perhaps when it did, it was too late and the first arrivals had established themselves too well. It has had the result of giving the centre, with some exceptions, shopping that is of one level. Shoppers looking for the specialist range go to other towns for it, so a demand appears to exist. Another reason for the absence of these stores and shops may be the rents, because all the buildings were new, and rents must reflect this. It has prevented some of the city's own small traders from taking new premises, when they have been moved from old shops because of redevelopment. There is no place for instance, for the master cobbler, who moves out to the suburbs.

Of course, shopping is not all that the new centre offers. In 1958 Coventry made its impact in the theatre world, when its £265,000 Belgrade Theatre was opened by the Duchess of Kent.

The theatre, in Corporation Street just outside the precincts, was the first professional civic theatre built in this country since the war. The building itself makes an interesting contribution to the street scene, with a generous expanse of glass, so that passers-by have a view of part of the interior—the foyer and staircase—which provides a spectacle when the lights are on at night. The theatre can seat 911, and there is a resident cast. Like other Coventry projects, the 'Belgrade' has a touch of the unusual about it.

In this case it was a gift, not of shrubs and plants, not even a mural, but timber, from Yugoslavia. Coventry has a friendship link with Belgrade and Sarajevo, and there have been exchanges of gifts, and visits. Some of the timber was used in the theatre, whose name, and the bas-relief on the frontage, marks the bond of friendship. The 'Belgrade' is part of a block of shops, and above them are twenty-one bed-sitting-room flats, some let to local residents, others reserved for members of the theatre company. The theatre has a restaurant which is in general public use, and there is a pleasant outlook over Belgrade Square, an ornamental area with a fountain—not a dainty affair, but one that throws up its 'water spout' to the heights, to fall with a splash, as if reflecting the progressive spirit of the post-war city.

For the theatre-going public, the opening of the 'Belgrade' marked the end of a post-war era of drama at the Technical College Theatre, which itself put on a noble act in coming to the rescue, to fill the gap caused by the loss of the Opera House. At the college, plays were presented by the Midland Theatre Company, who were accustomed to the shortcomings of small theatres, for they also went on tour with their productions to perform in small towns around Coventry. The 'Belgrade', however, has given us a professional theatre, with a company that recalls the old 'Rep' at the Opera House. The theatre's first director was the late Bryan Bailey, and he opened with *Half in Earnest*, Vivian Ellis's musical adaptation of Oscar Wilde's *The Importance of Being Earnest*. Since then, under him and its successive directors, the theatre has gained a high reputation, and has presented a wide range of plays, including new works. It gave Arnold Wesker an outlet for his plays before he became well known.

It has a theatre club; a theatre-in-education scheme which encourages drama in schools; a young stagers' association; and it gives free lunchtime entertainment to the public. Support for the theatre has fluctuated, with popular plays receiving best attendances, while new and way-out plays trail behind. There is no lack of enterprise. One idea was the sending out of publicity and an offer of concessionary price tickets, with the rate demands. It is a civic theatre and this was a civic touch. All-in luxury-night-out offers of taxi, theatre, meal, and flowers, have been another idea.

Another cultural building, and again the first of its kind to be built in this country since the war, is the £445,000 Herbert Art Gallery and Museum at Jordan Well, opened in 1960 and, as the name implies, built with a generous gift by Sir Alfred Herbert, who first made his offer before the war. The stubby white-walled building used now as toilets at Bayley Lane was the beginning of the pre-war art gallery, halted at that level by war. After it, as in the other parts of the centre, the bombs had laid bare sites not previously available, and there was a change of plan and a move to a new site where it was possible to build larger premises, Sir Alfred adding to his pre-war offer. The building (designed by Herbert, Son, and Sawday, Leicester) has a light and modern interior, altogether removed from the rather formal and fusty atmosphere of older galleries and museums. As behoves a museum in Coventry, it has a fascinating array of early and late bicycles, motor-cycles, and cars, and some of today's engineering marvels of Coventry, like multi-powered jet units. But it has not overlooked the ribbon trade, and there are displays of Stevengraphs and Cash's woven-silk pictures and labels, and reminders of the watch and clock makers.

Upstairs, via a staircase where pictures of Lady Godiva hang, the galleries are open wide to cater for the local public. On the one hand, Lord Iliffe's loan to the gallery of the Graham Sutherland collection of sketches made for his great cathedral tapestry, next door, perhaps, a gallery filled with the work of Coventry schoolchildren. National exhibitions which go on tour are shown here, but so are the works of Coventry area societies, and once a year there is a selection of the work of local artists in general. The gallery has given us a new dimension, for we did not have one before the war, and there is good use of it. Another facility is its 180-seater lecture theatre, available for public use, in an area that has not been well equipped with meeting places in the past.

It would be pleasant to mention the fine new library next to the

The Belgrade Theatre
An engineers' strike meeting in the Precinct

art gallery, in Bayley Lane, but as only one instalment has been built, and that several years ago, with no sign of the next, we can only say that bookworms have taken a back seat in planning! The council debated library or baths as to order of priority, for the finance available in each year's programme limited the programme of new projects. To be fair, the swimmers, who won, were worse off than book borrowers. The library did eventually get a start, and stage one of it housed the reference library, gramophone records library, Coventry and Warwickshire Collection, and head offices. Long ago the members of the Drapers' Club found new headquarters and evacuated the Drapers' Hall, which had to be demolished to leave its site for the completion of the new library, but the hall still stands, partly in use for court work. The war-damaged Gulson Central Library was still in use in 1981, more than 100 years after John Gulson presented it to the city.

But the swimming baths, in Fairfax Street, are a wonderful asset to swimmers, and at the same time are a spectacle from the street, with the huge 'walls' of glass that give a view of divers and swimmers, and that eye-catching 'flying wing' of a roof. The baths cost £1,300,000 and accommodate over one thousand spectators. An electronic communication signals system for timing races and recording on the results board cost £16,000. The Olympic-size main pool is blue and inviting. All the facilities, like those for entering and changing, work on a very scientific system, for reasons of cleanliness and hygiene. There is a special diving pit, and there are smaller pools for club use and for learners. You can have meals in a restaurant—the 'Priory'—and watch the swimmers below. Coventry Baths are said to be among Europe's finest. They are the Midland region centre for competitions, and international matches are televised from them.

By contrast the pre-war central baths in Priory Street, almost on the same site, dated back to 1894 and were cramped and totally enclosed. We walked round the edge of the pool in our shoes, and we changed in small cubicles, with short doors, so that every now and then someone dived and sent a shower of cold water into the cubicle, where you stood on floorboards because the stone floor was saturated. The baths were always so busy that the best time to go was Sunday morning about 6 a.m.! In winter, the baths could be covered by flooring, and were useful for various events—all-in wrestling first made its début there. The building was destroyed in the war, and the only other public

Inside Coventry Baths

baths were those at Foleshill, in Livingstone Road, which had also been severely war-damaged. They were repaired and re-opened in 1946, with one pool to cater for a whole city! So the new baths were really needed. Before they were built an idea considered by the council was to build several small pools, dotted round districts, instead of having one in the centre.

The super baths won the day, and they have been located so as to be convenient for everybody by car or bus. The unseen River Sherbourne has a role in the operation of the new baths. The swimming pools are emptied into it. The filtration system in the building can deal with a quarter of a million gallons of water an hour and a complete turnover of water every three hours. Coventry had to wait until 1966 for its new baths, but when they came they made amends for twenty years of frustration! Here the City Council run an advanced swimming coaching scheme, and the City of Coventry team is among the best in the country.

Fairfax Street, in which the baths stand, was made in recent years, and is developing with shops and other premises. Flowing underneath in culvert is the River Sherbourne. High above the street level is the new cathedral, which we were able to admire from Pool Meadow and other vantage points around. Gradually, it has been built in, so that the views have been lost. New buildings around it block the view, but not on Pool Meadow where we still wait for a new bus station. The Fairfax Street frontage is infilled by the De Vere Hotel, and by the second hall of residence of the Lanchester Polytechnic, and together they enclose Cathedral Square. This is a pleasant paved open space with public benches, trees, and an imposing flight of stone steps leading to Priory Street. The De Vere's frontage looks on to the square, and the rear has access direct from the multi-storey car park. The hotel's 200 bedrooms are a big boost to the tourist and conference hopes of the city. Since *Portrait of Coventry* appeared in 1972, Broadgate, at the top of the town, has changed.

Coventry Corporation, so progressive elsewhere, have now dealt with the row of 'temporary' shops that fronted Broadgate near to Holy Trinity, the only side of Broadgate that had not been redeveloped. When the shops were erected after the wartime damage, nobody could have imagined that they would still be pulling in the customers thirty years later! The Corporation even took one into use themselves as their information centre, boosting the new Coventry from premises that should have gone long ago. But now they have gone, and a grassed area has been laid.

Near to Broadgate are Holy Trinity Church, the cathedral ruins, St. Mary's Hall, and, round the corner, Priory Row. This is a popular area for tourists and the pride of Coventrians when they show their visitors round. Small boys who climb the steps of the cathedral tower shout gleefully down to their friends below. It is an area that has seen many generations of small boys up there, in fact it is five hundred years since the cathedral spire, 300 or 303 feet high (it is varied in the different accounts of it) was built. It is higher than the 237-foot spire of Trinity and that at Christ Church, 211 feet, which is the oldest. The area has had its influence on surrounding development. No new scheme has been allowed that might mar the new cathedral.

Opposite it, in Priory Street, stands the twenty-storey, 157 study-bedroom tower block for residents of the Lanchester Polytechnic, built only after controversy about the effect it might have on the new cathedral. The plans were approved by the Royal Fine Arts Commission after changes had been made to alter its outline, making it more fluted than it had appeared in the original design. Both the Cathedral Council and the architect, Sir Basil Spence, approved the plans. The Fine Arts Commission were also consulted over the design of the De Vere Hotel, and the second hall of residence. The general layout of the Lanchester buildings, set among lawns, trees, and walks, makes a pleasing blend with the cathedral, and it is so quiet an area that it does not appear to be close to a busy centre. It is part of a civic area, with the art gallery, library, council offices, police headquarters and telephone exchange, swimming baths and law courts, in a group.

Coventry's central area does not sprawl, it is all planned with a purpose—civic area, precincts, offices—and its 450 acres are neatly enclosed by the city engineer's inner ring road. This in itself is a major redevelopment achievement, and has been marked by the praiseworthy way the council's officers have handled the problems of those hundreds of people who have had to move from homes, shops, and businesses on account of it. Long before work on the road began, the officers were informing, negotiating, making arrangements for relocations. There might have been uproar, instead it was remarkably peaceful. The odd businessman protested, that was all. Much of the property was old, and was doomed anyway. The occupiers moved to more modern homes.

Construction of the ring road was completed after fifteen years. It sounds perhaps a long time to make 2¼ miles, but difficulties, planning, technical, and financial, delayed each stage.

There were changes of ideas, and of traffic growth. The first short stage between London Road and St. Patrick's Road, which was opened in December 1959, was hailed as progress, a milestone, yet it was already out of date when the last stage was being built, twelve years later, to absorb it and fit it for present-day needs! It was estimated, in 1959, that the ring road would cost £3 million, but the final figure (inclusive of land charges), was £13 million. There were to be nine roundabouts, but now there are mainly overpasses and underpasses, and even some multi-level junctions. It is a spectacular sweep of road, rising and falling, and has two- and three-lane dual carriageways. The ring road, and the radial arms that have been made linking traffic to it, have swathed through property, stopped up roads, brought us subways and overbridges. We have built another defensive wall like the old city wall, this time to keep the through traffic out!

The city centre benefits enormously from the road. At each successive stage there has been noticeable traffic relief. It is quicker to skirt the city by the ring road than go through it. Quick, yes, but not at the expense of road safety. One of the bonuses of the new road has been its good accident record. Since its completion, traffic management has gone a stage forward with the intro-duction of a traffic control centre that monitors traffic flows on main roads and meets demands by altering the frequencies of traffic lights.

Coventry is proud of its centre, but, equally important, great progress has also been made to meet other needs of a community lacking houses, schools, clinics, and hospital facilities, after the war. So outside the ring road there have also been wholesale changes, and, because the city plan requires more road schemes, there are future changes in store. The greatest need that faced the city council was for housing. War damage had made inroads on the housing stock, and the population had grown rapidly because of the influx of workers. There was also a high birth rate after the war.

Many of the people, mostly young, had arrived to do war work, and a large number lived in industrial hostels, and in prefabricated bungalows. The end of the war brought no relief, for migrants were flowing in, having heard of Coventry as a 'boom city'. The factories were busy on peacetime production, with universal demand for their products, and were paying well over average rates. It made a serious housing problem worse. For a short time when they were desperate for shelter, some people 'squatted', breaking into houses that were still empty after being requisitioned during the war, and temporarily living in them. The council, pushing ahead with the centre because it was also much-needed and it was good for public morale to see it developing, had to mount an all-out housing drive for the 14,000 applicants, plus their families, on the waiting list. But building-trade labour was in short supply and brick construction was impossible. Speed was the vital factor. It was found in the 'no fines' concrete houses and flats built by the contractors, George Wimpey.

The system needed no reinforcement in the concrete. It was poured into shuttering to build walls, and houses and blocks of flats went up at a phenomenal rate at Tile Hill, where the rapid progress so pleased all concerned that one of the roads was named Jardine Crescent in honour of the Wimpey site supervisor of that name. The estate, though quickly built, won a Ministry of Housing and local Government award for its layout, and has remained a pleasant and well-maintained council estate, a corporation showpiece. Wimpey went on to some other districts and built housing estates by the same method. Altogether they constructed about 10,000 dwellings for the city. The large estates were provided with district centres on the precincted shopping principle. The £1 million district centre at Bell Green won a Ministry commendation for good design in 1965, and at Willenhall Wood Estate there were Ministry and Civic Trust awards. It was here that Coventry pioneered in this country the Rayburn system of housing. The houses have their frontages to green walks instead of roads, and all services are at the back. Several other awards have been won.

Coventry Corporation now own about 27,000 properties, of all types—houses, flats, special bungalows for the disabled, old people's bungalows, and tower blocks. There are clusters of ten-storey blocks at Spon Street and Hillfields, distinctive with their rooftop ventilation units which have the appearance of wings. Tower blocks were one answer to the housing shortage and to the high cost of sites in built-up areas, but they were an experiment in living for most Coventry people. There had been no structures of this kind before the war. Some people, especially those with young children, have not liked this form of accommodation, and would rather endure a longer wait in the queue until they could have a house, or perhaps a ground-floor flat. Tower blocks, even those of only six storeys, proved unpopular with tenants and the Council decided not to build any more. But the all-out housing drive did reduce the housing waiting list to fewer than 5,000 by the early seventies. And the Housing Committee was able to say that none of the remaining families was in urgent need. The crisis was over. They had built 20,000 dwellings. Another 24,000 had been erected privately. The tempo slowed down in the seventies due to policy changes and economies, and in 1981 the waiting list was up to 7,600.

With housing, the cry was 'more schools'. Progress has been remarkable in education with many new primary schools, a ring of comprehensives, colleges, and a university. Coventry was a pioneer of the comprehensives in the provinces, adopting this policy to cope with the explosion in school population. The old-style schools were mainly the brick-built, high-windowed, pre-war elementaries, in tiny hard-surfaced playgrounds among terraced back streets. They were renamed secondary moderns, given huts to help the accommodation problem, but were the same old cramped premises in the end. They catered for most senior children. There were a few other schools—the four grammars, the school of art, a junior technical school, a commercial school, and small private schools.

The grammar schools were the two independent schools for boys, Bablake, and King Henry VIII, and two local authority schools for girls, Barr's Hill, and Stoke Park. The boys' schools took in fee-payers, and some of these places were paid for by the local authority. The boys selected faced fierce competition in the examinations because there were hopelessly few places for the many who wanted them. It was not enough to do well in the eleven-plus. Only the boys right at the top of the pass list could go to grammar school. For the girls, all places at the two girls' schools were open. Faced with an even larger school population, the council had either to build more secondary moderns and grammar schools, which would have perpetuated the much-criticized eleven-plus examination, or build comprehensives, to which, when there was enough of them, all junior-school pupils could transfer without examination and be educated according to ability and aptitude.

The Education Committee were enthusiastic about the new schools, but there was a great deal of controversy, from people who saw the comprehensive as being too large, losing the personal touch, and its education as a levelling-down of bright children who would not be able to go to grammar school. And what would be the effect on the independent grammar schools? Were they doomed when, having provided sufficient places in comprehensives, the local authority no longer required the places that it was paying for? We now have the answers. The comprehensives gain academic and sporting successes. The independent schools flourish, Bablake and Henry VIII, now linked by the Coventry School Foundation, filled as before but now by fee-payers, plus some winners of special places, as yet unaffected by loss of Council-sponsored places.

The first two comprehensives, afterwards much-visited by other education authorities, were The Woodlands, Broad Lane, and Caludon Castle, Wyken, both for boys, and both opened in 1954. As the nucleus for the schools, boys of the old Junior Technical School transfered to The Woodlands, and those of John Gulson School, to Caludon Castle. Each school had a catchment area, and boys living in it were able to go to the comprehensive without having to pass an examination. In addition, each school accepted boys from other parts of the city who passed examinations. As the number of schools increased, catchment areas were adjusted, and more and more boys and girls were able to go to their local comprehensive, regardless of examination result. Now it was the turn of some parents, not the same as those who originally were anti-comprehensive, to complain that because of the area in which they lived, their children had less chance of going to one of the new schools! There were many petitions, and meetings. Some of the pioneers of the system in Coventry, now dead, would have smiled wryly at the situation. They had to address meetings where they were challenged on the wisdom of their policy. There are now twenty-one comprehensives, not all purpose-built. Barrs Hill and Stoke Park were formerly municipal grammars. The new schools, set in landscaped areas, with gymnasiums, swimming pools, sports grounds, laboratories, workshops, house blocks and assembly halls, are places where children can go as far as their talents will take them, staying if they wish into their late teens. The eleven-plus? It was abolished in 1971. The old schools remain, some as annexes to the comprehensives, some as junior schools, some as community centres.

Coventry has over 60,000 primary and secondary school-children, compared with 24,000 just before the war, and even in those days it had overcrowding problems, and some very large schools in terms of pupil numbers. Stoke Council School had 1,600, and there were 1,500 at Barkers' Butts. Frederick Bird had 1,256, and others over the one thousand mark were Holbrook Lane (1,154), Whoberley (1,057), and Folly Lane (1,032). Some schools had what were called central advanced classes with a four-year course for selected senior boys and girls. These schools were Frederick Bird, John Gulson, and Wheatley Street. To continue their education when they left school boys and girls could attend evening classes at various schools, where there were two-year courses in engineering, commercial and domestic subjects. These were linked up with higher courses continued at the technical college evening classes. The junior technical and the day commercial schools had two-year courses for pupils who entered in their thirteenth year to prepare for careers in engineering or commerce.

The Municipal Art School, in Ford Street—it has gone now—originated in 1844, when the silk industry was so important in Coventry as a 'school of design', catering for those who were expecting to make a career in art in trades, or to become artists or teachers of art. It had special courses for architects, illustrators, typographers, painters and decorators and sign writers, and others.

A school quite different from the others under the aegis of Coventry Education Authority is the City of Coventry Residential Boys' School, in the countryside of Shropshire, at Cleobury Mortimer. It was originally a wartime camp school under Government auspices, and Coventry boys went there as evacuees. It was so beneficial that some years after the war when the Government were no longer interested in them, as the need had passed, Coventry decided to buy the school at Cleobury Mortimer, and to continue it for boys whose parents wished them to go, paying according to income towards the cost of upkeep. It ran successfully, but numbers fell, and the City Council decided to close it in 1982 as it was not educationally viable.

It was college, singular, before the war, with only the technical college in Coventry; but the expansion in higher education since then has been remarkable. The technical college was heavily overloaded, with 14,000 enrolments a year of part-time students, plus hundreds full-time, and an annexe was opened in a wartime hostel at Haynestone Road. Later there were more annexes at the old Leigh Mills, Hill Street, and then in the vacant Winfray factory in the Butts. The Henley College of Further Education, at Bell Green, and Tile Hill College of Further Education on the other side of the city, were built to help cope, but the 'Tech' continues to be at full stretch, still needs annexes and has added another department, that of the School of Music. The Lanchester College of Technology, at a more advanced level, was started almost in the city's High Street, at Priory Street, its first buildings being taken into use in 1960. The Hereward College for the physically handicapped, at Tile Hill Lane, the Coventry College of Education at Canley, and the University of Warwick at Gibbet Hill Road, add up to an impressive array of higher-education facilities, and Coventry has become a student city.

The College of Education was first on the scene. It began life as a hostel of huts for war workers, but the shortage of teachers, and need for quick training of recruits to the profession, led to its use as a teacher-training college. It had the accommodation for students, and the assembly hall and communal buildings for teaching purposes. From this modest beginning it was gradually redeveloped, with permanent buildings. In 1978 the college merged with the university and is now the Faculty of Educational Studies. In the 1960s a look at education in the city would have included Coventry College of Art, but it seemed doomed right from the start. It began with great hopes in Cope Street shortly after the war, opening with the school of printing, and in time was to be extended into a full college. But at about the same time 'big brother'—the Lanchester College—was being built and the two were to be side by side. The Lanchester could not stop growing; it dwarfed the College of Art, and then, because more accommodation was needed, 'swallowed' its neighbour.

So that its premises could be taken over, the College of Art moved out, to a new building at the corner of Gosford Street and Cox Street, and there seemed set for an independent career. In 1970, however, the Lanchester was redesignated by the Ministry of Education as a polytechnic, and merged with the College of Art and the Rugby College of Engineering Technology. So the College of Art became the faculty of art and design for the polytechnic. The polytechnic has continued to grow, dominating

Cox Street, Jordan Well, Much Park Street, and one side of Gosford Street, and bridging Priory Street with a hall of residence. It covers sites that were occupied by Coventry Baths, the Triumph Works, terraced houses, shops, and public houses of Cox Street, Cope Street and New Street, houses and old graveyards in Priory Street, business property of Jordan Well, the old Lea Francis works and property in Much Park and Gosford Streets. Student activity has changed the local scene, brought the novelty of a rag week and procession that raises large sums for charities, and infiltrated into the working population a cheerful young element in college scarves, who come from many parts of the country and from overseas. The polytechnic was named after Dr. Frederick William Lanchester (1868–1946), who was a pioneer of the British petrol-driven car, and one of the originators of the theory of flight. He became connected with Coventry when his firm was taken over by Daimler.

Henley and Tile Hill colleges of further education are chiefly for local students, but the Hereward is another education centre in Coventry that caters for students from far afield. It is a national college, purpose-built for the handicapped, with wide doorways, and ramps for wheelchairs and similar aids, and disability is no bar to the gaining of higher education qualifications.

There has been a transformation at Gibbet Hill Road in the arrival of a university. For this the councils of Coventry and Warwickshire jointly made a gift of 417 acres of pasture land on the city outskirts, spreading over the county boundary, so the impact on the city has been less marked and is confined to that area. From the Kenilworth Road—the main road joined by Gibbet Hill Road—the city dweller's impression of the university is of students waiting for buses or lifts, to the city or away from it. The buildings cannot be seen unless a special trip is made along Gibbet Hill Road, which used to be a little-used country lane between farms, and off the motorists' map. University blocks have infiltrated the rural scene, and occupy a long sloping site, but still in a green setting. It is about 3 miles from the city centre, and $1\frac{1}{2}$ miles from the town of Kenilworth. As it is an outpost, special efforts have been made to link the university with the community. There have been open days, courses for the public in certain subjects, and use of the buildings for conferences and meetings of outside organizations. The university's arts centre attracts the public. It has two theatres, with a regular programme of plays, music, and films, and is a welcome extension of the amenities in the city.

Lord Rootes, former chief of the Rootes Group, the car manufacturers, was to have been the first chancellor of the University of Warwick. He had been among those who put great efforts into the promotion of it, but he died while still chancellor-designate, and Lord Radcliffe was appointed chancellor, and Mr. J. B. Butterworth vice-chancellor. Lord Rootes's association with it is commemorated in the name of Rootes Hall, the first hall that was built. The university was opened in 1965, with an initial intake of 430, and with a planned expansion taking the number of students to 5,000 in about twelve years, and ultimately to 15,000. When they leave the campus, students have a choice of going into the city or out to the towns of Kenilworth, Warwick, and Leamington, all lying close; and the good communications of motorways, and bus and rail travel, can get them to London and other destinations quickly and conveniently.

Coventry's post-war programme did not overlook the special needs of the older people, and deprived children. Homes that are homely were the objective. The old people's homes are not large, they have separate and communal rooms, and they are fitted out very comfortably. Where people share accommodation it cannot be exactly like home, but if they accept that they must lose some of their independence, the old people have the best of conditions. As time goes on it is being found that the average age of residents is increasing and many of them become frail, and could not in any case look after themselves in their own homes. There are sixteen homes for the elderly, most with about forty places. The council have also built old people's bungalows and sheltered flats.

The children's homes are strictly anonymous, so that the boys and girls can grow up in a normal way among other children. Each home has about nine children who live as a family, with an 'aunt' and 'uncle'. Each home is indistinguishable from its neighbours; the children attend the local school, join the scouts, or other organizations, and 'uncle' goes to work. This is the next best thing to home for children who have perhaps lost parents, or one parent, or who have come into the authority's care for other reasons—perhaps a broken home. The corporation rely a lot on foster parents to take many of the children they look after, which is another way of giving them a family.

Hospital services in Coventry have improved very much after years of struggling under great difficulties, trying to deal with a much-increased population, in buildings that were inadequate. After the bombing they were repaired, and there were extensions —but not at all on the scale that the new Coventry needed.

Long waits at out-patients' departments at Stoney Stanton Road; long lists of people awaiting admission; hard work for doctors and staff, doing wonders in unsatisfactory conditions for more people than they should have been expected to deal with; in some hospital wards, long rows of beds, and some 'overflow' beds occasionally parked down the centre of a ward. Coventry people had to wait, but in 1968 came the opening of Walsgrave General, and the maternity hospital, a project of more than £6 million by Birmingham Regional Hospital Board, and the 'last word' in hospital accommodation. The general has 614 beds, the maternity 203. A psychiatric block has been added. The site is almost out of the city, at Clifford Bridge Road, in the countryside. Wards are spacious, divided into cubicles with varying numbers of beds, and separate sitting-room-dining-room areas for the walking patients. Telephones—and for meals, choice from a menu.

The internal planning includes operating theatres placed close to the wards. There is storage space for patients' belongings. These seem obvious facilities, but Coventry people had not known such luxuries before. We stayed in bed or sat alongside it, without anywhere like a sitting-room to potter off to. We accepted our fare from the trolley like men, and we were wheeled along passageways and lifted up and down steps—quite a trip!—before we reached the operating theatre. Keresley branch hospital was closed with the opening of Walsgrave, but what memories some Coventry folk have of it! Whatever the weather, patients were wheeled out of the wards and across the grounds to the theatre, for the wards were separate blocks. The Queen performed the Walsgrave opening on June 30, 1970, talking to staff and patients on her tour of the wards.

New churches, public houses, and clubs are also part of post-war Coventry, a happy hunting ground for builders since the war. One building that Coventry badly needed was a better railway station, to replace the small and dingy station that survived the war, with its one platform up and one down. It was so inadequate that holidaymakers had to stand in long queues outside the station. The modern station has four platforms, is all glass and light, with a large airy booking hall, clean and bright shops. Outside are taxis and the large car park, and a railbus that connects with train arrivals and departures. British Rail were kind to us, and Beeching economies had not begun when this station, costing £1 million, was planned. Any visitor arriving by rail has an immediate impression that he is about to see a modern and pleasing city.

IV

CATHEDRAL OF OUR TIME

AN ESTIMATED ten million people in ten years visited the cathedral after it was consecrated in 1962. In the first two years 4½ million queued. There have been visitors from all over the world—royalty, peers, heads of state, ambassadors, bishops, tourists, and the everyday folk from various parts of England, brought by coach, car, and train. At the height of the rush, British Rail ran sixty special trains in a year, bringing in people from all points of the compass. The attraction was such that when a London coach operator applied for a licence to run trips to it, he explained that he had found that people taken to see Kenilworth Castle—5 miles away—were slipping away and catching the bus to Coventry to see the cathedral! The queues were huge then, but the attendances now have steadied down, although an estimate of 660,000 a year shows what a draw this cathedral is.

And is there anywhere a link-up quite like that of the beautiful ruins of the old cathedral, with the new one designed by Sir Basil Spence? The ruins are open to the sky with their sturdy walls, pinnacles, and the graceful tracery of the windows; the altar made from stones and rubble heaped up after the raid; the charred cross from the half-burnt timbers; the cross of nails, formed from large nails that lay around after the firebombs had done their work, and the words "Father Forgive". The ruins, treated to make them weather resistant, are a mute, but eloquent, reminder that war is waste. Here, when they were filled with debris, stood King George VI when he came to Coventry after the raid—a stone pillar, the King's Pinnacle, marks the spot. People walk, look in, take photographs, sit on benches in the sun, and seem, one and all, spellbound by the ruins.

Bishop Neville Gorton, remembered with affection by everybody as a benign, unconventional saintly man, was enthroned in the ruins in 1943. He died in 1955, before the new cathedral was above ground level, and fittingly for the ruins were his only cathedral—he and his wife are buried here. His successor, Dr. Cuthbert Bardsley, a breezy, forthright personality, was also enthroned in the ruins, and for him the great moment was when he consecrated the new building. The ruins have had a powerful message, for from them have gone crosses of nails, more than one hundred of them, across the world, given, and accepted, in the spirit of reconciliation and hope. They were formed from the fourteenth-century hand-made nails, of varying size, found in the rubble when the timbers had burnt away. Some were picked up and bound with wire in the shape of the cross and later silvered. So the idea was born.

Crosses of nails have been given to royalty and bishops, statesmen and missionaries, cathedrals and churches. There are several in Germany. One of the first to be given was that which Provost Howard took with him to Kiel immediately after the war in a gesture of friendship, and in return he was given a stone from Kiel Cathedral, which was destroyed. This is the Kiel Stone of Forgiveness in the Chapel of Unity. At Dresden, in East Germany, there is a cross of nails; also in East and West Berlin, and in Lubeck in north Germany, home of Herr Willi Brandt, the West German Chancellor who has great interest in the cathedral at Coventry. There are crosses of nails in many parts of the world, in great cathedrals and in small parish churches in remote parts of the globe. The 'cross of nails centres', as they are called, are jointly working for reconciliation, in all its aspects—between divided nations or peoples, between races—a network of prayerful effort, a means of communication. Apart from the nails, the burnt timbers had a use. Thousands of small crosses were made from them and sold, raising nearly £200 for the cathedral rebuilding fund, and masonry was also sold for the fund.

The ruins are seldom without some activity. Today it is the steady stream of visitors, and in the past there have been great occasions. The victory of Alamein, celebrated by ringing the bells in the tower on 15th November 1942, was one of them. It was not permitted to sound bells until then, because church bells were to be a signal of invasion. There was VE Day, 1945, when Coventry people in their thousands surged joyfully into the ruins which were bedecked with flags and flowers. The Festival of Britain and the Coronation of Queen Elizabeth II were celebrated here. Many special services have been held in the ruins, and it has become an open-air theatre. Before the rubble had been moved a play was performed. In 1949 the stage was built. Young German members of a group for reconcilliation came and worked on a voluntary project, restoring war-damaged vestries. These now form the tiny international centre, in one corner, where anyone is invited to enter, mingle, and have refreshments. For foreign visitors there are shelves of books in their own languages. Here, chat and cups of tea are the simple formula for making friends.

In his book, *Ruined and Rebuilt*, Provost Howard comments on the very great interest which German people have shown in the cathedral, and he says that many of them, visiting the ruins, had earnest talks with him and afterwards went away "with a sense of release and joy". Provost Howard wasted no time on recrimination after the bombing, but straightaway gave expression to his theme of reconciliation, even before the last of the heavy raids. The Cathedral Council matched this in their own sphere, for early in 1941 they met to consider plans for the rebuilding, and passed a resolution to build on or near to the site of the ruins. They formed a rebuilding commission to make plans, and the commission invited Sir Giles Gilbert Scott, who had designed Liverpool Anglican Cathedral, to design the new building for Coventry. Not to rebuild was unthinkable, evidently, although, with the splendid and large church of Holy Trinity just a few yards away, there was a voice suggesting that this might well become the new cathedral for Coventry.

Sir Giles submitted designs for a building on the site of the old, planned round a central altar, and the Cathedral Council gave their approval, but the designs failed to receive the approval of the Royal Fine Arts Commission. The upshot was that Sir Giles withdrew. He felt that in any case it would be several years before work could begin on any scheme, and that he would be too old to be involved by then. It was 'back to square one' for the Cathedral Council, who now appointed a commission to advise them. The commission came to the conclusion that (a) the ruined walls could not support a new structure and (b) that an open competition should be held to select a design. The competition, held in 1951, was open to the members of the Commonwealth, and it received 219 entries. The winning design—to preserve the ruins and to build a new cathedral alongside—was that of Basil Spence, an architect who had offices in Edinburgh and London. He wrote long afterwards that too little thought had been given

The University of Warwick
Whitley Abbey comprehensive school

by the competition organizers to the best way of handling the news about the winning design.

News of the decision was announced before he had time to prepare a suitable perspective drawing for the Press, for the rules of the competition did not allow one to be submitted and therefore only technical drawings were available. These appeared in the Press and the result was unfortunate. They did not reproduce well and there was a lot of talk about a "concrete monstrosity". The design became the subject of criticism and national controversy and the architect, elated first at his success, was now heavily criticized and received abusive mail. The consequences were drastic, for he did not receive another commission for two years and had to dispense with the services of some of his staff. He has said that he was near bankruptcy. It was a heavy price to pay for winning the competition.

Happily, it ended in success, for later he received numerous commissions, was elected president of the Royal Institute of British Architects, and was knighted. The cathedral impresses visitors, although readers of a magazine, *Design and Components in Engineering*, in 1967 voted Coventry Cathedral the ugliest building in the Midlands, and the sixth ugliest in the country! Basil Spence wanted the exterior to be simple, but some have described it as "stark". Far from being a 'concrete monstrosity', it has walls of pink-grey sandstone, as he had intended in the beginning. This required 34,000 stones—the Hollington stone from Staffordshire.

Quite apart from the design, there was opposition to the building of any kind of cathedral, from Coventry City Council. They did not think it was an opportune time to build a cathedral, they said, when there was a shortage of labour and materials and a great need in the city for houses, shops, schools, and other buildings required for the community. It was a view fully appreciated by the Cathedral Reconstruction Committee, but they did not regard it as being valid, because the cathedral would be of stone not needed in housing, and the craftsmen who built it would not be from the labour force engaged on housing. Sir David Eccles, Minister of Works, received a city council deputation to hear their views, and later gave his decision in favour of the cathedral. His letter giving permission made the point that the cathedral was not the concern of Coventry alone.

The echo of the bombs on Coventry had gone round the world.

Award-winning housing estate at Henley Road

"We cannot tell how many people are waiting in this country and abroad, for this church to rise and prove that English traditions live again after the blitz," he wrote. Building work was controlled by licence because of the scarcity of materials, and Sir David gave a permit to spend £985,000. The final cost of the Cathedral was £1,385,000. Preliminary work began in June 1954, three years after Spence's design had been chosen. First of all, graves had to be cleared and this took many months. The main building contract was given to John Laing and Sons Ltd., in stages. The first, for the foundations, was in January 1955. Work on the superstructure began in 1957.

Laings regarded the cathedral project as an honour, and approached it with the belief that they should produce work that would compare with that of the cathedral craftsmen of bygone days. They sent a letter to the senior employees chosen to do the work, reminding them how Sir Christopher Wren, in the building of St. Paul's, personally examined the stone round the coast of England to find that which stood up best to the effects of tide, frost and sun, and stressing that they too, should be as careful, in all they had to do for the cathedral. It was to be, the letter said, a building that would endure a thousand years, and from the standpoint of beauty it should compare with cathedrals built about the year 1200.

This was the spirit that animated all who were engaged on work for the cathedral. In eight years of work, with hundreds of men involved, no hint of labour unrest was heard. They seemed to realize that it was a unique experience—a cathedral of our time using the skills and techniques of the day, on trial as an example of twentieth-century workmanship. Yet it had to owe something to the past. The great tapestry of Christ in glory was woven on a loom 500 years old, in a French workshop. It had to be woven in one solid piece and it was found that it could not be done in Britain because of the size—about 74 feet 8 inches by 38 feet wide. There was a loom 40 feet wide at the works of Pinton Freres at Felletin, near Aubusson, where there had been skilled workers in the craft from the Middle Ages. Ten weavers were engaged on it continuously for two years, using wool from Australia, some local French wool, and doing their own dyeing using water from the local River Creuse.

The firm have guaranteed the tapestry for 500 years! The full title is "Christ in Glory in the Tetramorph", the tetramorph being the name given to the four figures, representing the four evangelists and referred to in the Book of Revelation, Chapter Four: the eagle for St. John, the ox for St. Luke, the lion for St. Mark, and the man for St. Matthew. The lower part of the tapestry forms a separate design of the crucifixion, and serves as the reredos of the Lady Chapel. The tapestry is a mass of glowing colours—the panels outlined in yellow on a background of deep green. It weighs about a ton, and was flown from France in an aircraft subsequently renamed *City of Coventry*. An anonymous Coventry donor paid for the tapestry, which cost £20,000.

Spence, and the reconstruction committee, were determined on engaging the best talent for the cathedral, and for the tapestry they chose Graham Sutherland, war artist, landscape and portrait painter. It is the largest tapestry in the world, and the dominating feature that meets people as they enter the building at the west door. From a great height the calm gaze of Christ in majesty greets them. The figure of Christ is so large that another figure of a man, between his feet, looks puny, although it is life-size. A tapestry was visualized by the architect from the outset, when he first visited the ruins and was thinking of entering the competition. Within five minutes, he wrote, he knew what he wanted to build there and how it would look. Back he went to Edinburgh—and did his first plan within the next twenty four hours.

He was inspired, he felt, on that first visit, which he found to be a stirring and moving experience. He saw the ruins, a "lace-like screen of masonry, buttresses and pinnacles", as the Christian sacrifice, while the new cathedral would represent the triumph of reconciliation. The new would have a simple exterior of pinky grey stone, and a rich interior "and huge tapestry behind the high altar". As for the zig-zag walls, they were an amendment to the original design, which he says he dreamt of while he was under the anaesthetic at his dentist's!

This proved very effective when the building was completed, with the wall line regularly broken, and it enabled the stained glass windows to be aligned as they are, looking towards the altar. On the Priory Street frontage the other point of contrast is the Chapel of Christ the Servant which is rounded, as opposed to the angular main wall, and projects forward of it. Entrance from this approach is by the massive flight of stone steps, where, fixed to the wall, is Sir Jacob Epstein's striking 25-feet-high bronze sculpture of St. Michael and the Devil. The famous sculptor died

in 1959 while the work was being cast, and it was unveiled by
Lady Epstein. On the other side, from St. Michael's Avenue, the
exterior of the cathedral is treated like that in Priory Street,
with the Chapel of Unity projecting from the main building. It is
an arresting shape, like a Crusader's Tent, and is finished in
green slate.

But the best approach to the new cathedral, to get the impression of old merging into new, is by way of the ruins: descending
the twenty steps that lead down to it, passing under the high
porch that acts as a physical link between the two, to the west
door. The whole of the west wall is of plate glass, weighing seven
tons, with ninety-six panels engraved with figures of saints and
angels, designed by John Hutton. With such a wall, there is no
feeling of separation of the ruins from the new building—they
merge and belong. There is a through-view, into the nave and to
the sanctuary of the new cathedral, while from inside it there
is a view into the ruins. Here, clearly, is a cathedral where nothing
takes place behind closed doors!

Space and height are the first impression inside the building,
then the tapestry rivets the eye, as do the radiant lights of John
Piper's beautiful and colourful baptistry window, particularly if
the sun is shining in. The window is 64 feet high and 84 feet
wide, and has 195 separate panels. They are abstracts, and were
made by Patrick Reyntiens to Piper's design.

If the cathedral is toured from the left-hand door, the first
opening is also on the left, into the Chapel of Unity, an idea
pioneered by the cathedral and requiring special approval of the
ecclesiastical authorities. This was given only after a reasoned case
had been argued, because when it was planned there was not the
same thinking that exists today about the need for church unity.
The chapel is interdenominational, born out of Coventry's
wartime experience of close co-operation between the Church of
England and the Free Churches.

While it is a physical part of the cathedral, the chapel is run
separately, by a joint council, and the aim is to use it as a centre to
bring about closer ties between different denominations. It has
joint chairmen of the Church of England, Roman Catholic
Church, and Free Churches. Unusual in concept, the chapel is
also unusual in structure. Its Crusader's Tent shape alludes to the
crusade it is waging for church unity. The ground plan, a star,
alludes to the star of Bethlehem which leads to Christ. The

chapel was dedicated on Whit Tuesday 1962 by Dr. W. A. Visser, general secretary of the World Council of Churches. Everything has a meaning. "That they may be one" is the inscription on the threshold, and the Cross is black, to signify mourning for the division of the Church. The Church of Sweden paid for the inlaid floor, designed by Einar Forseth, a famous Swedish artist; and a gift from Germany paid for the long, narrow, stained-glass windows between the buttresses, designed by Margaret Traherne.

On the walls round the cathedral from the chapel are the large 'Tablets of the Word', irregular lettering of texts, by Ralph Beyer, and below them, the pilgrim seats. The primitive lettering is said to be symbolic—the texts those which the early Christians passed along by word of mouth, the symbols like those carved on the walls of the catacombs under Rome, so linking the church today with those early Christians. Prominently displayed alongside, calling attention to today's circumstances—an appeal for donations with the message that it costs a lot of money to maintain the cathedral!

Passing the Tablets, now, steps lead down to the undercroft, but this is open to visitors only three times a day, when parties are taken down by a guide. The treasury and museum here attract great interest. There are about one hundred relics, some on loan. They include medieval objects like brooches and buckles and brass pins found during excavations of the first cathedral and the priory, and modern articles like the trowel and mallet used by the Queen at the foundation stone service in 1956. There are designs and paintings done by John Piper, and cartoons by John Hutton, for their windows; fragments of glass, charred coins, and other items picked up after the destruction of the cathedral in the raid. There are robes and vestments and some of the cathedral's valuable plate.

The undercroft, now divided into small rooms, was first a large area designed for use as a storeplace. The idea of using it for services led to its adaptation as the Chapel of the Cross, and, after its first service on New Year's Eve 1958, it was used for cathedral services for nearly four years, while up above work continued on the superstructure. The clergy use some of the rooms in the undercroft for a vestry and social centre and there is a library furnished by a gift from Kiel. A modern building for a modern age, the cathedral has its television control room and sound broadcasting studio here.

Returning to the ground floor, the Lady Chapel is at the foot of the tapestry. Behind the High Altar, a plain solid block, is a view of the five pairs of nave windows. These cannot be seen on entering the cathedral because they are fitted into the zig-zag of the walls so as to face the altar, and they are aligned so that they receive the full benefit of the morning and afternoon sun, streaming through the coloured glass into the nave. But from the High Altar they can be seen in their full glory. They represent, in pairs and in colour pairing too, the stages from birth to after-life. They are the work of Lawrence Lee, Geoffrey Clarke, and Keith New, of the Royal College of Art department of stained glass.

Much of the interior work in the cathedral is strange to anyone accustomed to seeing orthodox furnishings inside cathedrals and churches. It is full of surprises. There are no memorial tablets or regimental colours in view. There are no pews. It is a place of clinical cleanliness, with shining marble floor, rows of chairs. The eye never rests. It alights on the High Altar, unadorned and severe, the massive candlesticks that match it, and the Cross with a surrealist shape which was inspired by the charred cross in the ruins. Cupped in the Cross, as if in a hand, is the cross of nails that was carried on a pilgrimage throughout the diocese before the cathedral was consecrated. And all those birds—on closer examination what first looked like birds in flight are found to be massed thorns, the crown of thorns over the Bishop's throne and choir stalls. Equally striking, but in a different way, is the beautiful little Chapel of Christ in Gethsemane.

This small chapel for private prayer by those with intense personal problems and sorrows—since it was in the garden of Gethsemane that Christ suffered great torment—stands out for many as one of the special treasures of the cathedral. It is viewed through an iron screen which represents the crown of thorns, made to Spence's design by the Royal Engineers, who gave it, and on the back wall are ceramics by Stephen Sykes, depicting the angel and the chalice. There is a mosaic on the right, portraying the sleeping disciples. The chapel was designed to catch maximum light and to deflect it on to the angled wall, so that those who pray there will always find some brightness.

The cathedral has not gone so 'mod' that it has made a clean break with tradition. The city's churches had chapels in them for the craft guilds. The modern concept of this is the Chapel of Christ the Servant, or the industrial chapel; and the modern counterpart of the medieval craft guilds are the city's employers and trade unions. The cross in it was made, and given, by the Coventry Apprentices' Association. The industrial chapel has clear windows, and there is a reason for it. They are a reminder to those within, of the constant activity that surrounds them. The inscription, "I am among you as one that serves", reminds them that Jesus is constantly with them. The cathedral is very conscious that it has a role to play in industry, and its staff are in constant touch, making works visits, mixing with employers and working men.

As remarkable as any of the furnishings in this surely unique cathedral is the font. It is a 3-ton boulder in its natural state, with the basin carved out at the top. It is a bit of Bethlehem in Coventry, for it came from there and made its journey in a wonderful way. It was transported stage by stage, by land and sea, at the instance of many people of various religious beliefs and races, as a goodwill gesture, without any charge to or any organization on the part of, the cathedral. And it arrived at the time of goodwill, on Christmas Eve, a timely gesture indeed. The idea was that of a London architect, Frankland Dark. From then on, there was generous co-operation from all parties. The boulder font, standing at the foot of the baptistry window, is a symbol—albeit a bulky one!—of how doctrine and prejudice go overboard when men are inspired by a noble thought.

And a lot of people have been inspired to give something to this cathedral. The bulk of the cost was defrayed by a £1 million war-damage payment in respect of the destroyed cathedral and contents, and another £150,000 was given through the Bishop of Coventry's diocesan appeal. In Canada, a tour by Provost Howard, Canon Ross, and Mr. Spence, raised £22,000. Choirs and organists over there also gave £10,000 towards the cost of the organ. Lord Kenilworth (the first) gave £100,000 as an endowment for fabric maintenance and support of clergy, choir, and vergers. Lord Iliffe gave £35,000 for reconstruction. The West German government gave £4,250. The Russians sent an ikon. Women in the diocese did the needlework on one thousand kneelers. An anonymous donor paid for the sculpture of St. Michael and the Devil and for the ten nave windows. A pro-cessional cross was given by the Dowager Marchioness of Reading in memory of WVS wartime service. Many other gifts were made. It is a cathedral founded on goodwill.

The foundation stone of the cathedral was laid by the Queen in 1956, when she was accompanied by the Duke of Edinburgh. The Queen, this time accompanied by Princess Margaret and Lord Snowdon, was again present at the consecration by the Bishop of Coventry, Dr. Cuthbert Bardsley, in 1962. It was a great occasion for Coventry, for the nation, and for other countries. The destruction of the old cathedral, twenty-two years earlier, had been a blow, a victory for an evil cause, and now good had triumphed, and wounds had been healed. It was a day of splendid and colourful processions; of robed archbishops in cope and mitre; bishops from places as scattered as Australia and Canada, Iran, South Africa, America, India and Pakistan, and West Africa, with those of England, Wales, Scotland and Ireland; of ambassadors, from numerous lands; Ministers of Governments, Members of Parliament, deputy-lieutenants of the county, mayors, town clerks; the leaders of all kinds of churches—a gathering of the world the like of which Coventry had never seen before, and may never see again.

There were designated buildings for robing, there were specified routes each procession would take, all converging with perfect timing in the May sunshine on that central place which had captured world attention—the new Coventry Cathedral. The Queen, Princess Margaret, Lord Snowdon, and the Lord Lieutenant of the county, Lord Willoughby de Broke, made their arrival, however, at the ruins, where those presented to the Queen included some of the people who had been instrumental in the rebuilding scheme. Then the Royal procession made its way through the nave of the old cathedral and by Queen's Way and St. Michael's Porch, to the west door of the new. Here the bishop stood at the top of the steps, to pray with the large crowd of people outside the cathedral, while inside it the choir were singing a psalm in praise of Christ glorified—appropriate, with the great tapestry of Christ in Glory dominating the scene. Then the bishop entered the cathedral, heralded by a fanfare, for the service of consecration. There were 2,300 people in the new cathedral, and 2,000 others seated in the ruins. The Archbishop of Canterbury preached the sermon.

Just as the consecration had been preceded by the Cross of Nails pilgrimage through the diocese, every parish being visited,

The cathedral from Priory Street
The cathedral and Holy Trinity
(overleaf) *Graham Sutherland's cathedral tapestry*

so afterwards there followed a great festival of celebration lasting three weeks and covering a wide range of activities: special services for industry, for agriculture, for youth, and so on; Sir Malcolm Sargent and the BBC Symphony Orchestra at the Coventry Theatre, where the Covent Garden Opera presented the world première of Michael Tippett's *King Priam*; Yehudi Menuhin playing Bach in the cathedral, which also gave the première of Britten's "War Requiem" and Sir Arthur Bliss's "The Beatitudes"; the Royal Ballet at the theatre; plays at the Belgrade Theatre and in the cathedral. There was a historical pageant about Coventry in the War Memorial Park. There were special sports events. The festival, which took several years to prepare, involving twenty-four committees throughout the diocese, had something for everyone spreading all through the diocese. Canon Ross was the man who pulled the strings, working in his festival office. Sir Stanley Harley was chairman of the executive committee.

Provost Howard did not have a principal role in the service of consecration, so did not see the cycle completed, as provost, from the night of the raid to the advent of the new building. He effaced himself in a typically modest way by retiring four years before consecration, so that a younger man should take over in good time to see the new cathedral develop. He had been provost for twenty-five years, a kindly but resolute leader in the church, in spite of some difficult years. He battled with the bombs, kept a cheerful face, and was an enthusiast for Spence's design, backing him up through thick and thin. He was succeeded as provost by the Very Reverend H. C. N. Williams, rector of St. Mary's, Southampton, who after 23 years retired in 1981.

There was a building debt of £120,000 on the new cathedral when it was consecrated. This was cleared in the first seven months by donations from the great rush of visitors—2½ million of them in the first year. And having been consecrated, Coventry Cathedral was not to lapse into a humdrum, routine church life. It was to be an outward-looking, 'with it' cathedral, playing a full part in the community, using all the modern media such as television and radio, drama, the arts. When it appointed a drama director, it was the only cathedral to have such a person on its staff. Plays are presented several times a year using the nave theatre where, at the entrance to the Chapel of Unity, up to 300 people can be seated. Plays such as *The Firstborn* by Christopher Fry, *Christ in the Concrete City* by Philip Turner, and *Waiting for*

(overleaf) *Epstein's St Michael and the Devil on the wall of Coventry Cathedral*
Ford's Hospital and the new Eventide Homes
The canal basin during the annual rally in 1971

Godot by Samuel Beckett. The cathedral's porch plays—twenty-minute plays performed at lunchtime on the steps in the cathedral porch—attract on-the-spot audiences during the summer. They are brisk little plays with point about life.

When in 1971 the daughter of the precentor of the cathedral, Canon J. W. Poole, was married there, eight girls from a dancing academy, where she had been a pupil, led her up the aisle and then danced. The cathedral is like that. Its policy brings creative artists to communicate to people in the popular form of the day—through drama, through music. There have been world-famous musicians, folk-singers, dancers. The cathedral has its St. Michael's Singers—nearly one hundred men and women—and its choir has recorded and made overseas tours. The choirboys are choral scholars at King Henry VIII School.

Typical of the cathedral outlook is its industrial mission, with full-time chaplains visiting factories and making contacts at all levels, listening, discussing, becoming more knowledgeable about the role of the church in the world of industry. There is a cathedral chaplaincy to the police, identifying with the problems of the force, leading perhaps to better understanding with the community.

There is liaison with city stores—visits to the Co-op and Owen Owen, Woolworth's, Marks and Spencer, British Home Stores, and conferences with their personnel on themes like "Shops, People and Values". There have been short services for Council House staff before work, using the Council Chamber. The cathedral is making a big impact on youth. From Bardsley House at Hill Top come the sounds of pop music. To John F. Kennedy House, a residential hostel for international youth, young people come from various countries to attend 'Service and Study' courses. They will be found, during their course, visiting old people's clubs and entertaining the pensioners with guitar and singing. During holidays, 'Cathedral Workshop' gives opportunity for drama activity for young people. Is there a way of drawing people in that the cathedral has not found? I doubt it. In the grounds there are exhibitions of sculpture. In the ruins a permanent fixture is "Ecce Homo" (Behold the Man) by Epstein, a 9-ton sculpture given to the cathedral and said to have been carved in 1934–5 from marble so hard that tools broke on it.

The cathedral's annual running costs are about £100,000, and visitors' donations and bookshop sales were stated a few years ago

to meet about two-thirds of this. Money is always a problem, and
there was an appeal for £250,000 to enable the cathedral's widely
varied activities to be maintained and extended. The cathedral's
departments cover international work, race, training of ministers
to deal with social problems arising from urban development,
music, education, and ecumenical work, in addition to all that has
already been mentioned.

The association between Sir Basil Spence and the cathedral
administration ended when his resignation as consultant architect
was announced in 1967. Denys Hinton and Associates of Leamington became consultants for the cathedral, and Mr. A. H. Gardner
of Coventry for the ruins.

An early requirement at this period was the replacement of the
metal 'flying cross' that had been lowered spectacularly on to the
79-feet-high rooftop flèche of the cathedral by RAF helicopter
in 1962. There was a crash when the 12-hundredweight flying
cross was blown down on to the roof in 1967, and the question of
replacing it with one made of lighter material was under discussion
when Sir Basil resigned. It was replaced subsequently by one of
fibreglass, weight 3 hundredweight, which was placed in position
without the requirement of a helicopter as it was not so heavy.
The cathedral also had some early trouble with acoustics; music
critics complaining of "muddled sound" and inaudibility.

If there have been critics, there are so many more who have a
feeling of indebtedness to the cathedral. Music lovers, for example
—where else in Coventry might they hope to hear the Hallé or
the Berlin Philharmonic? Drama we have already mentioned. It
is an outward-looking cathedral that is part of the daily life around
it, that can present photographic and horticultural exhibitions,
dance and mime, to mark its anniversary, and great works of
music and theatre at homes and on gala days for visitors. There
are many special occasions when people of various denominations
attend for civic, or similar services. They are arranged so that
with service papers they are easily followed. Nothing drags;
the pace is brisk. It seems fitting in a new building like the
cathedral.

It is the third Coventry Cathedral. The first was that of the
Benedictine Priory, thought to have been a beautiful building of
great proportions—about 425 feet long. The piers of its west wall
can be seen at 5a Priory Row. Other traces of it were found when
the new cathedral was being built. This first building was

demolished in the sixteenth century at the time of the Reformation, and from that time until 1918 Coventry did not have a cathedral. In that year there was a reorganization which created the Coventry diocese covering the whole of Warwickshire, except Birmingham, and the parish church of St. Michael was designated as a cathedral. It was of Norman origin, and was rebuilt and extended in the fourteenth and fifteenth centuries, so that its length was 300 feet—the height of the spire. It was considered to be one of the finest parish churches in England and owed much to the wealthy local Botoner family, wool merchants and clothiers, some of whom were mayors of the city.

Their generosity is reflected in this jingle:

> William and Adam built the tower,
> Ann and Mary built the spire,
> William and Adam built the church,
> Ann and Mary built the quire.

There were six bays in the nave, and with its arcade of pillars and archways St. Michael's was most impressive. It had guild chapels and one of these, the Cappers', has been restored in the ruins and is used, about once a year, to maintain the tradition that goes back hundreds of years. The tower was built towards the end of the fourteenth century and the spire in the early part of the fifteenth.

The steeple is a splendid sight as it is approached from Cuckoo Lane, screened first by the churchyard trees; then, suddenly, there is the sturdy brown sandstone tower that has defied time and Hitler's bombs, effortlessly supporting the spire that seems about to take off into the sky. The tower has windows, various openings and carvings, flying buttresses, and in its niches a number of effigies—it has been said that there are forty but some may have gone—which include members of the Botoner family, Edward III, and Leofric and Godiva. The tower steps can be climbed to get a view of Coventry from the battlements. The bells are not rung, but every day their chimes and their hymn-tunes sound over a wide area of the city centre, played mechanically by a carillon, penetrating offices and shops.

The sound is part of the charm of Coventry's centre. All this new building, busy people rushing ant-like about their business, and every now and then the clear notes of the bells, in keeping with the cathedral's policy of being involved in the outside world.

V

KEEPING THE PAST

VISITORS to Coventry, especially from America, are delighted
when they are shown older parts of Coventry, and tours arranged
by the corporation's information centre in Broadgate have been
popular. There are quite a few Coventry people, too, who make
interesting discoveries on the walks round the centre. The future
looks secure for some of the old areas because of the national
policy on conservation areas, and under this umbrella of protection
Coventry has designated several areas which will be guarded
against undesirable development. Included in these are areas at
Allesley, Kenilworth Road, Stoke Green, Greyfriars Green, Hill
Top and the cathedral, Lady Herbert's Garden, and Spon Street.
The most central is that at Hill Top where there are ancient
buildings—Holy Trinity, Priory Row and St. Mary's Hall, the
cathedral ruins. Everybody knows Holy Trinity since it faces
directly on to Broadgate. Its impact is immediate: the aged
bulwark of the church, stone walls, stained glass, churchyard
trees, cheek by jowl with modernity.

The church dates at least from the thirteenth century, when it
replaced an earlier one, and contrasts sharply with the stores and
the office blocks, not to mention the Wimpy Bar on its doorstep.
Trinity slows the tempo for a moment. It has an aura of mellow-
ness around it and at most times of day there are people sitting
or standing by the flower beds in front of the church that have
been maintained so well by the Parks Department.

Its spire, crowning its glory, is 237 feet high, but it is not as old
as the other Coventry spires because there was a great gale in 1665
that blew down the original one, and this spire was built to
replace it. The experts say the church is a mixture of styles. Inside,
it is large, and the full extent of this reveals itself in a walk down
the long aisles, passing the pillars and the archways, and the
monuments and brasses, the stone font and pulpit, and the choir

stalls that came, it is recorded, from the Whitefriars Monastery church when it was dissolved. Holy Trinity once had fifteen altars, and was packed with chapels used by the craft guilds. It is interesting to think that this secluded, yet prominent, building, which has not only visual appeal but large congregations for worship, will stand, rocklike, while buildings of today will probably change their shape and use, as has happened with buildings in its vicinity in the past.

Alongside the church is the tiny lane called Priory Row, and the black-and-white timbered cottages which include the verger's house, a remarkable dwelling house for late twentieth-century occupation, with small chambers, varying levels, and beamed ceilings. Under the verger's house are remains—the piers—of the first cathedral, and in the background the old Blue Coat School. This is a corner of the city centre—there are several—where, a few yards from the main streets, there is tranquillity and the aura of history.

Along Priory Row, stepping away from the Broadgate traffic, the new cathedral comes into view, and on the left is Hill Top, the cobbled 'short cut' walk down to Fairfax Street. Priory Row offices include the handsome Georgian house, No. 11, that was severely bomb damaged and then carefully rebuilt after the war. Its garden has masonry said to be from the old priory, and the site it stands on was the priory burial ground. From Priory Row there is a quiet walk behind Holy Trinity, passing the ruins of the cathedral, to Bayley Lane, where St. Mary's Hall has its entrance.

The Merchant Guild of St. Mary built the first hall, called the 'Hall of our Lady', in 1342; and after the merging of the guilds into the Trinity Guild, the great hall was built to complete it. It has been owned by Coventry Corporation since 1552, when, after the suppression of the monasteries and guilds, the corporation appealed and were allowed to buy back some of the property that had been surrendered to the Crown, including St. Mary's Hall. It has been modernized in recent years to improve the heating and the catering arrangements, changing the appearance of the kitchens where there were huge fireplaces for the cooking of the guild and civic feasts. It has long been the centre of civic events. A splendid medieval hall, it is higher—34 feet—than it is wide (30 feet), and has a wonderful oak ceiling with many carved angels and bosses on it. The angels play instruments, and the bosses are heraldic in design.

The hall is 76 feet long, with a 500-year-old Arras tapestry under the north window at one end, and the minstrel gallery, hung with armour, at the other. In the great hall portraits of royalty look down on the functions that take place, including the installation of mayors each year. One mayor-making ceremony, however, did not take place in the hall. In 1711, the political factions were feeling particularly hostile and there were signs of trouble breaking out at the ceremony. To avoid this, the new mayor was sworn in on a cushion placed in the street, on his way to the hall! The sword and mace were used. They had been spirited away and hidden in a nearby house for the purpose.

Of the original St. Mary's Hall, parts remaining are the kitchen, Mayoress's Parlour, the porch, the old Council Chamber, the Prince's Chamber, and the armoury. Caesar's Tower, which dated from 1393, was destroyed in the raids and has been rebuilt. The council chamber also has a tapestry, but it is more modern work. There is carved oak panelling from the former 'Coventry Arms', and, dating from about 1450, a guild chair which has seating for two and was used when the mayor and the guild master sat side by side. In the base of Caesar's Tower is a thirteenth-century treasure chest, which was damaged and has been restored. The door to the tower has three locks, indicating that for security three people each had a different key, and all had to be present to open the door. There is a tradition that Mary, Queen of Scots, was imprisoned in an upper room in the tower when she was brought to Coventry. She was imprisoned in Coventry from November 1569 to January 1570.

In the courtyard of the hall is the crypt, which looks like a dungeon, and is said once to have been a tavern. It was originally a store for food and building materials and for gunpowder and muskets during the Civil War. In our time it has had store use and has also been used for a short time as an overflow courtroom, very cramped, surrounded by a clutter of medieval remains, where the magistrates heard the first stages of a murder trial. But now it is modernised and is used for receptions and for cocktails for guests before they go into the great hall for dinner. Having been involved at the trial and at receptions, I find the crypt has very much a 'then and now' atmosphere.

The hall, which had its roof bomb-damaged and repaired, has been used as a theatre, for fish fairs, as a soldiers' billet, for council meetings, and for one Quarter Sessions sitting. When the weaving trade was in decline the kitchen became a soup kitchen for distressed weavers. Nowadays the hall is used for important civic dinners, or luncheons—as when royalty visit the city—and it can also be hired for private events such as meetings or wedding receptions. Near the hall, at 22 Bayley Lane, is a sixteenth-century half-timbered cottage, and the 'Golden Cross' inn, which is said to have been a Royal Mint long ago. County Hall, alongside, was built in 1784 and was used as an Assizes Court until 1842. Now it is used for Crown Courts.

Lady Herbert's Garden, also a conservation area, is alongside The Coventry Theatre, a landscaped area of $1\frac{1}{2}$ acres with trees and shrubs where people sit and rest or have their break at lunchtime; and it is administered by trustees who also have responsibility for the cottages that are in it. They are let to elderly ladies, who have garden all round their homes. The best of the remains of the old city wall stand in the garden, in parts festooned with rambler roses and other climbing plants. The wall connects with the two surviving gates: Cook Street, at the top, given to the city by Sir William Wyley; and Swanswell Gate, at the lower end, a gift of Sir Alfred Herbert. The Cook Street gate is still a passageway, although the inner ring road has put an end to through traffic, and today only pedestrians go under it. Swanswell Gate had its passageway closed, and it became a dwelling house. Now it is a store for the gardeners' use.

Walking through the garden, under trees with a view of the spires, is a pleasure—especially as before the garden was laid out, in the thirties, it was the site of slum property called the Chauntries.

Another central conservation area is Spon Street, and one of the most interesting of the schemes being carried out as part of the redevelopment of the central area is taking place here. It is the Spon Street Townscape Scheme. The street is being re-created, and may extend over Queen Victoria Road towards the city centre. Old shop and dwelling properties from various parts of the centre that were dismantled to make way for new schemes and stored, are being re-erected here beam by beam. Spon Street is itself very old, and some of its timber-framed properties are being restored *in situ*.

It will not be a museum street. The restored shops will be in business, and will be an extension of the central shopping layout. The first restored shop, opened in 1970, dates from the fourteenth century. When completed, Spon Street Townscape Scheme will be a place of considerable interest, although it will not appease those who have criticized Coventry about old buildings. According to the Society for the Protection of Ancient Buildings, 120 timbered buildings survived the war, and now there are only 38. Nor does the society look kindly on a policy of dismantling old properties and re-erecting them on different sites.

The properties that are being saved, and given new life, range in date from the fourteenth to the seventeenth century; so when the project is finished, this shopping precinct will be a fascinating contrast with the modern precincted shopping area close by. St. John's Church, which is also in this conservation area, will look out once more on buildings of a former age that it knew when Coventry was a town of wealthy merchants, living in large timber-framed houses like that in Spon Street of the Wilmas Gallery. St. John's is an ancient building, pleasing the eye with its warm brown sandstone walls, in parts showing the wear of time. It has stained-glass windows, and that chunky tower with the odd-shaped outline that is part of the skyline, along with the spires elsewhere. The frontage is to Corporation Street, and traffic swirls quickly past, while pedestrians making for the shops or going to work spare hardly a glance.

But at the rear there is absolute seclusion, and beyond the small churchyard there are the old Bablake and Bond's Hospital, timbered buildings that are also in the conservation scheme. St. John's is not as large, inside, as the outside walls suggest. It is lofty, with graceful fluted pillars and delicate archways, but compact, and has a number of memorials. It was built in the fourteenth century as a chapel for St. John's Guild on land which was given by Queen Isabella, and it was suppressed at the time of the dissolution along with monasteries and guilds. It came into the ownership of the corporation along with other property they bought back from the Crown; but it was nearly 200 years before it was used again as a place of worship in 1734. It had been neglected and damaged in the meantime. There are several empty niches on the exterior walls from which effigies were probably removed at that time. The church was even used as a lock-up for Royalist prisoners-of-war, and probably had damage at that period. It was restored in 1877.

Old Bablake and Bond's are entered from Hill Street, behind St. John's, and look on to a triangle where a visitor feels as if he has stepped back centuries. Bond's is on the right—timbered, elaborate with gables and carved barge boards, a perfect specimen, it is claimed, of early sixteenth-century domestic architecture. This is a home for elderly men; twelve can be accommodated, each having a bed-sitting-room. Thomas Bond, who founded it in 1506, was a city draper and former mayor. Improvements have been made. It has interesting small rooms, a common room where there are settles for the residents to sit and smoke their pipes, and a boardroom with handsome old furniture in it.

Old Bablake was endowed by another ex-mayor, Thomas Wheatley, in the sixteenth century. He is said to have received from Spain, by mistake, a chest of silver ingots instead of steel wedges. When he could not trace the owner, he sold the ingots and gave the money to endow Bablake Hospital, as it was called, for twenty-one boys, and a nurse. The boys were to be clothed, educated, and to take up apprenticeships. This was where Bablake School, now at Coundon Road, began. At one time the building, which, like Bond's, is timbered, was a small museum. The building is now offices for charities and land agents. To turn into the courtyard from Hill Street and enter Old Bablake's cloistered walk is to step suddenly from the twentieth century to the Middle Ages.

This might also be said of Ford's Hospital, in Greyfriars Lane, except that the front of it is in view as it is approached, whereas at Bablake the surprises are hidden behind a long wall. Ford's—not in a conservation area—was founded and endowed by a Coventry merchant, William Ford, in 1509, and was extended later by his executor, William Pisford, as an almshouse for poor men and women—later it was for women only. After it was damaged in the wartime raids a careful restoration was carried out using salvaged materials; and as most of the timber framework survived, it is still a fine specimen of sixteenth-century building.

Greyfriars Green, flanked by Warwick Row and the curved line of Victorian properties in the Quadrant (also in the conservation area) is surviving as a jewel of green space and gardens, despite being crossed by the new Greyfriars Road, and overshadowed by the ring road, and it has had its area increased. It is a popular spot for office and shop workers to take a lunch-hour break, and a pleasing visual amenity for passers-by. Up to the middle of the nineteenth century the Great Fair was held on the green, sometimes spreading into Hertford Street. The

levelling and planting of the first small park was completed in
1876. It covered two acres and formerly belonged to the Coventry
Freemen. Coventry does not have many monuments, and
two of them—to James Starley, father of the city's cycle trade, and
Sit Thomas White, a London merchant who was a benefactor to
Coventry—belong here on the green.

Lady Godiva's statue is on Broadgate garden island, and the
Coventry Boy is in Priory Street, but there is one memorial that
many people never see—the Martyrs' Memorial, in Quinton
Road. The Starley Memorial, erected in the 1880s, and the
Martyrs' Memorial, unveiled in 1910, were put into store when
stage six of the ring road began, to be replaced later. On the
memorial to the martyrs are the names of eleven Protestant men
and women who were burned at the stake between 1510 and 1555
in that vicinity, when it was called Little Park, because they
would not recant their faith under the Roman Catholic régime.
Anniversary services have been held at the memorial, and descendants of one martyr, the Reverend Lawrence Saunders, have
made pilgrimages to it and placed wreaths there. The martyrs
are also commemorated in a mosaic in a recess beneath the Bridge
Restaurant, in Broadgate, but this too is not prominent and is
probably not noticed by many visitors. A descendant of Joan
Ward, one of the martyrs, was disappointed to come from
Australia on a visit in 1971 and find that the mosaic was not only
'hidden away', as it appeared to her, but bore no plaque of any
kind. Although the martyrs died four centuries ago, some still
have families who remember them.

The Kenilworth Road conservation area will preserve this
beautiful approach to the city, starting from the boundary. It
includes extensions at Cryfield Grange Road, Stoneleigh Road,
Canley Ford, and Stivichall Hamlet, embracing spinneys,
common, and greens, and it extends along Warwick Road to a
point about half a mile from the city centre. Coventry people are
very proud of this approach, 3 miles long, and almost a continuous
strip of woodland. It was all part, originally, of the Stoneleigh
Abbey estates. When the monasteries were dissolved by Henry
VIII, the abbey and the estate was sold, to Sir Rowland Hill and
Sir Thomas Leigh, for £1,950.

Stoke Park and Stoke Green are areas of character. Stoke Park's
large houses are enclosed by a wall, in a manner not found
anywhere else in Coventry; and the green, which extends on

each side of Binley Road, is a pleasing open space with trees. The Bull's Head Inn and properties fronting the green are included in the conservation area.

Allesley Village, the remaining conservation area, has come into its own as a result of the opening of the Allesley By-pass. Previously the Birmingham Road traffic thundered through the village and rocked it, and because of the bottleneck at one end there were long hold-ups. Now it is a peaceful backwater, pleasant with brick houses and cottages; and off it are lanes leading to green-belt land. The parish church, originally twelfth century and later rebuilt, and the Stone House, which dates from the sixteenth century, are part of what is now the only village group within the Coventry boundary.

Coventry has many interesting old buildings that are part of the past, and some of them have surprising modern uses. For example, the gateway of Cheylesmore Manor House remains. It has been restored and couples now go there for registry-office weddings. The manor house was once the home of the earls of Chester, and passed to the Black Prince, who became lord of the manor. He frequently stayed there in the days when the Cheylesmore area was a great park. The Black Prince's link with the city gave it the motto of *Camera Principis*—'the Prince's Chamber'; and his crest of three feathers, taken from the coat-of-arms of King John of Bohemia at the Battle of Crécy in 1346, found their way into the Lord Mayor's crest and have adorned it ever since.

Coventry's own coat-of-arms, by the way, has a cat-a-mountain or wild cat, for watchfulness, as its crest; a helmet—that of an esquire; and shield coloured red and green, with a device of a gold elephant beating a gold castle on its back. Red and green are the traditional colours of Coventry. In 1959 supporters were added: the eagle of Leofric on one side and the phoenix rising from the flames on the other—symbols of old and new Coventry. The supporters were suggested by a resident, Mr. Reg Trotter, and the idea was taken up by the city council because of the opportunity to symbolize the city's rebirth after the destruction by war. The right to bear arms was conferred on Coventry by Edward III. The elephant is said to be a symbol of strength and security, but Mary Dormer Harris, the Leamington historian who took such great interest in Coventry and spent between ten and fifteen years transcribing and editing the Leet Book records, thought that the elephant which is found on early Coventry seals, was chosen from the ancient bestiaries, which treat animals as religious symbols, and that the elephant would be seen in early times as a symbol of Christ's redemption of the human race.

Coventry Corporation have preserved some of the city's past by carrying out a modern restoration of Christ Church (formerly Greyfriars) tower and spire, which seems always to have been doomed to stand in splendid isolation. After the suppression of the monasteries by Henry VIII, the steeple stood alone for nearly 300 years, until, in the nineteenth century, local people decided another church should be added to it, and this was completed in 1832. Then in the wartime raids the church was once more flattened, and again the steeple remained, sentry-like, at its post. No rebuilding of a church this time, however. The destruction of property and post-war development plans meant that there would not be a sufficiently large parish there, and a new Christ Church was built in the Styvechale district instead, where there is also a replacement for West Orchard church.

Whitefriars Museum is near the inner ring road, at Gulson Road. It is a remarkable building comprising one of the cloisters, with dormitory above, of what was a cloister square of White-friars 'monastery'. There was some destruction of parts of the square when it was turned into a residence for John Hales, when he acquired it at the dissolution of the monasteries, and there was some damage too when Charles I's marksmen were firing at the city wall. In modern times the cloister has had some strange uses. Before restoration it was a dining hall for men staying at the Salvation Army hostel. Earlier it was part of the old workhouse. Queen Elizabeth was a guest at the 'monastery' in 1565, after it had become the home of John Hales.

Not far from the Whitefriars Museum in London Road is another old building—the Charterhouse. The Carthusians settled in Coventry in the fourteenth century at this spot, and Richard II granted the land, and laid the foundation stone of their church. The house was suppressed in 1539. The surviving building, which became the home of Colonel Sir William Wyley, may have been the prior's lodging, or the guest hall. In 1940, in his will, Colonel Wyley bequeathed the Charterhouse to Coventry City Council, and the surrounding park, for public use, but little use was made of it because of the cost of restoring and adapting the old building for a suitable modern purpose. It has had repair and is in regular use now as an education and art centre. A wall painting of the Crucifixion was found behind panelling in one room.

One of the oldest buildings in the city comprises the remains of the Hospital of St. John, now known as the Old Grammar School, at Hales Street. The hospital was founded in the twelfth century, and the remains are of its fourteenth-century church. At the time of the dissolution, the property passed to John Hales and he changed its use to that of a grammar school, naming it after King Henry VIII. It was the forerunner of the grammar school at Warwick Road. It was a free grammar school until 1885, and then had use as a church mission room. It has had a variety of uses since—for sales of work, tradesmen's sales, as an extension of a store to cope with the Christmas rush!

A corner of Coventry that has kept its character to a considerable extent is Spon End, where the bridge over the Sherbourne was built in 1771 with materials from the demolished Spon Gate. The remains of an old chapel, that of St. John and St. Christopher, have been preserved nearby, and some of the shop properties alongside the river are several centuries old, with heavy beams to the ceilings.

While there are various remains of old Coventry, there are only names to remind us that once the city had a castle. Broadgate, according to historians, was the 'broad gate' of a castle that stood in the centre, built by Hugh, Earl of Chester, after the Norman Conquest. Bayley Lane, it is said, may have been named from the bailey of the castle.

VI

COVENTRY IS A COMMUNITY

COVENTRY people today are almost classless, for it is a city of people working for a living, and management has had to learn to live on equal terms with labour, often in the past in short supply, and able to call the tune through strong organization. The war, too, when the man making munitions was every bit as important as the director, and when life was as precious to each when the bombs fell, helped the levelling-off process. Who was superior then? Coventry's company directors and executives are usually men who in any event rose from the shop floor, and their roots are among the machines. If they want to live more ex- pansively they have a habit of moving house, towards the boundary, or beyond. People do not choose Coventry to live in, unless they have work to do in it. People do not retire here. It is not a Cheltenham or a Bath.

It is a place with a lot of energy—factory traffic, noise, too much litter, and vandalism—and quite a number of its residents, when they retire, move from it. They choose somewhere more quiet. Those who stay put have the benefit of being among people they know, and they can benefit from local welfare schemes to a more- than-average extent. Sometimes they welcome back to their midst old friends who have changed their mind and come home again, because they missed the comradeship when they tried to make retirement homes by the sea. Coventry's population in the post-war years of plenty was lively, confident, affluent. The eighties find them in a trade depression, jobs have gone, the future is uncertain.

The image of a city often hit by strikes has been with us for a decade or so. Wage rates were good and the factory workers were strongly union, seemingly ready to down tools at the drop of a hat. From the factories at the end of the shift they drove home in long bumper-to-bumper lines of cars, and in many cases their wives were also making their way home from work. Many factory workers on high wages, perhaps with the wife bringing in another wage packet, were leading the executive life without the executive responsibilities. Many couples were able to dine out, take holidays abroad regularly. Workers called the tune when unemployment fell after the war to a figure of under 2,000, considered irreducable because it included people on the move, and unemployables, and factories on high pay obtained their workers by signing on skilled tradesmen for the assembly lines. The Standard assembly lines could supply enough bricklayers, plasterers, carpenters and electricians to build houses complete! As a result of the flow, house-building lacked workers and so did all the services. Women could easily get employment. Recruitment drives were organized all over the country and in Ireland, to get bus crews.

The bus services are an example of the flow of labour into the city and into the factories. There was enormous difficulty in keeping enough vehicles on the road because of lack of crews, and after the recruiting drive we had the era of Irish conductors, until they too found their way into the factories, as all newcomers do when they have settled down and looked around. Now we have the coloured crews, with conductors who are quiet and courteous and a success at the job.

It has become a joke in Coventry that, as a result of people coming into it for work, there are hardly any Coventry-born people! It is a very cosmopolitan place, and if a native actually meets another amongst the Scots, Welsh and Irish, the meeting is made into an occasion. People who came long before the war, in the depression of the early thirties, regard themselves as Coventrians—and, of course, their children and their grandchildren were born here. Coventry has been like a kindly mother to a lot of people migrating from areas of acute depression in providing them with work and homes. Many have come from overseas to better their lot. About one-tenth of the population were born outside the United Kingdom. The biggest migrant group are Irish—estimated at about 20,000.

Coventry's 'local' people have not had to make a conscious effort to accept newcomers—at least not while there has been work for all. It began with the Geordies and the Welsh families pre-war, and the city is used to it. The locals are on the whole easy-going and peace-loving, and integration of migrants has been achieved to give a very mixed community.

There are people from the Ukraine and Poland and other Iron Curtain countries, coloured immigrants from the West Indies, India, Pakistan. Conversation in the bus can be quite unintelligible to the local passenger. The conductor is probably from Jamaica, and the new local doctor will probably be from India. The hospital nurse is almost certainly Irish, and behind the grille at the post office counter you may be served by a clerk wearing a turban. Most of the coloured migrants live in Foleshill and Hillfields, and the Hillfields news-sheet has some of its space filled by writing in Indian or Pakistani. The corporation, who run classes in English for migrants, also have to issue notices in foreign languages. Coventry has accepted them, one and all, provided them with jobs and shelter, and welded them into the community. Sikh and Moslem temples are opened by the Lord Mayor, Indian games are played at well-supported rallies on the parks. Coloured children, born here, are as local as their white friends.

There are all sorts of clubs and societies—for the Irish people in the community, who have done marvels in building Roman Catholic churches and schools; for the Scots, for the Indian and Pakistani people. Some are in converted premises, like cinemas, and others in buildings which have been purpose-built. If there is a club specially for Welsh people I have not heard of it; it appears that they have been absorbed into other clubs, such as the working men's clubs that grow so fast and thrive so well in the city— there were thirty-one in 1951, and now there are over seventy! The Latvians and people of other nationalities, much smaller in their numbers, take a pride in holding on to their traditions, far from home, and teach their Coventry-born children how to wear national costume and perform national dances.

Everything considered, the city has a colourful community, the like of which it never knew in all its long history before the war of 1939-45. Probably it owes some of its vitality to those who have migrated to it. Some migrants take an interest in civic affairs, and are elected to serve on the city council. There are Welsh, Irish, and Scottish members, and they rise, if they serve and become senior members, to wear the robes of Lord Mayor.

This was the case with Alderman Tom Meffen, a Scot, in 1971-2. He arrived in the city as a colliery engineer to help his firm sink a shaft at Binley Colliery, and decided to stay, transferring to the colliery work force. He was elected to the council in 1947, and in 1971 was Lord Mayor—the first Scot to hold the office. But in his regard for Coventry, just as much a Coventry man as any native, and this applies to many others who came for employment, liked what they found, and settled in it, at their journey's end. And when they raise their families, the roots are established.

Although so mixed, Coventry has a community spirit. This is manifest in its arrangements for the welfare of elderly people. After a visit to the city in 1971, one pensioner wrote to a Manchester newspaper about some of the benefits old people enjoy in Coventry. "It's worth a lot to be sent to Coventry," was the message in her letter. Since 1943, pensioners, regardless of their income, have had cheap travel on the buses. Once they were issued with blocks of tickets, and their rides were free until the block was used up for that period. A simpler system followed this, with the issue of permanent passes, which enabled the holder to travel for 1p. In 1970 the Conservative-run council offered free travel. To their surprise, pensioners were indignant! They declined, rather, they said, than be a total burden to other ratepayers.

But free rides for senior citizens did come, and Coventry pensioners have for years enjoyed a mobility envied by those of other towns. And in 1974, when Coventry became part of the West Midlands County, this was continued and adopted for pensioners in the whole of the West Midlands. There's a refreshing absence of red tape, too, about the concession, an applicant receiving a permanent travel pass which has his or her photograph on it. Pensioners in Coventry also have reduced price admission to cinemas and theatres, and the Belgrade Theatre has a keen following of elderly people who attend their special afternoon performance. All over the city there are old people's clubs, where members of the Women's Royal Voluntary Service and other voluntary workers, cook and serve cheap meals, organize social activities and outings. The way that some clubs have been launched indicates the helpful attitude of the public, as well as of the local authority, to the welfare of the elderly.

One club, the Triple Triangle at Jardine Crescent, Tile Hill, was suggested and paid for by employees of the Massey Ferguson factory at Banner Lane. Another, Wava Hall, Barras Heath, was paid for by Stoke Philanthropic Society and has its name from the initials of one of their officers who thought up the idea. There are over thirty old people's organizations, and clubs formed and run by people in their own districts, using premises like church halls. Until it had to close for financial reasons, the Corporation had a holiday hotel at Deganwy, North Wales, where elderly people were taken for low-price holidays in free transport. An unusual amenity which surprises people from other places is the *Pearl Hyde* narrow boat, a voluntary project, that plies up and down the canal with parties of old people. It is operated by a voluntary (and rather hard-up!) trust set up by the late Alderman Mrs. Pearl Hyde, and in principle the trips are free. But the parties are usually made up of members of organizations, and they have almost always preferred to pay something towards the expenses.

The *Pearl Hyde* boat service is unique. Mrs. Hyde was Lord Mayor in 1957 when the Inland Waterways Association held their rally of boats at Coventry, and she was so delighted by her trips on the water that she had the idea of a boat that would give this pleasure to the old people, in whom she was very interested. Her idea became reality because of the co-operation of others who made gifts of money and materials so that when an old Ovaltine company working boat—it carried coal—was purchased, it was possible to convert it, providing a superstructure under which passengers can sit if there is rain, rather than stay—as they also can do—in the open. Coventry Climax not only gave a particularly fine power unit and fitted it, but afterwards maintained it. Its name was changed from *Albert*. The *Pearl Hyde* has given great pleasure to thousands of people, who are taken into the countryside at Stretton, near Brinklow, and back again. Sometimes they are steered by volunteers, sometimes by paid crew. They have cups of tea, but usually provide their own refreshments. Mr. Bill Woodhead, Chairman of the trust for many years, frequently downs tools at his monumental mason's yard to act as steersman, and other people help as crew. In 1981 another canal boat, *Lady Godiva*, was launched, a gift of the Rainbow Trust, for handicapped children to have canal holidays.

Another service for the elderly, run by the corporation, is a free coach, which has volunteer drivers. Apart from taking parties on trips, it links up with the boats, collecting people and taking them to the canal, and meeting them for the journey home.

Various organizations—Rotary, Lions, Round Table—

churches, clubs, and public houses, make efforts for old and needy folk in the city; but an unusual fund that has helped them for many years, the 'Canine' Fund, deserves special mention. Who was 'Canine'? It was a well-kept secret for thirty-seven years. Each year he made his appeals through the newspapers for funds and with the money helped hundreds of pensioners to pay for renewal of dog licences, so that for lack of a few shillings they would not have to lose their pets. Then the fund was widened to help them pay for radio licences, then it helped with 'tobacco money', and Christmas gifts of 10s. (50p). Inevitably, came TV, and a rise in calls on 'Canine', who, when a Coventry man left a bequest to him of no less than £1,800, decided it was getting too big for one man to manage. He called in friends to form a trust to administer it, and in the process his identity was revealed— Alderman Harry Weston, ex-mayor, a long-serving Con- servative member of the city council, and local businessman. Alderman Weston revealed that the fund started in 1920 when he spoke to an old man in the street who was looking particularly miserable. He was taking his dog to be put down because he could not afford the licence. The fund now has fewer calls on it for licences for dogs, because, as flat dwellers, many old people are not permitted to have them. But on the other hand television plays a big part in the lives of those who are old and lonely.

A long list could be made of the various ways in which other help is given in Coventry. There are meals on wheels and home helps, which are corporation services; WRVS welfare work and Toc H; and there are college students doing practical work, decorating or gardening; and the old Coventry charities which provide cash gifts and goods vouchers, and which have helped to make the city a community. In a typical year the trustees of the General Charities may disburse £7,000 or so in pensions and allowances, and some £3,500 to students, in grants for books, clothing, equipment, and scholarships. Help is also given to needy young families who cannot be helped adequately by the State.

A good example of community feeling, is the strictly anony- mous Coventry Boy Foundation, a title that sums up its origin. In the early twenties a few Coventry boys made an agreement that when they had succeeded in their business lives they would set aside part of their good fortune for charity and to help make the local countryside and Coventry a better place. Over the years they have carried out this purpose, and some, still anonymous, have died. The foundation is a registered charity, administered through the National Council of Social Service, with local advisers, its objects being preservation and improvement in the county and in Coventry, but the identity of the 'boys' remains a secret, and the only contact with the foundation is via Messrs. Browetts, Solicitors, 23 Bayley Lane, Coventry. The foundation has considerable assets and their gifts have varied: the establishment and upkeep of new church walk alongside Keresley Church and the ornamental garden through which it passes; beautifying and improving Shelton Square fountain, in the city centre, at a cost of £1,000; the "Coventry Boy" statue, life-size, which stands in the landscaped area of the Lanchester Polytechnic, Priory Street, "a boy with bare feet symbolizing a humble beginning, rolled-up sleeve showing capacity for hard work, and the other cuff turned down to show he has risen to managerial level". There have been grants to Corley, Ansty, Stoke (Coventry), Baginton, and Sherbourne for churchyard improvements; a grant towards repair of the bells of All Saints' Church, Sherbourne; a tree-planting scheme for Keresley area; a statue, "The fisherman and the Nymph", for the lake at Coombe Countryside Park; a silver centrepiece for the civic dining table in Coventry "in appreciation of the women of the city from the days of Godiva to the present time", a sum of £2,250 for planting of trees in the city's lower precinct and Shelton Square; £450 for the plinth for Epstein's "Ecce Homo" in the cathedral ruins; the building of a replica of the 50-feet-high Coventry Cross in the city centre to restore a link with Coventry's history. These, and gifts of seats, are certainly in keeping with the intentions of the Coventry boys who thought about and cared for their city. After Alfred Harris died, it was revealed that he was the main benefactor. Changes are being made in the fund's administration.

Coventry has been well blessed with many individuals and organizations who clearly care about it, by giving money for trees and seats and other amenities. Some gifts have been very large indeed. The library, the Charterhouse, Cook Street and Swanswell gates, Swanswell Park and pool, Spencer Park, are just a few of them. Some people say that Coventry has not got a soul and that it is too materialistic, affluent, and car-conscious. Attendance at church is not all it might be. Factories work on

Good Friday—a habit that began when the cycle boom was on and there was a peak demand at Easter. But there is no lack of support for good causes, and factory workers will quickly have a 'whip round' for a case of distress. A child with cancer, and its mother hoping for a miracle cure at Lourdes, resulted in a flow of cash that would have sent several children on the trip. And an appeal for a CAT scanner at Walsgrave Hospital brought in £425,000 in a year from people in the city and in Warwickshire. It was installed in November, 1978.

A criticism often heard is that there is "not much to do" in Coventry. There is lots to do, but not of the late-night type—few sophisticated nightclubs, and not much going on in the central area at night. But leisure-time interests of all kinds exist around the city if anyone wishes to get involved. Coventry lacks a concert hall, but has a thriving School of Music, which has hundreds of members, and many sections. It is an organization that began as a band of a RAF cadet unit in the war period, and which was nurtured very tenderly by dedicated local people—the mainspring was Mr. John Parbury—to blossom forth into a large organization that was finally taken under the wing of Coventry Education Committee, to become part of the technical college. It has its headquarters in the former St. John's C.E. School, an old building with a pleasant little spire, and here, and at Cheylesmore School, many musicians are trained. There is a symphony orchestra, a brass band, a corps of drums that has won many prizes, recorder classes for children, choirs, and a drama section. Soon the school will have to find larger premises.

The School of Music is just one instance of the growth of musical activity in the city, much of it due to the comprehensive schools which are large enough to have their own orchestras. Now there are several junior and senior bands, and the 13th Coventry Scouts band have been national champions and have often played before Royalty. Once labelled 'a cultural desert', Coventry is now well blessed with cultural activities. The cathedral, university, polytechnic, and civic theatre have all had an influence on this. Greyfriars Arts, who meet at the Charter-house, cater for all tastes—art, literature, music—among them.

The city has a network of societies of all kinds—operatic and dramatic, artists; orchestras; choirs; community centres; keep-fit classes; townswomen's guilds; horticultural, historic and archaeo-logical societies; clubs for chess, bridge, motoring, rambling,

Morris dancing, angling; leagues of all kinds for indoor and outdoor sport; uniformed organizations; and thousands of people of all ages, as busy as ants, going to evening classes. There is a cruising club, and a canal society whose members are dedicated to preserving and maintaining the canal in good order for recreational purposes.

'For those who take part, and those who only watch, Coventry is nearly a 'Mecca' for sport! It provides first-division football, first-class Rugby football—but hardly any first-class cricket. Coventry City FC are the big crowd attraction, the highlight of the weekend for many when the offices and factories are closed— and when they re-open on Monday the Saturday match becomes the main subject of conversation. The rugger enthusiasts are a smaller band, regular supporters of Coventry FC, whose ground at Coundon Road is as well known in Rugby football circles in England and Wales as Lord's is known to cricket fans. Two important clubs. But what about the cricket? Warwickshire County Cricket Club, of course, have their headquarters at Edgbaston, Birmingham, and they ration Coventry to two games a season, played at Courtaulds ground, Lockhurst Lane. If rain happens to spoil one or both, Coventry does not see much of the county side, and fans must travel to Edgbaston, Birmingham, to see the county side who have had few Coventry players as regulars in the first eleven. But we did supply Tom Cartwright, Fred Gardner, and Aubrey Hill, in recent years.

But sport-lovers cannot grumble. They might, after all, still be waiting to see first-class football too, but for the two men— Chairman Derrick Robins, and Manager Jimmy Hill—who were responsible for the club's promotion drive, from the third to the second division in 1964, and into the first in 1967. Mr Robins appointed Mr. Hill in 1961, and gave the club £30,000 to help buy players for a promotion team. Mr. Hill found the players, inspired club spirit, inflamed the lukewarm supporters, put the players into a new strip, and gave the club a new image with its title of Sky Blues and its club song. The drive, the support, the gimmicks too, worked wonders. The team won matches, the gates grew bigger—a record 51,452 saw Wolves on 29th April 1967—and going to a Highfield Road match was like going to a show, with perhaps a display on the pitch by gymnasts, or a ladies' netball match, music, and announcements, before the whistle blew for the kick-off. Sky Blues razmataz maybe, but it led to a huge expansion programme, with new stands and other improvements. And how many football clubs have a bishop as their president?

Mr. Robins became a director in 1954, when to be a Coventry City director was to risk the wrath of the disgruntled shareholders and supporters. Lowly City had been struggling, changing managers almost every year, and the directors had been resigning. From 1945 the managers of Coventry City had formed an unhappy procession: Harry Storer, Len Bayliss, Billy Frith, Harry Storer again, Jack Fairbrother, Jesse Carver, George Raynor (caretaker manager), Harry Warren and Billy Frith again, until 1961. Supporters, each time with great hopes of a new era, could not understand why managers left so soon. Some stayed for a season or less. The fault, they felt, lay in the boardroom, and this seemed to be borne out by the resignation of Mr. Erle Shanks, the president, immediately after Harry Storer departed in 1953. Six directors resigned in 1954, and in the reshuffle three, who had agreed to stay on as caretakers, were, with others, elected. Mr. Shanks returned as chairman. Unnoticed, a young local businessman, Derrick Robins, had joined the board. In 1958, when Mr. Shanks resigned again, disappointed at the lack of progress; Mr. Robins became vice-chairman, and, in 1960, chairman.

Mr. Robins, having appointed his chosen man as manager, and having helped with money, kept to a simple formula: no interference by the directors with the management. He had seen it all happen before, when so many managers came and went before they had time to prove themselves. Mr. Hill had a free hand. There was nobody to countermand his orders, or to remove from the transfer list a player put on it by him. Soon Coventry football supporters were recalling the promotion days of the mid-thirties, when the Clarrie Bourton team took the club from the third to the second division—only for the club, after the war, to drop back to the third, and for one season, to the fourth! Now it is a new look Highfield Road, with Jimmy Hill as chairman, becoming the first Football League ground in England to have seating for all spectators in a bid to stamp out hooliganism, and with T for Talbot shirts!

The history of Coventry City, like that of the city itself, is linked with the era of the cycle trade. It was at a cycle works, founded by Mr. George Singer, a mayor of Coventry, that a works football team, Singers, was formed. It began to make a name for itself in the Birmingham area. In 1898 it became Coventry City playing on land at Hillfields—now built-up—and acquired Highfield Road ground in 1905. The club became a member of the Southern League, and after the 1914-18 war was elected to the Football League. And as the former Singer Car company was absorbed into the Rootes Group, and the group was taken over by Chrysler, and is now Talbot, it seems logical enough that Talbot should now be sponsoring the club. And the club, in its ups and downs, has certainly put colour into our lives.

The habit goes back for generations: the walk or the drive to Highfield Road, the familiar ground surrounded by terraced houses and other property; the music; the "Oohs" and "Aahs" and the 'thunder' for a home goal; then the return journey with dejected faces or beaming smiles announcing the result! In the old days there were children taking coppers for the privilege of "minding your bike", storing it in the family forecourt or yard. Now there are cars in their hundreds, lining the back streets up to a mile away.

Few Coventry City players, born in Coventry, have played for the senior England team—goalkeeper Reg Matthews was one—but it has been 'caps' galore on other heads at Coundon Road where most players are local men, and where they often catch the eyes of England selectors. There have been at least twenty-seven England rugby players who came from the city. We are told that the best Lions' team ever to tour New Zealand was that of 1971, when England won the series. A Coventry player, David Duckham, was in the team. Two Coventry players—Ivor Preece, a 1940s player with twelve caps, and Phil Judd, a 1960s player— have captained England. Judd who wore twenty-five England jerseys, was captain five times. Oddly enough both men came from the same nursery, Broad Heath School. In 1946 five Coventry men played in an England team against Scotland. They were Pateman, Preece, Stock, Greasley, and Harold Wheatley. A great year, too, in 1963, when six players won England caps: five were chosen for the Australia and New Zealand tour; three for the Barbarians; and thirteen for the Warwickshire fifteen that won the county championship! To get into a discussion about Coventry City is one thing—the club players are from various places in the UK and they are pro-fessionals—to fall into one about the rugger club is quite another! Among members and players are the partisan old boys of local schools, and it's almost a declaration of war to claim the virtues of one above another, in terms of rugger. The enthusiasts remind listeners of the wonders performed by old schoolmates, and the rugger tradition of their old schools. South Street is a typical case. Today it is not even a senior school and is not playing rugger, but will its old boys let us forget their Wheatley brothers, and Roberts, and Jimmy Giles, and Alan Clarke?—all England players from this school, at Hillfields. Drawing on talent from the schools, most of them playing only rugger in those days, Coventry became a leading Rugby Union club, enjoying a continuing run of success.

Coventry has had its rugger club for a hundred years. Early matches were played in 1873 and the club began in 1874. They played at the Old Bull Fields, and then on the Butts ground, using, after it was built in 1907, the Albany Hotel dressing rooms. The early Coventry were a force in their day too, several times winning the Midland Counties Cup. They had gates of ten thousand to twelve thousand for attractive games. A crisis, however, arose a few years before the 1914–18 war, over alleged professionalism, and for about two seasons Northern Union (Rugby League) was played on the Butts ground. Those staying true to Rugby Union played on a ground at London Road, near the Charterhouse, and on various other temporary pitches. Before things returned to normal at the Butts the 1914–18 war began, and after the war, Coundon Road ground, then a field, was bought.

Coventry FC play in front of much smaller crowds than those at Highfield Road, and the atmosphere is very different. No 'crowd roar' here—instead, the occasional shouted "Come on, Coventry," "Now, Cov," and the ripple of hand clapping. Key matches are another matter, a visit, perhaps by Cardiff or a representative touring side, sending up the gate attendance and arousing the latent enthusiasm of men who were bred on rugby but have perhaps wandered away to Highfield Road. With the advent of comprehensive schools, with more boys to choose from and ample recreational facilities, both football and rugby are now played in them.

In addition to the two senior clubs, Coventry has a wealth of junior soccer and rugger clubs, many of them works sides, and others which are independent or belong to old boys of various schools. Soccer, and cricket, is organized in leagues, and for nearly every sport there seems to be an *Evening Telegraph* cup competition! With other competitions, soccer players spend half the season cup-tied, and if they get knocked out of one competition they may still be winners in another.

Trinity Guild RFC, whose headquarters are at Coat-of-Arms Bridge Road, an independent club who can field five teams, are probably the oldest Coventry junior rugger club, dating from 1899. Another independent club, able to put out four teams, are Earlsdon RFC, who play at Kirby Corner Road, where the Coventrians RFC, also an open club, have their ground.

Coventry and North Warwickshire CC, who play at Binley Road, are the 'senior' cricket club, and were founded as long ago as 1851. Since 1947 they have been amalgamated with Coventry and North Warwickshire Squash Rackets Club, and later they were amalgamated with the Coventry and North Warwickshire hockey and tennis clubs—but the old title has been retained, covering all these activities.

The club has had many well-known players, including R. E. S. Wyatt, a native of Meriden, and old boy of King Henry VIII School, who was the club's first life member. He was captain of Warwickshire County Cricket Club, captain of England sixteen times, and played in forty Test matches. Aubrey Hill and Fred Gardner were others who graduated to the county side as regulars. Several others have played for the county. The club played for many years at the Butts, moving to their present headquarters at Binley Road in 1900.

Most people interested in athletics in the British Isles have heard of the city's Godiva Harriers, while Coventry people not particularly sport-minded have seen the dedicated few, running purposefully on circuits round the streets, in training. Some of them keep it up into their old age! Godiva's first run was on 5th October 1879, from the Bull Fields in the Butts, when two 'hares' were sent off, wearing high hats so that they would be distinguishable from the 'hounds' that followed their paper trail. Most of the young runners were watchmakers and they aroused excitement as they pounded over the fields of Earlsdon with one of the whippers-in sounding his hunting horn. It did not greatly please a farmer to see them scattering paper and careering over his fields and he laid about him with a muck-spreading fork. But running with the Godiva Harriers had come to stay.

Godiva have won many honours and have produced internationals, men and women, in every field. They are regarded as one of the best athletic clubs in Britain. Names like those of Heatley and Kilby, Adcocks and Taylor, and David Moorcroft have made sporting news. Godiva have had several Olympic representatives. They have been well served by officials and one name that almost means Godiva Harriers is that of the Ashby family, whose members have been runners and officials for generations. Mr. Jim Ashby joined in 1904, was club champion, and then chairman for thirty years until he retired in 1957. A brother, Arthur, represented Great Britain in the 1908 Olympics. A nephew, Stan, represented Great Britain in the 1928 Olympics, and later became an official, giving a lifetime's service recognized by the presentation to him of the rare Coventry Award of Merit. His daughter, Roma Ashby, was a Godiva star on the track.

Coventry has three golf courses. The only central course is at Hearsall Golf Club, a club with over 500 members and a waiting list, and still with eighteen holes after defeating a Council plan to build a school on it, reducing the course to nine holes. Hearsall have been at Beechwood Avenue since 1908, a well-used and busy club which used to have ex-Ryder Cup player Ralph Moffitt, as pro. The club's history starts in 1895 when play was on Hearsall Common. They found the greens excellent, since they had been "cut out of centuries-old turf". But there was an extra handicap, for people would picnic on the greens! For safety of the public, golfers had to wear red jackets. There was also some bother about wanting to cut long grass to save the loss of golf balls in it, and a farmer objecting as he wanted it for hay.

Experiences of this kind caused the club to move to Beechwood Avenue, taking with them their wooden clubhouse from the common. It was destroyed by fire in 1922, and the new one, built the following year, had a similar fate in 1967, soon after completion of a £24,000 extension. Starting with 60 acres, the club course was extended to 84 acres in 1925, and a policy of acquiring the freehold of it resulted in the club becoming outright owners. Like Hearsall, Coventry Golf Club, whose eighteen-hole course at Finham is just outside the city boundary, had a course on a common, at Whitley. But going back still further, to 1887, they had a few holes and rough greens at Pinley. Soon they moved to Whitley Common, and a writer some fifty years ago enthused about it, saying that Whitley "Links" were "very near the best inland course in England". He was writing in retrospect, when the club had moved to Finham, and could cheerfully speak of the difficulties that made it such a good course, the tricky placing of its hazards and large beds of whins (gorse) requiring skill with the irons.

He said that the links, 5,000 yards long, were "very good in the days of the gutta ball", and added "but the rubber core ball coming along, shortened some of the holes rather too much and robbed them of their characteristics". This mastering of the course with the longer-hit new ball was not the reason the club moved from it. Too many problems were arising, as they did for Hearsall. The corporation had insisted that wooden blocks were placed in the holes when not in play, because of danger for cattle grazing on the common. Golfers accepted that. They put up too with the army drilling on the common, "doing as little damage as possible", although some of them with their guns were seen on the greens. The golfers did not like the corporation's tipping of rubbish, and they managed to have it stopped. But the city was growing and extending out towards them, and more people were using the common for picnics. The last straw was the arrival of footballers, ruining Saturday afternoon golf, and always, it seems, playing on Monday, which was ladies' day!

Perhaps it was the nuisance on ladies' day that led to action! Although they had established themselves and had bought a house as club premises and accommodation for the greenkeeper, plus a horse and new roller, the club now had to find a private course. It was made at Finham Park and opened in 1912, with two Open champions, Harry Vardon and James Braid, taking part in exhibition matches. Harry Vardon went round in sixty-eight. The club, membership over seven-hundred, have an interesting bit of golf history. Hugh Rotherham, a member—he was also a good cricketer and played for England—suggested in 1890 or 1891 that the scratch score of each hole at Whitley Common should be taken, this to be called the 'ground score'. It was done, and golfers tried to beat the ground score as they went round. Great Yarmouth Club adopted the idea. It happened that at the period a popular song was, "Hush, hush, hush, here comes the Bogey man". It was with this in mind, no doubt, that a player made the comment to the Yarmouth club secretary, when trying to beat the ground score: "This ground score player of yours is a regular Bogey man!" Ever since, the ground score has been 'bogey'.

The newest course is the eighteen-hole City of Coventry Club at Brandon Lane, developed by the City Council, opened in 1977. In the city's vicinity are the North Warwickshire (nine holes) at Meriden, the eighteen-hole at Kenilworth, and the Forest of Arden eighteen-hole and nine-hole, at Packington.

Coventry has not got a decent river, and the canal is spoiled by domestic rubbish and industrial waste. Hardly a place for anglers! Yet there are several thousand in the Coventry and District Angling Association, and it has won national championships several times. A noteworthy name in the sport was that of Billy Lane, who was national team captain, and world champion. The association do not worry about the lack of local waters. They have holdings on rivers and canals elsewhere, and these days most people have transport.

Boxing too has a following, with several local amateur clubs, and at one period the city was a prominent centre of the sport. Coventry watched the progress of Leamington boxer Randolph Turpin, from local amateur in Coventry club tournaments, to world middleweight champion when he beat Sugar Ray Robinson, only to crash, soon after, in the return match. Randolph's knock-out punching made him a great crowd attraction and on one occasion at the Butts Stadium a crowd of about twelve thousand saw him knock out the Belgian champion in the first minute. The introduction and the fanfares took longer! Dick Turpin also boxed in Coventry and became a British champion, and a third brother, Jackie, was frequently seen in local boxing rings. Boxing was probably at its peak in Coventry area in their day. Johnny Williams and Charlie Squires were popular local boxers; and among the amateurs at the top of club bills were Les Allen, Michael Stack, Mervyn Hill.

The Butts Stadium is inadequate by modern standards but has served Coventry well. It has been the venue for schools' sports finals, the scene of top-line cycling and athletic matches. Like boxing crowds, the support for these meetings seems to have declined perhaps due to the comfort of seeing sport on TV. For many years we had the annual meeting of the Rover Cycling Club, and meetings bringing international riders staged by Coventry Cycling Club, attended by big crowds. Godiva Harriers presented cycling and athletics. The stadium has few meetings now, and there are no extraordinary crowds. Cycling of course is not the pursuit of every youngster today, with cars in almost every family, but Coventry Cycling Club and others continue with the sport. The club have had some very successful members, but none to rival their Eileen Sheridan, who accumulated a string of British road records in her day.

In most spheres, Coventry has had its personalities. In swimming, among the country's top swimmers were names like Coventry's Symonds, Sykes, and Lord. In tennis, there was Coventry's Tony Mottram, father of England player Buster Mottram, a British star, now a national official in the sport.

Through sport and its many other activities Coventry is certainly blessed with a community spirit.

VII

FRIENDS EVERYWHERE

IF BY now a picture has emerged of an unusual city, shaping itself on individual lines, with a cathedral that seems 'way out', it will come as no surprise to learn that Coventry City Council have been pioneering the ideal of international friendship ever since the war ended. While the cathedral has been spelling out forgiveness and reconciliation, the council have been working on the policy that, to prevent war in future, ordinary men and women must learn to understand one another across the territorial boundaries that separate them. The council began, energetically, to forge links of friendship, and now has twenty-five of them—some quite active, some, due to distance mainly, goodwill ties in intent only. Nowadays we don't talk of Stalingrad, the Russian city that fought a great battle with the invading Germans, because when Stalin was denigrated the town had its name changed to Volgograd; but, regardless of name, Coventry has a bond of friendship with it that goes right back to the period when backs were to the wall.

In those days people became allies for the purpose not of making peace, but war, as when the women of Stalingrad sent a message, signed by 6,819 of them, to the women of Coventry. It was prepared in June 1942 but not handed over until months later, by Madame Maisky, the wife of the ambassador. It sent warmest greetings to the women of Coventry, "valiant British patriots", and expressed thanks for a message of friendship and solidarity they had received from Coventry. After speaking of the battles in which they were engaged, and the part the women were playing in war work, it said: "Valiant sisters, daughters of the great English people! Our friendship grows stronger every day. We are united by the feeling of holy hatred for the enemy, we are united in our resolution to destroy the Fascist barbarians. Let us fight on then with all our strength, with all the means in our power to gain a final victory over Hitler's bands in 1942 . . . Long live the women of Coventry who are playing a valiant part in the struggle against Fascism!"

Six thousand Coventry women had signed the earlier message of greetings and encouragement. It said: "From this city, scarred and ravaged by the arch enemy of civilization, our hearts go out to you, who now face slaughter and suffering even more fearful." It was sent in 1941, and in 1942 the Mayor of Coventry sent a telegram to the Russian city congratulating the defenders on their heroic resistance. In 1943, King George VI offered a sword of honour to Stalingrad in admiration for their courage, and it was on show in the ruins of Coventry Cathedral before it was handed over. While on show the sword and its scabbard were hung in the base of the Cathedral tower and had a guard of honour of two of the city's Home Guardsmen. Thousands of people queued to see it. Other links have been the ikon sent from Stalingrad Cathedral to Coventry Cathedral, and a cross of nails from Coventry Cathedral to Stalingrad.

Coventry did a great deal to show support for the Russian city, apart from messages. It raised more than £20,000—not bad for a city that had been 'destroyed'—for medical relief, and when the Stalingrad hospital was rebuilt, one of the wards was named "Coventry". A bond forged in war became a peacetime friendship when the war was over, and quite a number of Coventry's civic leaders, and other people, have visited the Soviet city. They find that the fact that they are from Coventry opens all doors there. They receive warm hospitality, are taken to the war museum where a tablecloth from Coventry, on which many women embroidered their names, has a place of honour, having been sent as a goodwill token.

When—not so often—Volgograd parties visit Coventry, it is treated as a special occasion, with a civic reception and dinner and a programme which shows them aspects of the city and how Coventry people live. When their deputy mayor came in 1951 he stayed, for example, in one of the city council's new flats. A party of six came in 1955 and their programme included informal meetings with workers, one of them in a public house. The two places co-operated in 1954 when the hydrogen bomb was a matter of such widespread concern, Coventry City Council suggesting that the two cities should make a joint appeal calling on the United Nations disarmament sub-committee to ban it.

Stalingrad—as it then was—invited Coventry to send a civic party to talk it over, and six people made the journey. This resulted in a joint declaration calling for the banning of the atom and hydrogen bombs and it was sent to UNO. Coventry's tie with Volgograd has been watched with interest by the Foreign Office. Sir Patrick Reilly, when appointed British Ambassador to Russia, visited Coventry before he went. As a result, when he visited Stalingrad in 1957 he was able to give them greetings from Coventry, and no doubt it was a useful introduction. In 1971 the Lord Mayor, Alderman S. J. Cordery, visited Volgograd and came back with ideas for strengthening the link, by sporting events, exhibitions, and more student exchanges of the kind already operating.

Friendship with the Russians behind the Iron Curtain did not prevent Coventry's close friendship with a West German city—Kiel. Civic parties, schoolchildren, organizations, are regularly visiting Kiel, and Kiel sends parties to Coventry. It is a friendship that began strangely. Mr. Gwilym Williams, from Coventry, an architectural engineer who had twice been bombed out in Coventry raids, and who was a Home Guard officer at the Daimler factory, later joined the Control Commission and became British officer in charge of the department of reconstruction at Kiel. He did such a good job in Kiel, and was so well regarded, that in 1947, out of gratitude, they formed a Society of Friends of Coventry.

Coventry children helped the goodwill along too by sending chocolate—a rare luxury in Germany then—to Kiel children, and when Mr. Williams returned home and suggested that a Friends of Kiel Association should be formed in Coventry, it was readily taken up. The inaugural meeting at the Council House was attended by some German prisoners-of-war encamped near Coventry, and their impressions can be imagined. One said it was remarkable that Coventry, so badly damaged by his people, should form such an organization. It began as a citizens' affair, not as a civic link, and a party, led by the mayor Alderman George Briggs, went over to Kiel's 'reconstruction week'. Provost Howard represented the cathedral, and he took a cross of nails. Mr. Wilfred Spencer represented the Trades Council, of which he was secretary.

When Councillor W. H. Malcolm became mayor in 1948 he kept up the good work with a visit to Kiel, and ever since Kiel has invited Coventry's civic heads to attend the annual Kiel Week, while they sent representatives to Coventry at intervals. The friendship has flourished, with holiday exchanges of school-children, and meetings at football, swimming, and athletics. The official civic link-up, made in 1956, was at the invitation of the Foreign Office, who hoped it would lead to children's exchanges. Boys of King Henry VIII School dramatic society went to Kiel in 1958, and during a thirteen-day visit gave per-formances of *Hamlet*. When Kiel boys visited Coventry in return there was an athletics match. In 1961 Kiel visitors attended the Coventry mayor-making ceremony in St. Mary's Hall, and in the same year Kiel made a gift of £900 to furnish the library of the new cathedral.

The corps of drums of Coventry School of Music have happy memories of Kiel, where they have made successful visits and have performed before as many as six thousand people. A Coventry Schools FA party went there for matches, staying with families in Kiel, and there was a similar arrangement at Coventry. When parties of young people from Kiel were accommodated in the Charterhouse, London Road, during stays in Coventry, they affectionately nicknamed it, 'Kiel Castle'. Kiel announced in 1967 that they were to name a street or square after Coventry. In that year Coventry Folk Workshop were over there giving folk music concerts at Kiel's 725th anniversary celebrations. Swimming galas, home and away, have been held between swimmers of the friendship towns, and there has been an organ recital in Holy Trinity, Coventry, by the Kiel Director of Music. A Kiel police delegation was in Coventry in 1971. Among gifts exchanged has been a ship's bell from Kiel—an appropriate gift from a port, but where it should hang, in an inland city like Coventry, was a poser. It will probably finish up in the crypt of St. Mary's Hall, to ring out for silence and the announcement to the gathering that dinner is about to be served in the Great Hall!

It is surprising how many of the friendships have their basis in war experiences. Perhaps it is a case of the 'ill wind'. Coventry formed an informal link with Caen (France) at Christmas 1946, when the BBC arranged an international Christmas Day broad-cast to link up the war-damaged cities of Coventry, Caen, Arnhem, Warsaw, and Stalingrad. As a result of this, the mayors of Coventry and Arnhem were invited to visit Caen in 1947, and in 1948 there were further visits, the mayors of Caen and Coventry visiting Arnhem and those of Caen and Arnhem visiting Coventry. There was no further exchange until 1957 when the Lord Mayor of Coventry was invited to attend the inauguration ceremonies at the rebuilt Caen University. There have been exchanges with Caen, but not regularly as Coventry has a very thriving link with another French town, St. Etienne.

Nor did the BBC-inspired link with Arnhem have much result, but again Arnhem has its friendship tie with Croydon. Coventry and Arnhem are content to keep in touch. In 1955 on the tenth anniversary of the liberation of the Netherlands, and again in 1958, Coventry delegations went to Arnhem, and in 1971 Arnhem's deputy mayor and deputy mayoress paid a visit to Coventry.

Apart from Kiel, St. Etienne is the most active of the Coventry friendship ties. It was sponsored by Le Monde Bilingue, and the first official visit from Coventry was made in 1955. Each year, parties of schoolchildren of each town make holiday exchange visits, each of three weeks. Hospitality is on a reciprocal basis, the children staying in private homes. The visits have been well supported and popular, and many lasting friendships have been formed—one or two marriages have even resulted. The friendship had a great boost at an early stage when the late Alderman John Fennell and his wife, a homely, unpretentious couple past retirement age, were Lord Mayor and Lady Mayoress of Coventry. They made a highly successful visit to St. Etienne. The Mayor of St. Etienne made the comment that their visit had been not just a success—"it had been a triumph". Yet the couple spoke no French.

On the way to St. Etienne, in Paris, the Lord Mayor was invited, with his wife, to meet the President of France, M. René Coty, in the Elysée Palace; and Alderman Fennell received a further honour when he was invited to rekindle the everlasting flame at the tomb of the unknown soldier at the Arc de Triomphe. He was the first civic head, outside France, to have this duty, and it was carried out with full ceremonial. The visit to St. Etienne was of such significance for the people of the town that their newspaper had a cartoon showing the little alderman stepping across the Channel. With their unaffected manner, the couple were a 'hit' in St. Etienne. Alderman Fennell, head of a property-repair firm at home, showed his skill during a school visit, taking a piece of wood in the woodwork shop and planing it, then autographing it. On a visit to a cycle works, he mounted a racing cycle and rode it up and down the street to the cheers of the factory workers!

When Alderman Fennell returned to Coventry he proudly recalled the words that the President of France had used to him: "Coventry sounded the tocsin for the whole world, and remained a symbol of heroism and endurance in the face of atrocities." Similar tribute was paid in 1965 when a St. Etienne delegation visited Coventry and looked at the reconstruction. The French mayor, M. Michael Durafour, commented: "Coventry is living and radiant," and went on to refer to the "traditional tenacity of the English people". Coventry and St. Etienne were both engaged in ribbon weaving at one time, and were centres of the trade in their respective countries. It was a native of St. Etienne district, Joseph Jacquard, who invented the famous loom of that name that revolutionized the trade throughout the world in the nineteenth century.

Coventry is also linked with Lidice in Czechoslovakia, the village that was completely destroyed by the Germans and rebuilt after the war. The "Lidice Shall Live" campaign, launched in 1942, was strongly supported by Coventry, and in 1946 the city was officially represented at the laying of the foundation stone of the new Lidice. When a rose garden scheme for Lidice was organized in 1954, Coventry sent 1,000 rose trees for it from the Parks Department nurseries, and in 1955 and in 1957 the city council were again represented at Lidice ceremonies.

Civic leaders of Lidice have several times visited Coventry, and there have been exchanges with the Czech town of Ostrava, and with Prague. The City of Coventry Brass Band visited each of these in turn on a tour to mark their twenty-fifth anniversary, and Coventry has staged various Czechoslovak events such as plays, dances, and Czech trade missions have visited local factories whose products, such as tractors, interested them. Coventry has also had an exhibition about itself and its products, in Ostrava. So from friendship there may have come benefits in trade.

Some links seem unable to get off the ground, but at least the goodwill has been shown. An example is the town of Graz, in Austria. This link was initiated by the Educational Interchange Council in 1948, and a Graz delegation came to Coventry and made a successful visit. A return was made from Coventry in 1949. Very little has happened in recent years, and the contact has been mainly at a personal level, through Councillor Dennis Berry, who was a prisoner-of-war there and has friends with whom he keeps in touch.

Alderman Fennell's meeting with the President of France was not the only instance of a Coventry friendship tie leading to contact with the head of state. When Alderman Harry Weston led a civic visit to the friendship towns of Belgrade and Sarajevo in 1952, the party was received by Marshal Tito. Coventry has made gifts—a new Coventry-made car was one, another was some roadmaking equipment—to the two Yugoslav towns, and a joint party from them has visited Coventry. Other links have been of exchanges of children's holiday parties.

Dresden in East Germany has a friendship with Coventry dating back to 1956 when the German city sent gifts from its Coventry–Dresden Friendship Committee, apparently formed because of common experience of wartime air-raid damage. In Coventry a similar committee was formed, not connected with the city council, and a delegation visited Dresden. Later, the link was taken up by the City Council. Dresden was anxious to play some part in the reconstruction of Coventry and decided to hold a competition among its artists for a mural to go into Coventry's new retail market. The mural was brought to Coventry and the panels fixed in place by the artist. There have been several exchange visits, by other parties, such as teachers and trade unionists.

Friendship took a practical form too in 1965, when a working party of young people from Coventry Cathedral went to Dresden and helped to clear thousands of tons of rubble to enable work to be done on the rebuilding of a church hospital. A Coventry Service of Youth theatre group gave performances in Dresden in 1967, in schools, works, and clubs, presenting a 'mixed bag' of music, drama, and comedy. Civic parties from Dresden visited Coventry in 1959 and 1968, and a Dresden hygiene exhibition was staged in the Herbert Art Gallery and Museum in 1970.

A three-way link between Coventrys was forged in 1971. Coventry, England, and Coventry, Connecticut, U.S.A., who had been linked in friendship for several years, extended the link to include another American Coventry, that at Rhode Island. The link between Coventry, England, and the Coventry in Connecticut has been growing with exchanges, by charter flight, of large parties of parents and children from certain schools; and, arising from American interest in Coventry, the prospect of more general parties of tourists from the States, taking advantage of cheaper rates in charter flights, is being explored, the idea being that Coventry, England, would be their base.

Three Canadian towns, Cornwall, Granby, and Windsor, are linked with Coventry, but the ties are not very active. Others are with Ostrova and Galatzi, Rumania; Bologna, Italy; Kecskemet and Dunaujvaros, Hungary; Cork, Ireland; Warsaw, Poland; Parkes, New South Wales; and Kingston, Jamaica. New Coventry, a township in New South Wales, Australia, has had contact with Coventry, England, but it is not a friendship link, as one already exists with Parkes. There is talk of a link with China!

Some friendships are obviously limited because the two places are at great distance from one another, but they are a means of introduction when any visitor from those towns visits Coventry, as some have done; and sometimes council officers, such as fire officers, come to Coventry for a period of training. Friendships are fostered by one of the Coventry City Council committees, and there is also an independent Coventry Committee for International Understanding, which pursues these and other ties on its own account. It forms parties for organized visits, such as those made to Meschedes, Germany, and provides hospitality for visitors. It encourages young people to go abroad, finds hosts for young people who wish to come to Coventry to study, to holiday, or to work. Coventry must be one of the best known of English cities, through the many contacts that have been made!

The path of friendship has not been altogether a smooth one. Council visits abroad were regarded as jaunts at public expense, and those to Iron Curtain areas were seen as politically-motivated. Even moderates could not see much useful purpose in the journeyings of civic delegations when decisions of moment were, anyway, matters for heads of state! Yet an occasion did arise which indicated that by getting together the representatives of ordinary people do have a voice, a voice for peace. This was in 1961, when tension was at its height about Berlin, the big powers at flash-point. Coventry took the initiative in an attempt to get everybody to cool down. It sent out an invitation to its friendship towns—including those behind the Iron Curtain—to meet in Coventry to have talks. The invitation went from a Coventry meeting of civic, church, and industrial representatives, so it was broadly-based. It reminded friendship towns that Coventry had been grievously bombed in the war and it appealed to people of the world not to abuse those with whom they disagreed and not to indulge in "a trigger-happy attitude that war is inevitable . . .". It announced a day of prayer to be held in Coventry churches. Then the Lord Mayor, the late Alderman William Callow, made a 2,000-mile dash to Italy, Yugoslavia, and Austria to discuss a suggestion for a peace conference of friendship towns, in Coventry. This took place in the Belgrade Theatre in September, with delegates from towns in seven countries, including Stalingrad, Warsaw, and Lidice from behind the Iron Curtain. The conference sent out a call for relaxation of tension, and for peace, and the resolution to this effect was sent to the appropriate powers.

It was a gesture from civic leaders of different nationalities, and nobody knows what effect it had; but the fact that they could get together at a time of crisis and give expression to the fears of ordinary people and their desire to live in peace was surely a justification for friendship links. It was better than doing nothing! Because of its special place in the world, on account of its suffering in the war, Coventry has felt that it has a responsibility to give a lead in international friendship activities. As a result, it represents to people of many lands the ideal of unity and friendship.

This was evident in 1955, when—a proud moment for him— the late Alderman T. H. Dewis, then Lord Mayor of Coventry, stood before the members of the Council of Europe in their Strasbourg headquarters and received their award of the European Prize, a shield, to Coventry as the municipality which had done most in that year to promote the ideal of European unity. Alderman Dewis, a Co-op buyer at Foleshill, and the Lady Mayoress, were afterwards guests of honour at a dinner attended by political leaders of the various countries. The feeling that my city, so badly hit in war, had gained inspiration for good motives from its experience was uppermost in my thoughts as the representative of the *Coventry Evening Telegraph*, sitting with them while the politicians rose and toasted the "City of Coventry".

Coventry canal basin awaiting redevelopment
Bayley Lane and St. Mary's Hall, a conservation area

VIII

THE CITY COUNCIL

THE drive and direction in the creation of the new Coventry has come from the Council House, in Earl Street, which had damage in the raids and was repaired, and became the centre of the urgent action that had to be taken to cope with the situation after the blitz. Built of brown sandstone, gabled, with figures of Leofric and Godiva and Justice, heraldic shields, and its clock tower, it is a handsome-looking building and a worthy seat of the city's local government—although the expansion of staff to cope with the growth of Coventry has made it necessary to build new 'glasshouse' blocks of council offices across the road. The Council House was taken into use in 1917, but, due to the war, the official opening was not until three years later. It was opened by the Duke of York, afterwards King George VI, who in the Second World War was to enter it again when its windows were boarded up and lighting was by candles. He was to know Coventry well after opening the Council House. He came again in 1935 and opened the technical college; then visited Coventry three times in a few years, as King, during and after the war.

The Council House is not a building where many callers are at leisure to look around. Mostly they are on business—a matter of the rates, perhaps a petition. But there is quite a lot of interesting interior detail, such as stained-glass windows, decoration of ceilings, and along the lobbies on the first floor the collection of paintings by H. E. Cox of bygone parts of Coventry, such as Butcher Row. Older people in Coventry who have not seen them, would get much pleasure from the collection. At present, the main invasion by the public is at mayor-making time, when the Parks Department array the stairways and corridors with exotic plants and blooms from their hot-houses, and people go in to admire the show.

The Coventry boy statue, Priory Street

Schoolchildren learning civics are taken in parties to see the Council House, and into the council chamber, and arrangements can always be made for parties of interested citizens. It is a dignified place. The members' seats form a semi-circle, looking to the Lord Mayor's dais. Seats are of Warwickshire oak —carved with acorns and birds because Coventry is in the one-time Forest of Arden. On the walls hang pictures of the first Lord Mayor and the first woman Lord Mayor, which were presented to the city; and there are small shields going right round the chamber walls bearing the name and year of office of successive mayors and Lord Mayors.

A few minutes before the council meeting there is a buzz of conversation as members—there are fifty-four—take their places. Then, a sudden hush, and the Lord Mayor's short procession enters with everybody on their feet. With him, two bewigged and berobed men carry the civic sword and mace which they place in racks before the Lord Mayor. Now he is in charge, with his insignia of office as token of authority. The sword is said to be of the fifteenth century, and the mace dates from the seventeenth.

The public seating is in an upstairs gallery, at the back of the chamber. From time to time, while the meeting is in progress, lights flash on, and like traffic lights they are red, amber and green. They are switched on by an official who times the speakers, according to the time limit set out in standing orders. As their limit nears, on goes amber. When red appears, the speaker sits down, unless he is asked by popular vote to complete his remarks.

All the council meetings take place here, except the annual meeting in May, which is in St. Mary's Hall, where more members of the public can be seated than in the gallery of the chamber. There is a bridge from the Council House giving access to the armoury of St. Mary's Hall. This was once a storehouse for harness and armour belonging to the city and to the Trinity Guild. Now, suitably restored and furnished, it is used for committee and other meetings, and as an overflow from the great hall when extra guests turn up who cannot be accommodated down there for dinners. Outside the armoury, looking over the hall, is the minstrel gallery where music is still played for the entertainment of the company gathered below.

The annual meeting, and the annual civic church service, which starts the municipal year, are usually the only occasions when robes are worn—it used to be red for aldermen, but this office was abolished in 1974 under local government reorganization. Councillors wear blue and the Lord Mayor, in general elected from their ranks, wears a costly ceremonial black and gold robe that was presented to the council in 1956 by the engineering employers association jointly with the engineering unions. Annual meetings make a colourful spectacle in a setting like St. Mary's Hall, and are the occasions of warm and friendly speeches for the outgoing and incoming Lord Mayors.

Less happy meetings do take place, as they did in 1967, and in 1937, and, it appears, will be repeated. As in most councils, membership is divided, Labour versus Conservative, and in Coventry from 1937 to 1967 Labour had a heavy majority. For thirty years they held such solid control, including responsibility for the redevelopment, that it seemed unlikely that there would ever be a change. Then suddenly, it ended. There was a mighty national swing against Labour, and in Coventry the Conservatives made substantial gains—not enough to give them power in normal years, but enough in 1967 because it was one of the years in which nine of the aldermen were due for re-election after completing a six-year term. The aldermen were not voted in by a public poll. They were elected by the councillors, from their own ranks, and the retiring aldermen were usually re-elected for another six years. But in 1967 the Conservatives had a majority of councillor seats, and eight retiring Labour aldermen were at their mercy.

The annual meeting was a 'blood bath', the axe falling on nationally-known Labour veterans—the late Alderman Sidney Stringer, leader of the council, who had guided post-war policy, and Alderman George Hodgkinson, his deputy, both former mayors, each with thirty-nine years' council service, Alderman Stringer as the education figurehead, Alderman Hodgkinson as the planner. Each had received the freedom of the city, a rare honour, and now they were swept from office, from the council, into the backwater of retirement. Four past Lord Mayors, and a former Lady Mayoress, with service ranging variously from seventeen to thirty years, were also axed, and one alderman in ill health had announced his retirement in advance.

Local councils have become the arena of party politics, with very few exceptions, and in politics there is, they say, no place for sentiment. The Conservatives, who then proceeded to elect their own members to the vacant aldermanic seats, had a precedent for their action. In 1937, when Labour first gained control from a mixed majority of Conservative, Liberal, and Progressive members, they had been equally ruthless, and had sent long-serving aldermen and ex-mayors packing. The Conservative leadership, having won a majority on the councillor benches had to consolidate as much as possible by securing aldermanic seats.

In 1970 another nine aldermen would have completed the six-year term, and seven were Labour; but more 'bloodshed' was avoided because, before then, two died, two announced their retirement, and one, Alderman G. W. Sheridan, did not wait for the axe to fall on him, standing instead for a councillor's seat in the municipal elections, and winning it. Two Labour aldermen remained, and they were re-elected—so the Conservatives had sixteen of the aldermanic seats and a thumping majority, and the Labour Party had the other two and their thinnest representation on the council for thirty-three years. The aldermanic share-out was no surprise to them, for it was roughly the pattern that they they had set when they held power. The Conservatives, despite building a reserve of aldermen since 1967, then gradually lost ground at successive annual elections, with Labour making gains in councillor seats. They regained power in 1972, and now local elections are fought without the cushion of a majority of aldermanic seats to keep one or other party in power, regardless of the votes cast.

Whoever rules at the Council House, it is a less glamorous and much less exciting job than it was in the busy years of reconstruction when big decisions were called for. The changes made in 1974 took away much of the powers of the council, along with aldermen who had been at the heart of the reconstruction, and the new system of paying allowances to councillors for their hours of service took away the voluntary status they had enjoyed when they served the city for the love of it and at some cost to themselves. And when we admired them.

One great reward for service on the City Council is that of becoming Lord Mayor, highest office of all, to which the member senior in length of service is elected, with his wife as the Lady Mayoress. For one glorious year the pattern of their life is transformed by a daily round of engagements: receiving visitors, sometimes royalty, in the Parlour; performing openings and presentations; making hundreds of speeches; showing the civic flag in visits to schools; travelling at home, and sometimes abroad. The Lord Mayor may be a shop-floor worker, a shop-keeper, a company director, it makes no difference. For a year he is "My Lord Mayor", respected and honoured. To enable any elected member to undertake the office, there is remuneration, now over £5,000 a year, a hospitality allowance that works out at about £48,000 a year, and the civic car. Coventry has had mayors since 1346, and Lord Mayors since 1953. The first Lord Mayor was the late Alderman H. B. W. Cresswell, and the first woman Lord Mayor, the late Alderman Pearl Hyde. The first woman Mayor was Alderman Miss Alice Arnold, in 1937.

Local government has a stodgy image for the man in the street, who thinks at once of red tape, form-filling, rate demands, and of civic junkets and what he regards as unnecessary jaunts by councillors, paid for out of his, the ratepayer's, pocket. Coventry councillors were always on the move, and the unorthodox Labour council, with a big job to tackle in reconstruction and redevelopment, made it an exciting job to be involved in local government. There were always new projects to be carried out, ideas that made news. Their schemes always had to be the best, the biggest, and, said critics, the most extravagant! But they swept the Coventry public along in their enthusiasm, held exhibitions, public meetings, inviting citizens to put forward their criticisms and their views. An 'Ideas competition' was held. The public-relations side of it was excellent. People had to take notice. Some of the fever for building a city had to rub off, and it spread to the community, especially when they saw the buildings taking shape.

The council put planning first, the cost never overawing them. A £41 million road programme was approved in 1965. The civic debt, then about £90 million, seemed immaterial. "We have the assets," they said. Now the debt is £225 million.

Never afraid to try out a new idea if they thought it a good one, the council introduced cheap bus travel for pensioners. Later, although they were warned about the legal position by the City Treasurer, they decided to bring in free chiropody for old people too. They faced a showdown, with the showmen of the Great Fair, who brought the big guns of their National Guild to bear when the council put a limit on the charge for rides, and won. The biggest showdown, however, was in 1954, when, because they said it was a waste of time and money as then constituted, they abandoned Civil Defence! The Government acted promptly, appointing three commissioners, who took office in Coventry and proceeded to manage the Civil Defence organization.

The Civil Defence officer, instead of making his reports to the city council's Civil Defence committee, and receiving their instructions, reported instead to the commissioners at an office in Queen's Road! It worked, but it was expensive for the city council. All costs, including the commissioners' salaries, fell on them, whereas previously there had been Government grant and no salaries to pay. The position was maintained for a year, when the council said they had made their point, and capitulated. Fifteen years later the Civil Defence Corps was disbanded by the Government. There were few councils that were more of a nuisance to Whitehall than that of Coventry, persevering with deputations that pleaded for financial sanction for schemes, protesting against Ministry delays or refusals, refusing to take no for an answer—and aggressive with it!

Conservative rule, that followed in 1967, brought dignity, restraint, and order, the orthodox after the unorthodox, a concentration on management efficiency and budget control, streamlining of committees and departments, an effort above all to economize for the benefit of the ratepayer. The late Gilbert Richards, leader of his party and of the council, careful and studied in his remarks to the chamber, as expected of a solicitor, steadily pursuing a path leading to more private enterprise, and less interference by the municipality. Less council-house building, for example, until it stopped, and the release of some of the council-owned land to private builders. In the city centre, emphasis on commercial enterprise embarking on blocks of offices.

There was a general tidying up of the central area: the installation of litter bins, lady cleaners; at long last, the dustbin collection problem was solved by the use of plastic sacks; and, in the same sphere, there was a scheme for a £2 million waste-reduction unit to incinerate the refuse because of shortage of tipping sites. In another direction, tourism: more street signs, plaques for places of interest, and membership of the Tourist Board.

Changes in membership of the city council since 1967 had their parallel among the corporation's chief officers, due to retirements that came close together and broke up a long-standing team whose members were well known in local government. Sir Charles Barratt, the town clerk, died soon after he retired; his deputy Mr. K. B. Turner, Dr. A. H. Marshall the city treasurer and Mr. W. L. Chinn the director of education were among several stalwarts who stepped aside. As a result of this at chief officer level the corporation had a new look, and with it, a new structure. Sir Charles Barratt, who was a lawyer town clerk in the traditional mould, was succeeded by an accountant, Mr. J. D. Hender, who was previously city treasurer. In 1974 he became Chief Executive of the new West Midlands Metropolitan County Council.

At the same time, Coventry's water department went to the Severn-Trent Water Board, the bus service went to the West Midlands, along with the fire service and the police, and the health department became part of the National Health Service area health authority. Responsibility for roads, refuse disposal, and overall planning was taken over by the West Midlands. Yet Coventry City Council still run a big business. There are 18,000 employees, of whom 9,500 are in education, and there are 2,500 in the Social Services department. The annual budget is around £100 million, but £68 million of this goes on education, and £16 million on social services. And at the paying-in end are 135,000 ratepayers, other income coming from Government grants. The council own about 27,000 houses and flats, shops and offices, and 160 schools. Councillors claim about £43,000 in annual attendance allowances, and are also reimbursed travel and meal costs. Some claim more than £2,000.

Coventry local government history has had ups and downs. By 1451 Coventry had gone to the dizzy heights of being a county borough. This honour was granted by Henry VI when he had concluded an enjoyable visit, given and received gifts, and complimented the civic leaders on their well-governed town. For four-hundred years, Coventry was a major authority; but then litigation in a court action had the effect of removing the status it had enjoyed so long. It lost the Assizes, the Quarter Sessions, and its recorder, and had to give up the city gaol and county hall to Warwickshire.

In 1888, forty or so years later, Coventry regained its county status; but it did not have a Quarter Sessions and recorder again until 1928. The importance of this was marked by holding the first sessions in St. Mary's Hall. The year 1928 was one of widespread celebration, when schoolchildren had field days and free teas and commemoration mugs, because of a big extension of the boundary, trebling Coventry's size. Its area increased from a mere 4,147 acres to 12,878, partly swallowing Foleshill Rural District Council.

Since then, there have been other extensions and the area is over 20,000 acres and a population of 330,000. There was one Member of Parliament until 1945 when Captain W. F. Strickland, Conservative, represented the city, and there are now four. The late Richard Crossman (East) and Maurice Edelman (North) were Labour MPs for over twenty years from 1945. William Wilson (South-East), a Coventry solicitor, has been Labour MP since 1964 and is to retire at the first general election in the 1980s.

Mr. Crossman, who was succeeded by George Park, former Labour leader of Coventry City Council, and Mr. Edelman, succeeded by Geoffrey Robinson, ex-chief of Jaguar Cars, were contrasting types. Mr. Crossman was burly, dynamic, brusque, ex-Labour minister, appearing briefly at elections, and returned each time with a thumping majority. 'Maurice'—the party workers always use first names—the successful author and playwright, was handsome, quietly spoken, ever courteous, never in office in a Labour government. Mr. Edelman's charm, and Mr. Crossman's pugnacity, between them squashed flat a succession of Conservative candidates in post-war general elections.

In Coventry South, which covers more Conservative territory, there have been changes of representation. At one time Mr. Crossman was the doughty politician on foreign affairs, Mr. Edelman defended the industrial front, and a third Labour MP, Miss Elaine Burton (South) who later became Lady Burton, spoke up frequently for the housewife on domestic matters. At another period, we had a local man as South's Conservative MP. Mr. Philip Hocking had learned his politics in the Young Conservatives and had a spell on the city council. He became a junior Minister, but Coventry South was a marginal seat, and he lost it.

He was defeated by Mr. Wilson, so Coventry South had a Coventry-born man (Mr. Hocking had lived in the city from childhood but was born in Lancashire) as its MP. Mr. Wilson went to local schools, worked his way up to be a solicitor from a working-class home in Earlsdon, and after war service rose to be senior partner in the firm of Penmans. He could not get a seat on Coventry City Council because he stood in Earlsdon, a Conservative ward, but he succeeded in winning a seat on Warwickshire County Council and held it for twelve years. He was attempting the impossible when he stood for Parliament in Warwick and Leamington against Anthony Eden (later Lord Avon), but he tried four times, a David who never slew Goliath—though he once came near, reducing a huge majority to a mere 2,000. He was rewarded in Coventry South, although it was Conservative-held, beating Mr. Hocking, member of a family building concern, in 1964, by a thin 1,833-vote margin. Mr. Wilson held on to the seat in subsequent general elections; he is a veritable workhorse, continuing in practice and making appearances in court in the mornings, dashing by train to London for sessions in the House in the afternoon, often sitting into the night, and sometimes right through it to morning, but always appearing on duty each morning, a seemingly tireless man.

The fourth Coventry MP following the 1979 election is John Butcher in the South-West seat, the only Conservative of the foursome. The European MP is John Ling, Conservative, representing Midlands Central.

Voting for Members of Parliament used to be a rowdy affair in the city, and there was a time when only freemen could vote. Their vote, obviously, was very important. It led to some knavish tricks. City councillors who favoured a candidate for Parliament were not above rigging the elections, delaying the admission of freemen, 'swearing in' freemen of their choice, and rushing them to the poll! In fact, there were some unsavoury goings-on in elections, and Coventry had a name for brawling at the hustings. Daniel Defoe, who is better known as the author of *Robinson Crusoe*, wrote about the conditions he found here, in his *Tour through the Whole Island of Great Britain*. He said there was such heat and animosity that the inhabitants "engaged at one another, met, and fought a pitched battle in the middle of the street", and that "they fell on with such fury with clubs and staves" and "fought with such obstinacy that 'tis scarce credible". The astounded Defoe added that they were not the rabble of the town, but the burgesses and chief inhabitants, "nay, even magistrates, aldermen, and the like". He said it was not just one skirmish to determine a quarrel, but it "held on for several weeks". This makes our elections campaigns look mousy affairs!

Defoe was writing in the eighteenth century. In the nineteenth things were not much better. Commissioners sent to Coventry to report on a parliamentary election in 1826 found the hustings occupied "by a fierce and inebriated mob in the interests of Corporation candidates, who by acts of violence debarred all access to voters of the opposite party". They tore clothes, beat and kicked people. Their passions were inflamed by immense quantities of gin supplied from the shop of an alderman—and handed out by corporation constables from the police office!

In reporting elections in Coventry for a good many years, I have never seen as much as a scuffle, and never a spot of gin! The excitement has been when a seat has changed hands, producing a burst of clapping and cheering if the Tories win, and fervent singing of the "Red Flag" if the opposite applies. Once there was a slight to-do when a polling station ran short of ballot papers before closing time, so great was the interest in voting. Occasionally there is a little difficulty with the count when figures won't balance. It's pretty mundane, though, compared with what happened in the 'good old days'.

Also rather unhealthy in our local affairs, long ago, was the 'mix-up' over charities. It is kind to say the Corporation mixed up their own money with what was in their care for charitable purposes! Among other matters brought into the open by an enquiry, it was found that the corporation had made leases at low rents to council members, or to their relations of lands held in trust for Sir Thomas White's charity.

The upshot was that the corporation had to sell valuable municipal plate to make good the deficiencies. When the Municipal Corporations Act of 1835 came along one of its measures took charities out of corporation control, and they were handed over to trustees. The Act gave us the type of council we now have, openly elected after years of struggle for reform. Yet today it is hardly regarded as a privilege. Less than half of us vote in local elections, although all we have to do is go a short distance, because polling booths are placed fairly near to everybody. Coventry has been a municipality for over 600 years, since Edward III in 1345 authorized the men of Coventry to elect a mayor and bailiffs. They replaced the steward of the lord of the manor. By-laws that regulate our lives have been with us ever since! The rates have been levied since 1835.

IX

PIONEERS OF INDUSTRY

COVENTRY'S importance as an industrial centre, and its prosperity this century, came from the bicycle trade, although nobody in the city makes bicycles any more. But the bicycle pioneers became car pioneers, the skilled workers in cycle firms became the skilled craftsmen on cars, and the city enjoyed years of prosperity.

The story starts with a young man, Rowley Turner, cycling into Coventry in 1868 on one of those 'Parisian toys'—an early velocipede or boneshaker. A student over there, he had become interested in the velocipede, which was in vogue. He started a small business, and soon obtained more orders than he could meet. Rowley decided to bring a model to England in the hope that the firm at Coventry of which his uncle, Josiah Turner, was head, would manufacture 400 of them. He rode it from Coventry Station to the Coventry Sewing Machines Co. at King Street, and his uncle—in, without knowing it, at the birth of a national industry—had the firm's articles of association altered so that bicycles could be made. Coventry Sewing Machines Co. became Coventry Machinists Co. The company foreman, James Starley, who was an inventive genius and had been making improvements in sewing-machine design, now had a new contraption to grapple with.

The firm were not after all able to supply the 400 velocipedes required for the French market because the Franco-Prussian war intervened. It halted the cycle trade in France, and it gave the Coventry manufacturer, and those who joined in, a chance to expand the industry. Cycling rapidly became popular as the early bicycle was improved, mainly by the patents brought out by James Starley; and from being a depressed city after the decline of the weaving and watchmaking trades, Coventry ran into a boom and became the cycle city for the world. Coventry

Machinists moved to larger premises in Little Park Street. New firms were springing up.

Starley and William Hillman, another of the employees, patented a penny-farthing lightweight all-metal bicycle, the first, in 1870, and called it the Ariel. The two engineers went into business to make it, and one of their publicity stunts was a ride that occupied them from daybreak to midnight, from London to Coventry. The roads were not the smooth surfaces of today, tyres were solid, and the riders were middle-aged men. Not surprisingly they had to spend two or three days in bed recovering from the ride!

The Ariel was followed by Starley's patent of the tangent-spoked wheel, and many more patents. One of the most important, for the transport world, was the differential gear. This came about because when he was riding with his son William in a four-wheeler, sitting side by side and both pedalling, William out-pedalled him with his greater strength. The machine, forced to one side, overturned in a ditch. As he sat there by the roadside and thought about it, James Starley thought up the differential gear.

The most famous of Starley's machines was the Salvo tricycle, and Queen Victoria ordered two of these for use of the royal household. He was commanded to appear before her and demonstrate one of them, which he did, receiving a gold watch to mark the occasion. The model then became known as the Royal Salvo. James Starley, who had become a respected figure in Coventry, the city which owed its prosperity to him, died at the age of 51 shortly after this. The city's cycle factories closed down for the funeral so that workers could attend it, and a fund was opened for a memorial to 'the father of the cycle trade'. It was erected on Greyfriars Green, and the unveiling brought a gathering of thousands to hear mayoral and other tributes to him. Apart from the memorial, Starley Road, nearby, was named after him, and his widow moved into a house there. When new offices were built near Coventry Station after the Second World War, as headquarters of the British Cycle and Motor Cycle Industries Association, the building was named Starley House, and one of his machines was taken from the Herbert Museum and pedalled to Starley House for the occasion.

Coventry's cycle trade owed much to the name Starley, for his sons and a nephew carried on the trade and brought out many patents. His sons opened larger works employing 300 workers near the memorial, and opened a Paris depot. One son, William, who was in the Royal Warwickshire Territorials, introduced the cycle to the army, with suitable fittings to carry equipment. The nephew, John Kemp Starley, went into a partnership, that of Starley and Sutton. It is an instance of the way the motor trade developed directly from cycles that a first product of this partnership was the Rover cycle (it had small wheels and was similar in design to the modern cycle). After his partner's death in an accident James Kemp Starley formed the Rover Bicycle Co., which was forerunner of the Rover Motor Co. For his own use he designed, as early as 1888, an electrically-driven tricar, which he tested in France and averaged 8 miles per hour. In England the speed limit was 4 miles per hour, and a man had to walk ahead of a car holding a red flag.

Coventry cycle works, large and small, were many at the close of the nineteenth century. Coventry Machinists' Co. had their Cheylesmore Works at Little Park Street, a four-storey block where nearly 1,000 workers were turning out 700 machines a week. They had agencies all over the world, and their popular model was the Swift—later to give the name of the firm's successors, the Swift Motor Co. Another firm, Singer and Co., formed 1874, had large works employing 800 people, and claimed to have invented the diamond frame which became universal. Mr. George Singer was Mayor of Coventry from 1892 to 1894. The firm were noted in Coventry for their brass band, and for their football club.

The Coventry Cross Cycle Co. were also at West Orchard, at the Albion Mills, and also at Foleshill Road. The Premier Cycle Co. (Hillman, Herbert and Cooper Ltd.) were so successful that they established another factory at Nuremberg, Germany, to cope with Continental business. The company had been selling over 20,000 bicycles a year. The works had frontages to Read Street and South Street, Coventry, where the 'helical' tube was pioneered to save weight in the cycle frame. Clarke, Cluley and Co. were making Globe cycles at the Globe Cycle Works, Well Street and had about 150 workers.

Quinton bicycles were made by the Quinton Cycle Co. Ltd., whose works, employing 200 people, were not far from Coventry Station. Dr. C. W. Iliffe, who was coroner for North Warwickshire, was one of the directors. He had been founder of the

Coventry Co-operative Watch Manufacturing Co. A fellow director was Mr. Rowland Hill, J.P., also a watch manufacturer. Mr. Ernest Peirson was secretary and Mr. Samuel Gorton was general manager. Townend Brothers Ltd. began in Wellington Street and moved to Ford Street, and finally to works which had frontage to Paynes Lane and Gosford Street. They had 200 workers and produced models including the Townend Light Roadster, and Townend Racer. The Triumph Cycle Co. was first established in Much Park Street and was so successful that it added new works, built in Priory Street. Alderman Tomson, five times mayor, was chairman, Mr. G. W. Sawyer was vice-chairman, and Mr. S. Bettman and Mr. M. J. Schulte, managing directors.

Lea and Francis were making their Lea cycle at Lower Ford Street; W. B. Turner and Sons had the National Works in Spon Street; Bennett, Cotton and Co. made the Elk cycles; the Coronet Cycle Co. were in former watchmaking premises at Chapel-fields; J. H. Shaffir and Co. were in Hertford Street; and Humber and Co. Ltd. had their large four-storey factory at Coventry in addition to the Beeston and Wolverhampton works.

Rudge-Whitworth Ltd., formed in 1894 by a merger of two cycle companies, were in the six-storey factory block that is now used by G.E.C. at Spon Street. The works produced 100 bicycles a day in the busy season, went on to produce a famous make of motor-cycle and to develop the wire wheel. The factory block is one of the few reminders that Coventry was once the centre of the cycle trade. Coventry-Eagle cycles, and later motor-cycles, were a well-known mark. They were the last firm in the bicycle trade, surviving here until the 1960s, when labour difficulties, coupled with high local levels of pay, forced them to move away. Triumph bicycles, too, were made after the Second World War, the company moving from New Buildings to a new factory at Torrington Avenue, but soon closing down. Some firms, among them Rover, for many years produced cycles, motor-cycles, and cars; but as the motor trade grew, so the cycle trade declined. Only Middlemore's, component makers, remains.

Coventry, fittingly, has one of the largest collections of old bicycles in the world, but they could not be displayed properly until the City Council in 1980 opened its British Road Transport Museum in a former factory in Cook Street, where over 100 cars and commercial vehicles, 200 bicycles, and 50 motor cycles, carefully restored, are on show. It is appropriate that as the road transport industry in Britain had its origins in Coventry, the museum should be established in the city. It offers a walk, in effect, through road transport history as the displays are supported by information and material of the period.

While the cycle industry was booming, there was still a considerable textile industry. Leigh Mills at Coventry made serges, plain and fancy worsted coatings and trouserings. The spinning of the yarn was done at Stanningley, near Leeds, where all activities are now concentrated. Lord Leigh was chairman of the company. Lester, Harris and Co. made woven name goods at Great Heath. Dubock, Jones and Co. were elastic web and smallwares manufacturers at Wellington Street; and the works of ribbon manufacturer James Cramp were in Much Park Street. Other firms included W. H. Grant and Co., Livingstone Mill, Foleshill; Pridmore and Co., Foleshill Mills; Bates and Dalton, South Street Mills; G. Carey Franklin, Earl Street; William Franklin and Son, Bayley Lane and Much Park Street, Joshua Perkins and Sons who made coach trimmings at Britannia Mill, Paynes Lane, and Henry Spencer and Co. Earl Street. Textiles included medal ribbons, naval cap ribbons, hosiery, blouses, braces.

Those still in watchmaking included Smith and Sons at Hearsall Works, who made watch balances; John Hewitt in Holyhead Road; John Hawley and Son, at Reliable Works, Cow Lane, whose 'Collier's Friend' was for "colliers, railwaymen, and rough wear generally"; Thomas Kinder and Son, Richmond Terrace, Chapelfields; B. Bonniksen, patentee and maker of the Karrusel movements, at Norfolk Street; Charles J. Hill, Russell House; J. Masters and Sons, St. John Street; J. Player and Son, the Butts; Joseph White and Son, Earlsdon; A. H. Read, Hill Street; John Adams, Hertford Terrace, Queens Road; and Mr. R. Waddington, Earlsdon. Coventry Movement Co. Ltd., Spon Street, who supplied movements to watchmakers, survived the loss of that trade and became general engineers.

Having given a lead in the cycle industry, Coventry was also to play a useful role in the English production of the pneumatic tyre. Dunlop's invention was being developed in Dublin, but the Company had to leave when the local authority and the trades council took action against them because tyre manufacturing was causing a smell of rubber solution. The company moved to

England—to Coventry. They would have moved almost certainly
without the prodding, because cycle wheels were having to be
sent from English firms to Dublin to have the new-type tyres
fitted, and this was not a satisfactory arrangement. It was later
that the detachable tyre was to come along. The works in
Coventry were opened in 1890 and soon were making 1,000
tyres a week. The Dunlop Pneumatic Tyre Co., Coventry, of
which Mr. Harvey du Cros junior was managing director, was to
pave the way for the massive Dunlop tyre organization, the firm
moving eventually to Birmingham. It was the fore-runner of
Fort Dunlop.

Francis Barnett motor-cycles were made in Coventry, at
Lower Ford Street, after the war, but Triumph motor-cycles are
the last link with the motor-cycle trade. The factory is near
Meriden, just outside Coventry.

The arrival of the car in Coventry was similar to the arrival of
the bicycle in being an import. The car came from Germany,
when a financial group in Coventry formed the British Motor
Syndicate and secured the rights to make the German Daimler
in this country. Although engineers everywhere were designing
and testing out their individual petrol-driven cars, nowhere in
England were cars in production until Daimlers were made at
Coventry in 1896. It was the first real step in English car manufacture. Daimlers were driven—steered by tiller—to the top of the
Worcestershire Beacon in The Malverns, and one was driven from
John o' Groats to Land's End. A model was demonstrated before
Edward VII in the grounds of Buckingham Palace, and Daimlers
—ever a stately car—became favourite cars of the Royal Family.
One of the 1897 Daimlers is in the Road Transport Museum
and, with some of the other veterans, has been on runs like the
London to Brighton. Some cars are taken out on Carnival Day
and special occasions.

Publicity given at the launching of the British Motor Syndicate
described it as "the parent company of the horseless carriage
industry", and the *Investors' Guardian* in 1896 said: "In the
twentieth century when horses are kept only as pets, and when the
officers of the Royal Society for the Prevention of Cruelty to
Animals are driven to make speeches on Tower Hill demanding
work, the fame of Mr. H. J. Lawson will be great in the land. To
him, above all others, is due the astonishing rapidity with which
the horseless carriage has passed from the experimental to the

The velocipede of 1861
The early Daimler Wagonette with steering handle

commercial stage . . ." Mr. Lawson was chairman of the syndicate, and had been in the Coventry cycle trade. He had set about acquiring patents for car inventions to corner the trade for the syndicate, and had about seventy at that time. The syndicate had premises in Foleshill Road, near to the canal, known as the Cotton Mills. The Horseless Carriage Co. had one floor.

Mr. Lawson's fame has not lived on to be "great in the land", probably because his contribution was more that of a financier rather than that of an inventor and manufacturer. He was the businessman-opportunist. In the cycle trade he had patented the safety bicycle, but credit for its actual development has always been given to J. K. Starley. In the car world Mr. Lawson held the patent, dating back to 1880, of the first petrol-driven engine introduced into this country, but it was Gottlieb Daimler in Germany who master-minded it, and various British engineers, among them Frederick Lanchester at Birmingham, were working on their own original lines to bring out thoroughly British 'auto-cars'. Rightly today they are credited for their pioneering work, when the name of Mr. Lawson is almost unmentioned. His enterprise ensured, however, that the city was early on the car scene. Within a decade of the advent of Daimlers in Coventry the trade had 10,000 workers in it; in 1939 38,000; in the 70s, at peak, more than 60,000.

Daimler had financial troubles. In 1910 they were taken over by the BSA Group, but the Daimler name was retained. They made cars and buses at Radford Works. In 1931, the Lanchester car firm from Birmingham, who also had money troubles, joined Daimler in the BSA Group and production of Lanchesters was transferred to Coventry. That was not the last word in the take-over stakes, for in 1960 Jaguar Cars acquired Daimler from BSA, only for Jaguar, in 1966, to merge with BMC—now BL, who switched bus production away from Coventry.

In the early days of car development Coventry was filled by small car firms. They created their own public, with individual styles. Among them was Rover, rooted in the bicycle trade, which produced a car in 1904 at the Meteor Works—an 8-horse-power two-seater with canopy. The little car was a big success, and Rover had made their name. By 1907 they had won the Tourist Trophy Race in the Isle of Man, with a 20-horse-power tourer that averaged 28.8 miles per hour for 241 miles. Rover needed

The Daimler Sovereign
One of the three assembly lines at the Triumph factory

larger works, and these were found at Rover Road, off Queen Victoria Road. Their showrooms, now a mini market, were in Warwick Road. Rover, now in the British Leyland group, is still a popular name, with Land-Rovers and Range-Rovers. They pioneered the gas-turbine car. They moved their main works to Solihull many years ago, blaming Coventry's high rates. For Hillman cars, too, the springboard was the cycle trade, for William Hillman had been a partner of the great James Starley in those early days and later had his own cycle firm. He was joined by a French designer and they produced the Hillman Coatalen car in 1907, designer Coatalen marrying Miss Hillman. But he then joined Sunbeams, and Hillman continued on his own, making small to medium cars and later merging with Humber. The Humber enterprise was founded by Thomas Humber, who produced his first car in 1899. His firm had moved from Ford Street to the big factory at Humber Road, Stoke, Coventry. Humbers were interested in aircraft as well as in cars. As early as 1909 they made a small monoplane. But, with Hillman, they made their mark on the ground, with models that became everyday names—the Hillman Minx, the Humber Hawk, the Imp and the Hunter.

The Rootes Brothers—William and Reginald—who had built up a successful sales and distribution network, acquired Humber and Hillman in 1928, and set out to make a low-price economy car. The story goes that they told four of the biggest men in the factory to sit on chairs, as if in a car, and planned the car round them. This was to make sure the car would be roomy for any four people. For good measure, the 'guinea-pigs' had to wear sun helmets, to make sure there would be sufficient headroom for passengers. When the car was built, the management taught the works blacksmith to drive, and sent him off on a 10,000-mile test run in it, figuring that this would prove if it was easy to control! So the Minx made its début at the Stoke works in 1931, and at £155 it was the cheapest 10-horse-power car.

Rootes cars enjoyed a proud name for reliability. One of the most famous was 'Old Faithful', the Humber Snipe used by Field-Marshal Montgomery in the Second World War desert campaign. After its good service to Monty it was presented to Rootes, by the War Office, as a testimonial of reliability, and it is now in the Montague Museum. Rootes were taken over by Chrysler, of America, and when they found it unprofitable,

Talbot, of France, stepped in. Of the famous Coventry car names, only Alvis remains—and they are no longer a car firm!

William Rootes, who was knighted, and later became Lord Rootes, learned the trade in Coventry as a young apprentice at the Singer Works in Canterbury Street, and years later he and his brother Reginald, who also received a knighthood, took Singer into their Rootes Group. George Singer had worked with foreman James Starley at Coventry Machinists Co., had set up as a cycle manufacturer, and by 1901 his Singer Cycle Co. were making motor-cycles. By 1903 it was the Singer Motor Co., producing their first cars. In this they were linked with another Coventry firm, for they used a Lea Francis design. Lea Francis had their last car factory in the city at Much Park Street. It has since been demolished to make way for an extension of the Lanchester Polytechnic, which is suitably named in a car city for Frederick Lanchester was a brilliant car engineer.

The Rootes Group were happy to perpetuate the names of the firms they acquired—Humber, Hillman, Singer (the Gazelle, for example)—and when they also purchased Sunbeam Talbot, this policy continued. Sunbeam Talbot were transferred from Kensington to Coventry, and Rootes went into production with these cars at the large wartime shadow factory at Ryton, after the Second World War, as an addition to their Stoke plant. While Talbot now dominates the former Rootes Group firms, British Leyland bestrides other Coventry makes: the Triumph (formerly Standard) works, the Jaguar, and Alvis, plus other big local employers of labour such as Morris Engines. Numerous engineering firms, large and small, who supply components and carry out specialist work now depend largely on the two giants, instead of supplying a variety of firms.

The Standard (later Triumph) Motor Company, at Canley, was founded in 1903 in Much Park Street, Coventry, and, unlike so many other firms, it was founded to make cars, without any cradling in the bicycle trade. Its founder, R. W. Maudslay, saw it grow into a great enterprise, moving to Bishopgate Green (Foleshill Road), then adding a works at Cash's Lane, and finally establishing the factory at Canley, built in the First World War to allow the firm to expand its wartime production, which included 1,600 aircraft. Standard models after that war had strong local associations, with names of villages and towns in the area— there were Canley and Coleshill two-seaters, and Kineton and

Kenilworth four-seaters. Later, of course, came the Big and Little Nines, Flying Standards, the Vanguard, the Mayflower. In 1945 Standard purchased the Triumph Car Company, Coventry, whose premises in the city had been destroyed in the raids. Triumph had started making cars in 1923, and although they became part of Standard, the name lived on with the TR series, Spitfire, the Triumph Herald, and the Toledo.

Standard found themselves with a new activity after the Second World War, when they agreed to produce the Ferguson tractor at the Banner Lane factory, which had been a wartime shadow plant. Production of tractors started in 1946, and continued until 1959 under the aegis of Standard; but in that year there was a change of policy and Massey Ferguson took over the plant. It has continued ever since, producing tractors and a variety of tractor-use equipment for farmers—a welcome change of industry for Coventry. In 1960 Leyland took control of Standard and the last models bearing the Standard name were Ensigns in 1963. So ended sixty years of Standard cars, with whom many Coventry people will always associate the name of Captain (later Sir) John Black. He joined them in 1929, became managing director in 1933, and apart from reorganizing and revitalizing the company, made Standard workers the best-paid car men in Coventry in his day.

The Jaguar Cars story, so far as Coventry is concerned, began in 1928, when the Swallow Sidecar and Coachbuilding Co., from Blackpool, arrived at Holbrook Lane, Coventry, and took possession of part of the old White and Poppe munitions factory. They had specialized in sidecar body styling, but were attracted by prospects in the car industry, and naturally Coventry was the place for this. From car-body styling, which was carried out with marked success for several makes of car, the firm eventually became car manufacturers. By the time of the Second World War, there were over 1,000 workers, and SS Cars Ltd. as they were named were making 200 cars a week. In 1945 the name was altered to Jaguar Cars Ltd., and to meet demands for their models the firm moved to the old Daimler shadow factory at Browns Lane, Allesley.

From Brown's Lane has come a succession of successful Jaguar cars—the XK, the E-type, just to mention two—cars which have sweeping and graceful lines, plus speed, and a luxury touch. The firm had to expand to meet orders for models, and this led to the take-over of Daimler, Guy Motors of Wolverhampton, Coventry Climax Engines, and Henry Meadows of Wolverhampton, before, in 1966, the inevitable merger with BMC, now British Leyland, or BL. Jaguar retains its individuality although its founder, Sir William Lyons, has retired, whereas Triumph has wound down and BL plan to turn it into a car engineering and design centre.

Alvis, who were acquired by Rover, and so are also in the Leyland group, were another Coventry firm with distinctive and elegant cars, although their appeal in the years before the war was mainly on account of their racing sports cars. The firm was founded by Mr. T. G. John, and the first car appeared in 1920. Another name associated with Alvis is that of Captain G. T. Smith-Clarke, who became general manager.

In 1970 the Herbert Museum marked Alvis's golden jubilee with an exhibition, but Alvis cars are no longer made. Their Holyhead Road works now produce armoured vehicles, and BL are selling it off in order to concentrate their efforts on cars. The Alvis is in profit, and an offer has been made. Whatever the outcome, nothing will shake the pride of lucky owners of vintage Alvis models which made the name famous by scorching round Brooklands track long ago.

The old Siddeley Deasy, later Armstrong Siddeley, cars, are part of the Coventry story. They too have gone. Mr. J. D. Siddeley, who was knighted in 1932, and who became Lord Kenilworth in 1937, was the guiding hand at Siddeley Deasy after Captain H. P. Deasy resigned in a policy dispute. Under J.D.'s firm control—he was so keen on punctuality for instance that he once sent his own son home for being three minutes late— the company that had been stumbling along from week to week gradually became stabilized.

In the First World War they became so busy that they had to extend their works at Parkside, and they made among other things aero engines. In 1917 their Puma engine became the chief unit in British bombers and was famous for its reliability. The firm also produced complete aircraft, and this led to their decision when the war ended to continue in aircraft production, as well as returning to peacetime manufacture of cars again. In fact they were the first company to bring out a peacetime car, with their Siddeley Six which was an immediate success, and could not be made fast enough to meet demand. Expansion needs caused the firm to link up with the Newcastle firm of Armstrong Whitworth, and soon Armstrong Siddeley had taken the place of Siddeley Deasy. When the RAF station and airfield at Whitley, Coventry, became available, it was taken over by Armstrong Whitworth Aircraft Ltd., and Coventry, through the former Siddeley Deasy, now had a peacetime aircraft industry.

Between the wars, Whitley-built aircraft were mainly used on air-liner services. First there had been the Siskin single-seater fighter (1924), then came the civil aircraft such as the Atlas, Atalanta, and Argosy, while the Whitley heavy bomber (1936) became the RAF standard plane for night-bombing raids in the early years of the Second World War. Later, taken off bombing, they were adapted for Coastal Command. Among the aero engines produced at Whitley was the famous Cheetah, used in many aircraft. As with the car industry, mergers came in the aircraft field. Sopwith's Hawker Aircraft tied up with Armstrong Siddeley, to form the Hawker Siddeley Group, aircraft work was moved from Whitley to Baginton, still in Coventry, and there the Argosy freighters were built, until more reorganization ended aircraft production.

Like some of the other leaders of industry in Coventry, Lord Kenilworth played his part in public life. He was president of the Society of British Aircraft Constructors, treasurer of the Society of Motor Manufacturers, and High Sheriff of Warwickshire. His companies expanded from cars to aircraft, and their successors were to work on guided missiles, at Whitley and Ansty. Experimenting with the pneumatic-tyred railcar, his group formed the Coventry Pneumatic Railcar Co. for the purpose. They made two railcars and ran them on the Coventry–Rugby railway line. They were not commercially exploited, due to cost and other factors. Gas turbines are now one of the activities at Ansty, and Rolls-Royce Industrial and Marine Division, as Bristol Siddeley is now known there, have had sales of more than £100 million. At Parkside, Rolls-Royce Bristol Engines Division produce aero engines.

The Morris car was never made in Coventry, but the city has had a major role in supplying engines and bodies. White and Poppe at Holbrook Lane were early engine suppliers, but the Morris Engines branch at Courthouse Green originated in the Gosford Street works of the Hotchkiss company. The company came from France to escape the German advance in the First

World War and they made 50,000 machine-guns and other munitions at Gosford Street. When the war ended they needed peacetime production, and although they had no experience of car-engine manufacture, they approached William Morris, who was looking for a supplier to replace a Detroit manufacturer who had discontinued this. Hotchkiss made a sample engine to the design of the Detroit product, and was given the contract. In 1923 Morris bought them up, and ran the works as an engines branch, later moving to larger premises at Courthouse Green. The Gosford Street works are now Civil Service offices.

Hollick and Pratt, another Coventry firm, supplied Morris with specialist bodies. They were acquired by Morris in 1926, and Morris Bodies, Quinton Road, supplied bodies until the late sixties, when the plant was closed down. Carbodies, Coventry, are another firm linked with the Morris story. White and Poppe, mentioned earlier, were started by P. A. Poppe, a Norwegian, and A. J. Swift, son of a director of the Swift company. In 1899 they began to make carburettors, engines, and components, in Drake Street, Coventry, moving to Holbrook Lane in 1900. In the First World War they had as many as 12,000 workers, many of them girls whose hands were stained yellow by their work of filling shells—they were known as the 'W and P canaries', many were Irish girls and lived in hostels at Holbrooks. White and Poppe sold engines to the firm of Dennis, Guildford, after that war, and was wound up in 1934. Engine production went to Guildford. Many Coventrians went to Guildford with their skills.

The Coventry firm of Riley were makers of cars from early in the century. Riley were founded by William Riley, who had been a master weaver. He joined in the cycle boom, founded a Riley Co. in 1896 to make cycles, moved on to motor-cycles, and finally to cars that had a specialist following. The most famous model, the Nine, appeared in 1927. Nuffield Mechanisations took over Riley, at Durbar Avenue, in 1938.

The car trade and the firms who supply it and wait on it, are Coventry's chief industry, but industrial activity in Coventry ranges widely, from the ribbon industry to machine tools. J. and J. Cash, at Cash's Lane, Foleshill, have been in the ribbon trade for over 135 years and used to have the world's largest narrow-gauge Jacquard weaving mill. They also have an associate works in America. Cash's woven labels and ribbons are famous and they keep alive a traditional Coventry craft. Royal Wedding ribbons were made in 1981. Until recent years another firm, more than two hundred years old, kept the city's link with watch-making. This was Rotherhams, Spon Street, who now concentrate on other precision work.

The big textiles empire of Courtaulds, founded in Essex, came to Coventry in 1904, and now with their subsidiary, British Celanese, are employers of a large amount of labour in the city. The firm came when they had bought the British rights to manufacture viscose rayon yarn and chose Coventry for their factory. It was central, had ample water, available labour and a textiles tradition. For several years their chemists and tech-nologists wrestled with problems in spinning what later became the world's most successful type of rayon yarn. Their efforts founded the company's prosperity, and the main works at Foleshill became the 'capital' of a vast network of factories in the British Isles and in other countries. From Main Works went the 'colonizers' who established companies overseas—starting with the team who went to the United States in 1909 to found the viscose rayon industry there. Coventry is also Courtaulds' research centre, and rayon has been followed by Acetate, Tricel, Courtelle, Courtolon, Courlene, and other man-made fibres. From Main Works at Foleshill Road the company has spread along Lockhurst Lane and into Matlock Road, and to Little Heath. A noticeable aspect of their extensions has been the care taken to provide attractive surroundings, with landscaped areas and planting.

Coventry's earlier industrial history is one of adaptability, from wool and leather, metal work, to silk, watch, and bicycle trades. One of the nineteenth-century silk weavers, Thomas Stevens, is sometimes in the news today. His Stevengraph pure silk woven pictures of the last century, which could be bought for 6d. or a shilling each, are now collectors' pieces, and fetch pounds. ·The record is £520 for one of his pictures. Another was sold for £460. Stevens processed the pictures when the weaving industry was in dire trouble, hit by foreign competition. Silk weaving had been carried on for 150 years and half the city's population depended on it. When it failed, the hardship can be imagined, and in these conditions, and in order to survive, Foleshill-born Thomas Stevens devised a process for producing woven pictures that made them widely popular. He made bookmarks, pictures for Christmas and other occasions, birthday cards, portraits of celebrities, pictures of scenes and events, and his business prospered. In 1875 the Stevengraph works were built in Cox Street, and he had branch offices in London. His work was put on exhibition overseas. The works in Cox Street were blitzed in the air raids, and the company was acquired by Brough, Nicholson and Hall Ltd., of Leek, Staffs. Mounted pictures that were made by Stevengraph are sought by collectors. They are of subjects such as Kenilworth Castle and the Forth Bridge, the death of Nelson, Dick Turpin's Ride to York, and sports such as horse racing and fox hunting. Many Coventry homes had their Stevengraphs when they were worthless in terms of money. Constance Stevens, granddaughter of the inventor, used to cover her dolls with them. They had pretty edges and lovely colours. Collectors' interest in them dates from about 1967. There is a large collection of them at the Herbert Museum, Coventry, but the largest is privately owned, in America.

G.E.C. Telecommunications Ltd. with their headquarters in Coventry, controlling a manufacturing complex of sixteen factories and 30,000 employees—half of them in seven factories in Coventry—help to diversify Coventry's industries. They are the largest manufacturers of telecommunication equipment in the UK and one of the foremost in the world. They supply the post office with equipment: the bulk of its network of microwave-radio transmission systems that carry telephone circuits and television programmes, cable systems, new switchboard systems. Some of the factories they are using were once the workshops of the cycle and motor-car firms. GEC have been making tele-communication equipment in Coventry since 1920 and are the largest industrial employer in the city.

Like the cycle and car trades, the machine-tool industry in Coventry owes much to forceful personalities. The story of Alfred Herbert Ltd., the famous machine-tool company, started when young Alfred Herbert, son of a Leicester farmer, completed an engineering apprenticeship and came to Coventry to manage a small firm in the Butts, for £2 a week, doing mainly repair work. The firm also had steam-ploughing equipment, which they used on ploughing jobs for farmers, and their own steam roller, which they used on street works under contract to the corporation. Soon Alfred Herbert had the opportunity to buy the firm for a small sum, and he went into partnership with W. S. Hubbard. Herbert and Hubbard designed machines for the ribbon industry and then tools and mudguards for bicycle firms. By 1894 the firm had become Alfred Herbert Ltd. It grew, and in 1928 moved to Edgwick, where it already had a foundry and owned 38 acres.

Sir Alfred was chairman and managing director until he died, aged 90, in 1957, when the firm had 6,000 workers, in four separate factories—at Edgwick, Red Lane, Exhall, and at Lutterworth, and had become world distributors for other leading British machine-tool makers. In his lifetime it had become the largest machine-tool organization in the world. Sir Alfred made many gifts to Coventry, equipping a hospital ward for wounded soldiers of the First World War, when he was Controller of Machine Tools at the Ministry of Munitions; giving land in the Butts for a small park, Lady Herbert's Garden in the city centre, Town Thorns House as a children's home, £10,000 to the hospital, a £25,000 covenant to the cathedral reconstruction, and £200,000 for the Herbert Art Gallery and Museum. Two decades after his death, the firm have gone into a decline. A new firm, employing 800, keep the name alive.

'Herbert's' trained many skilled Coventry engineers, and several companies have been started by ex-employees. Coventry Guage and Tool, now T.I. Matrix Ltd., is an example. The founder, Harry Harley, later Sir Harry Harley, was a Herbert's apprentice, and was with the company for twenty-three years, becoming toolroom foreman. Together with a brother-in-law, he launched out, in 1913, at Earlsdon, starting the firm of Walter Tatlow Ltd. They had hardly got going when the First World War began, and orders for war equipment made them very busy. They expanded rapidly, and in 1916 changed their name to Coventry Guage and Small Tool Co. Ltd., dropping "Small" from the title in 1920. The Fletchamstead Highway works were built in 1936, and soon the firm in its larger premises was called on for the war effort again. For the duration, Mr. Stanley Harley, later Sir Stanley, son of the founder, was Controller of Jigs, Tools and Gauges at the Ministry of Supply. The Gauge and Tool company adopted the trademark of Matrix with such success that it was probably better known than the firm's name. The works were the Matrix, its canteen, Matrix Hall.

Another Herbert's 'old boy' was Axel Charles Wickman, who worked for them for six years and built up a precision gauge department, between 1919 and 1925. A year later he started his own business—now Wickman's, the machine-tool firm whose Wimet hard-metals tools are famous. He won the sales agency in Britain for the German tungsten carbide cutting tool then in its experimental stage, and this, together with the Wickman-designed multi-spindle machine tools that began to appear on the market in the thirties, was the turning point for the firm. They were acquired by John Brown in 1947. Wickman's have a 'factory in a garden' at Banner Lane, approached by a driveway bordered by flower beds, shrubs, lawns, and trees.

Among other ex-Herbert engineers, Alderman Harry Weston, who was an apprentice, founded the firm of Modern Machine Tools Ltd. in 1928. It became a public company in 1935. He formed and managed seven other engineering companies. Coventry has so many engineering firms that it is impossible to trace the development of all of them here: Dunlop's large wheel, rim, and brakes factories at Foleshill and Holbrooks; the Brico (British Piston Ring) at Holbrooks; Webster and Bennett, who were founded in 1892; Brett's Stamping Co. at Harnall Lane East; the Renold Chain works at Spon End (until its sudden closure in 1981 after trading problems); Coventry Radiator and Presswork ('Covrad') at Canley, are typical of the large employers. While all over the city, some in adapted workshops, some in purpose-built factories, smaller firms are making a versatile contribution.

Hardly any large-scale project is made without some contribution from Coventry, whether it is the QE2, the *Concorde*, the space craft in America, or a car specially prepared for a world speed attempt. The know-how that brought new industries to Coventry for development is still strong, and the apprenticeship system and the training available in the colleges should ensure that this will continue. Names like BTH have gone; the M–L Magneto is just a memory kept green by a few elderly ex-employees; the Swift Motor Co., the Calcott light car, are past history, as are W. H. Grant's woven labels at Livingstone Mills, Foleshill. The closing of these and other firms must have been shocks in their time, but Coventry has always weathered setbacks.

When it has not produced the men to provide new industries, the men have come to Coventry with their ideas, because of its reputation as a centre of skilled workers. The city provides work for many people living in neighbouring towns. Peak figures showed that 68,000 workers were employed in vehicle manufacture, 45,000 in electrical and general engineering, 15,000 in professional and scientific jobs, 13,000 in distribution, 7,000 in public administration, 7,000 in construction, and 6,000 in textiles. About 40,000 travelled to Coventry to work, and the total labour force was nearly 200,000 people. Fourteen large firms provided about three-quarters of the city's employment.

X

COVENTRY PERSONALITIES

COVENTRY cannot claim to be a famous birthplace. It has not produced a Shakespeare, a Dickens, an Elgar or a Constable. But it has produced brilliant engineers and clever businessmen, native and 'adopted', who have had highly successful careers and gained peerages and knighthoods. And it has been associated with people distinguished in their professions. Those dedicated people who honour the memory of Ellen Terry, the great actress of her day, may not accept the remark about a birthplace, for she was born in Coventry and they have kept her memory green. She was born in Market Street, off Smithford Street, in the city centre, on 27th February 1848, but Coventry was not actually the family's home town. Her parents were actors on tour who happened to be in the city at the time, and it was only by chance that the birth was in Coventry.

Ellen Terry inherited her parents' talent, and between 1856 and the early years of this century, had numerous stage successes, many of them as Henry Irving's leading lady. In 1906 her stage jubilee was celebrated, and in 1922 she was granted the honorary degree of LL.D. (St. Andrews) and in 1925 received the Grand Cross of the British Empire. She died in 1928. She performed in Coventry at its Theatre Royal, Smithford Street, in 1880, and at the Empire Theatre in 1908. Her greatest roles were said to have been as Ophelia, Lady Macbeth, Desdemona, and Volumnia in *Coriolanus*. Sir John Forbes-Robertson wrote of her: "I do not suppose there ever was such an Ophelia, nor do I think there ever will be again." Coventry has basked in the reflected glory of the 'Coventry-born' actress, as in 1906, when the red carpet was laid out for her arrival at the railway station, a huge crowd greeted her, and a civic reception was given. In 1935, to mark her birthday anniversary, there was an Ellen Terry Festival Week, and her daughter, Miss Edith Craig, was the guest of honour at a civic reception in St. Mary's Hall.

In recent years, the city's Ellen Terry Fellowship have marked her birthday anniversary with a short ceremony. Market Street has gone, and there is a plaque in the precinct which is as near as possible to the spot where she was born. The actual spot was a point of argument, because two shops in Market Street, one on each side of the road, claimed that their property had been the birthplace, and Ellen Terry did not know herself. One shop had a notice, "Birthplace of Ellen Terry", and the other said it was "the original birthplace". Mr. George Fearon, who was with the Opera House during the period of Coventry 'Rep', wrote that as one of the houses was a haberdasher's, and the other a tripe shop, Miss Craig, Ellen Terry's daughter, "with great dignity, placed a daffodil on a chair in the window of one shop, and another on a piece of tripe in the other". Ellen Terry wrote: "I have never been able to arbitrate in the matter, my statement that my mother had always said that the house 'was on the right-hand side, coming from the market place', being apparently no use." She added: "It is a delightful town, and it was a happy chance that made me a native of Warwickshire, Shakespeare's own county..."

George Eliot, the nineteenth-century novelist, had a strong link with Coventry. It was not her birthplace, but the city can justifiably lay claim to having played a formative part in the life of the famous novelist. As Mary Ann Evans, born at Arbury Farm, which lies between Bedworth and Nuneaton, she came to the city for her schooling in 1832. She attended a private school in a house at Warwick Row, run by Mary and Rebecca, the daughters of the Reverend Francis Franklin, minister of Cow Lane Baptist Chapel. She stayed at the school until 1836, the year of her mother's death, when she returned to Griff to be with her father. Five years later she returned to Coventry with her father on his retirement, and they lived in a house, Bird Grove, off the Foleshill Road, close to the Springfield Brook.

In those days Foleshill was blessed with fields, and the Coventry Canal, which ran through them, was busy with working boats tapping the Warwickshire coalfields through Nuneaton and Tamworth, and linking with other waterways to the Black Country, and with the Grand Junction (now Grand Union) canal for London. But the railways, that were to spell the doom of canal traffic, were already on the scene and had a service between the city and London. A paper on "George Eliot's Coventry", by

Alice Lynes, who for many years was in charge of the Coventry and Warwickshire Collection of the City Libraries, gives an interesting picture of life in Coventry at that period. In the ribbon industry, some factories had been introduced, but at the 'new town' of Hillfields, begun in 1828, the factory system was opposed. The houses with their 'top shops', where the master weavers worked the looms, were supplied with power by means of shafting, running through a row of houses from an engine in a yard below. Almost all the 'top shops' have now been demolished in the redevelopment of Hillfields, but a few are being preserved by the corporation as a link with those days. They can be seen in Holyhead Road, near Spon Street, and in the Chapelfields area.

Mary Ann made friends at Foleshill with the son and daughter of the Reverend John Sibree, minister of Vicar Lane Independent Chapel, and through her neighbour, Mrs. Pears, who before marriage was Elizabeth Bray, she became acquainted with Charles and Mary Bray of "Rosehill" in St. Nicholas Street, reached by a bridge over the canal and a short walk across fields. She became a frequent visitor there over the next nine years. They had many friends "of the better sort of literary people" whom she met. Charles Bray, who headed a weaving firm, was on the city council from 1845 to 1848. He bought the *Coventry Herald* in 1846 and was its editor until 1867. It was in this newspaper that Mary Ann had her work first published—reviews and essays, contributed anonymously. After her father's death in 1849, she decided to go to London and earn her living as a writer, and in her book, *Middlemarch* she penned many of her recollections of Coventry. The names of roads at Radford are taken from her novels— Middlemarch Road and Bede Road—for example. George Eliot Road, Foleshill, where Bird Grove stands, is so named because of its connection with the novelist.

Another writer who lived part of her life in Coventry was Angela Brazil, whose girls' school stories are still popular and are being reprinted. She was born at Preston in 1868, of a wealthy family. After travelling extensively abroad, sketching and painting, she came to Coventry in 1911, when her brother started in general practice as a doctor. With her brother, and a sister, Amy, she lived at 1 The Quadrant, now the offices of Mander Hadley, solicitors. The trio became well known in the city: Amy as an artist; Walter, the doctor, organizing musical events and being a sidesman at the cathedral—he started the Central Crusader Class, a Bible Class for boys—and Angela writing her schoolgirl stories that enjoyed a great following. She wrote them over a period of nearly fifty years. She died in 1947, the same year as her brother, and Amy died four years later.

Coventry has also had a link with Lord Northcliffe, the 'Napoleon of Fleet Street'. Long before he was proprietor of national newspapers he was a young journalist in the 'cycle city'. He arrived in Coventry in 1886 when he was 21, as editor of *Bicycling News*, published by the printing firm of Iliffe and Sturmey. Alfred Harmsworth, as he then was, lodged at 5 The Crescent, Holyhead Road, a small terrace house occupied by the former governess to the Iliffe children. A fellow lodger was curate of St. John's, and Alfred Harmsworth attended services there and at Queen's Road Church, where he accompanied the Iliffes.

In *Bicycling News* he had a feature called "Answers to Correspondents"; and when, later, he published a new weekly magazine called *Answers*, which became a national and popular journal, he said that it was from his column in the Coventry *Bicycling News* that he got the idea. In fact, first copies of *Answers* were printed by Iliffes in Coventry, until the magazine became a going concern in London, and set him on the path to fame and fortune through newspaper ownership. The Iliffe family were a Coventry family and from local enterprise became in their turn, newspaper 'barons', but their sphere was to be the Midlands, and—to Coventry's benefit—they have held to their Coventry connections. The *Evening Telegraph* was their first daily paper, and is still a family affair, an unusual arrangement for an undertaking so large. The family, as well as the paper, have been benefactors to the city in various ways, helping good causes, and contributing to local projects. The newspaper was founded in 1891 by Mr. William Isaac Iliffe, when the population of Coventry was only 50,000, a figure that would not support a daily paper today. He was owner of a weekly called *The Coventry Times*, and was a partner with Henry Sturmey in their printing and publishing firm. Alfred Harmsworth had left the firm two years before the *Telegraph* was launched. Coventry was then well served for weeklies. In addition to the *Times*, there were the *Coventry Herald*, *Coventry Standard*, and the *Coventry Reporter*. The *Coventry Herald* continued in circulation until the Second World War, and the *Coventry Standard*, eventually acquired by the *Evening*

Telegraph, closed in 1969. The other weeklies have long been out of circulation, but a new weekly, the *Coventry Express*, launched after the Second World War, later merged with the *Coventry Standard*. The *Telegraph* grew from small beginnings in 1891, and moved into works at Vicar Lane, off Smithford Street, at the back of the old Empire Cinema. Its front offices were in Hertford Street.

Iliffe and Sturmey catered for the cycling age with their publications, and for the motor-car era published the well-known motorists' magazine, *Autocar*, in 1895, before there was any actual car production in England! *Autocar* helped in the campaign to change the law which limited power-driven vehicles to a speed of 4 miles an hour, when they had to have a man walking in front with a red flag. This speed limit was put up to 12 miles per hour later. The *Midland Daily Telegraph* as the *Evening Telegraph* was first known used two of the early cars to take copies to outlying districts, with the news of the relief of Ladysmith in the Boer War. As the date was 1900 they were probably the first to deliver newspapers in petrol-driven cars. Mr. Iliffe, founder of the newspaper, who was a native of Coventry, died in 1917, and his sons, Edward Mauger Iliffe and W. Coker Iliffe, controlled the business, and developed the Iliffe Press, which owned numerous periodicals.

Edward, who became Baron Iliffe of Yattendon, Berkshire, was in the family business from the age of 17. Although he at one time was part-owner of the London *Daily Telegraph*, and then acquired, and was chairman of, the *Birmingham Post* and the *Birmingham Mail*, he had many activities including, at various times, chairmanship of the Coventry and Warwickshire Hospital; presidency of the Coventry Chamber of Commerce, and presidency of the governors of the Shakespeare Memorial Theatre. He had been Unionist MP for Tamworth in the twenties. Lord Iliffe was knighted in 1922 and became a peer, the first native of Coventry to have this distinction, in modern times, in 1933. He died, aged 83, in 1960.

His son, the Hon. E. Langton Iliffe, who succeeded to the title, was vice-chairman of the *Birmingham Post and Mail*, and chairman of Coventry Newspapers Ltd. (*Coventry Evening Telegraph*). He too is a native of Coventry and has shown his regard for it. His father gave Allesley Hall and 47 acres of land to the city for recreational use, and the new Lord Iliffe added 51 acres to it, twenty-six years later. He has made several gifts to the city, as quietly as possible, doing such things as defraying the £2,500 cost of the Belgrade fountain feature. He acquired the 157 drawings made by Graham Sutherland for the cathedral tapestry, and arranged for the collection to be shown at the Herbert Art Gallery. Lord mayoral portraits have been among paintings commissioned and presented to the city. The *Telegraph* shared Coventry's wartime troubles, having its works wrecked by bombs, and after a short period of publication in Birmingham, it was produced at Nuneaton for the remainder of the war, returning to Coventry, at Quinton Road, in 1946. The Corporation Street premises were opened in 1960, and today the paper has a 106,000 circulation.

Compared with the name of Lord Iliffe, that of Lord Lambury is probably known to comparatively few Coventry people, but he also was a native of the city who rose to the peerage in modern times. He rose in the motor industry. As Leonard Lord he attended Bablake School in Coventry from 1906 to 1912. His father was at one time superintendent of the Coventry Corporation Baths. Leonard Lord served an apprenticeship as a draughtsman at Courtaulds Ltd. engineering department. He worked at Coventry Ordnance, Daimler, and elsewhere and in 1922 became a jig and tool draughtsman with the Hotchkiss at Gosford Street, Coventry, until 1927 when the firm was acquired by Mr. W. R. Morris, who was to become Lord Nuffield. Morris acquired Wolseley Motors (1927) Ltd. and Leonard Lord was put in charge of its reorganization. His ability in this put his feet on the ladder to the top. By 1932 he was managing director of Morris Motors Ltd., where he reorganized production methods.

He had a brief 'retirement' when he was 40, having made a resolution to retire at that age, but a year later was back as manager of a £2 million trust fund set up by Lord Nuffield to aid the depressed areas, and in 1938 he became works director at the Austin Motor Company, rising to become joint managing director, and chairman in 1945. When six years later there was a merger with Morris he became deputy chairman and managing director of the British Motor Corporation, and in 1952 succeeded Lord Nuffield as chairman and managing director. He was knighted in 1954, for services to industry, and in 1963 was created a baron and became president of BMC. His title, Lord Lambury of Northfield, alludes to Lambury Point at East Portlemouth, in Devon, where he went to live in retirement, but later he moved nearer to the Midlands, to Cirencester. When he died, aged 71, in 1967, he had travelled a long way from the hard times he knew as a boy when his father died, and his mother had to work hard to keep him at Bablake until he was 15. Later, after the day's work, he taught higher maths at night school in Coventry, trying to repay his mother.

Another Coventry man who learned his job in the city and became a leader in the motor industry was Sir George Harriman. His story has close similarity to that of Lord Lambury. He began as an apprentice at the Hotchkiss when he was 16, and in the following fourteen years at Gosford Street rose to be assistant works superintendent. He was a well-known member of Coventry FC rugger team and played as a three-quarter, captained Warwickshire, and had an England trial. In March 1940 he joined Austin Motor Co. as manager of their engine factory, and five years later was made deputy managing director. After the creation of BMC he was made a director of the group, and in 1956, when he was 50, he became deputy chairman and joint managing director, with Sir Leonard Lord. The next step for Mr. Harriman, as he was at that time, was the post of sole managing director and, eventually, president of the enormous British Leyland Motor Corporation when a further merger had been made with the Leyland group. A parallel career in industry was that of Mr. Alick Dick, who from apprentice became head of Standard Motors, but ended his career with them on the change of organization when Leyland took over.

The first Lord Kenilworth was not a native of Coventry, but his son, who succeeded to the title, Colonel Cyril Siddeley, who died in 1971, was born in the city and held local public offices, also doing voluntary work for Coventry and Warwickshire Hospital. He was honorary colonel of the 7th Battalion The Royal Warwickshire Regiment (TA) which had its headquarters at the Drill Hall, Queen Victoria Road. He served with the regiment in both world wars.

At least one peerage created in the past has its roots in Coventry, for the Lifford family are descended from Viscount Lifford, who was Lord Chancellor of Ireland. He was born in Smithford Street, Coventry, a member of the Hewitt family, in the eighteenth century. A John Hewitt was Mayor of Coventry in 1755.

The earldom of Coventry does not appear to have begun with any family in the locality. It was created in 1697. The present earl, the eleventh, has his home at Earls Croome, Worcester, and is not connected with Coventry.

Another Coventry-born man who was given a knighthood is Sir Frank Whittle. His link with Coventry ends with his boyhood, but the city can claim to have been the birthplace of the inventor of the jet engine. He was born in Coventry on Christmas Day 1911, the son of an engineer. His schooling in Coventry ended when he was nearly 10, for his father then bought an engineering business in nearby Leamington Spa, and the family went there to live. Sir Frank's subsequent career in the RAF, and his work on the jet, are not part of Coventry's story, but the city was proud to honour him with the Award of Merit and to claim him as a distinguished son.

Sir Harry Harley, already referred to in connection with his firm, Coventry Gauge and Tool, was another Coventry man who was knighted, and his son, Sir Stanley Harley, was a prominent figure, not only in the machine-tool industry, but also in the public life of Coventry. Sir Alfred Herbert, also of machine-tool fame, was not a native of Coventry, but he spent most of his life in it, and was a generous benefactor. Sir William Lyons is another man who came to the city and prospered, and who was subsequently knighted. The same was true of Sir John Black, Lord Rootes, and Sir Reginald Rootes.

Harry Ferguson, who was an Irishman, and whose link with Coventry began after the Second World War, was said to have refused knighthood as he believed the honour was one for people such as politicians and servicemen who did not receive financial rewards for their efforts on the scale that happens in industry. He became a Coventry personality when he brought a new industry to the city and provided employment for thousands. Coventry was fortunate, but it often has been, and, after all, work has usually been brought to the city not to do it a favour, but because the expert labour and the capacity is known to be available. In this case, it was a quarrel between Harry Ferguson and the grandson of Henry Ford, in America, that helped Coventry.

Henry Ford made Ferguson tractors and implements from shortly before the Second World War until he died in 1947, when his grandson decided instead to make his own tractors. Harry Ferguson sued him, in America, built a rival plant in Detroit to make Ferguson tractors, and joined with Standard Motor Co. in Coventry to make them here, using the Banner Lane factory. It was about four years before the law suit was settled—against Ford. He was ordered to stop making a tractor which it was claimed infringed Ferguson patents, and he had to pay over £3 million for his use of the patents up to that time. Coventry was one of the places in England that were visited by an American 'travelling court', taking evidence in the case. Standard finally stopped making the tractors when Henry Ferguson linked up with Massey Harris in Canada, makers of combine harvesters, and production then continued under the new group. As well as a farm school at Stoneleigh, for courses on use of Ferguson system implements, Harry Ferguson started a research plant in Coventry, his aim—a car of completely new design. Work on this was continuing when he died in 1960.

The accolade of knighthood conferred on people associated with Coventry is not completely monopolized by the engineers. It fell on the late Mr. Charles Barratt, the town clerk; on Mr. Donald Gibson, the first city architect and planning officer; and on Mr. Alan Richmond, principal of the Lanchester Polytechnic. Sir Charles came to Coventry in 1941 as deputy to Mr. Frederick Smith, after the raids, and it fell to him, when he became town clerk, to persuade land and property owners in the central area to fall in with the plan to build the Broadgate garden island by allowing the authority to have sites. From then onwards, he was in the thick of the task of planning the new city, presiding over departments that tried to keep pace with the city's expansion. He concerned himself with life outside the Council House—in particular with Coventry School of Music of which he was president.

Donald Gibson was knighted later in his career when he had held a senior government post, and Wilfred Burns, who had been on his Coventry planning staff, also received a knighthood later on in his career, when in a government appointment.

Sir Alan Richmond started the Lanchester, officially opened as a college in 1961, and upgraded nine years later to a polytechnic. He steered it from the drawing-board stage, almost, to a student 'empire' that has an important role in advanced science, technology, management and business studies, and other courses. Previously he had been principal of the technical college, the post that brought him to Coventry.

Sir Frederick Gibberd, the noted architect, is a native of Coventry, and an old boy of King Henry VIII School. He

designed London Airport, and was planner and chief architect of
Harlow New Town; has prepared civic centre plans for several
towns, and won the competition for the design of the Cathedral
of Christ the King at Liverpool. His firm is in London, but some
of his schemes have been for Nuneaton, Leamington and
Stratford-on-Avon, places near Coventry. Coventry people who
attended the third Shelton Memorial Lecture in St. Mary's Hall,
in 1961, heard Sir Frederick lecture on the design of new town
centres. He said town centres in this country were a disgrace to a
civilized nation and would never be anything else until the
motor-car was brought under control. But, he thought Coventry's
town centre "really splendid", the work of a few people with
tremendous imagination and vision. On another occasion, at the
school old boys' dinner, he said Coventry was a "proud and
dynamic city" and that in it was taking place "one of the greatest
experiments in Europe". He was knighted in 1967.

Others honoured have included Lord Kearton, who spent much
of his industrial career with Courtaulds at Coventry, becoming
chairman of Courtaulds Ltd. in 1964. And Coventry solicitor
Edmund Liggins, who was president of the Law Society in
1975–76, was knighted in 1976.

Coventry personalities include those who have made their
reputation in the world of entertainment. Among them are John
Hanson, star of many musicals, and Reg Dixon, the comedian,
who at the height of his fame was a star on radio and television.
He was born in Coventry, and his signature tune, "Confiden-
tially", was as well known as any in the entertainment business.

John Hanson was not born in Coventry. His parents, Coventry
people, emigrated to Canada, where he was born. When they
returned they lived in the Home Counties, and, for a few years,
in Scotland where John sang as a boy soprano and was heard on
Scottish regional broadcasts. When the family finally came
back to Coventry he was given a week's engagement as a boy of
13 by Charles Shadwell of the Coventry Hippodrome Orchestra.
After a two-year rest while his voice broke, he began to sing as a
light baritone, worked as an engineer in Coventry, and, after
various engagements, became a professional singer, eventually
having his own shows. Hanson, whose real name is John Watts,
has made several appearances at the Coventry Theatre, starring in
shows like *The Student Prince*, and *The Desert Song*, and has had
big successes in London's West End. He married a Coventry

girl, Miss Brenda Stokes, at St. Barbara's, Coventry, where their two children were also christened.

Concert pianist Mr. Dennis Matthews, Professor of Music at Newcastle University, is a native of Coventry. He grew up in Leamington, and was educated at Warwick School. His early interest in the piano was fostered by attending Leamington Music Festival where he took part in piano classes. He entered the Royal College of Music on a scholarship at the age of 16. He is internationally famous, has toured many countries, including Russia, but often returns to the district of Coventry and Leamington to appear in concerts. He has recorded, and his autobiography, *In Search of Music*, was published in 1966.

Billie Whitelaw, the actress, who has had "Best Actress of the Year" (1960) and British Film Academy (1969) awards, was born in Coventry. When her father was transferred to Bradford by the GEC, she was a schoolgirl, and her connection with Coventry ended then. Popular singer Vince Hill was born in Coventry in 1937. He worked in a bakery and at Coventry Colliery before National Service in the Army gave him his break as lead soloist with the band of the Royal Corps of Signals. His 'Edelweiss' record topped the hit parade.

Coventry, as far as is known, has had only one holder of the Victoria Cross. He was Corporal Arthur Hutt, of the Royal Warwickshire Regiment, who died, aged 64, at his nephew's home at 277 Sewall Highway, Coventry, in 1954. He won the VC in 1917 at Ypres, when as a private he took command of his platoon after all the officers and NCOs had been killed or wounded under fire. Held up by a strong-post, he dashed forward and shot an enemy officer and three men and caused between forty and fifty Germans to surrender. He sent them back under escort and withdrew the platoon, sniping to cover the retreat; then, when the position was secure, he went out and brought in four wounded men under heavy fire. After Mr. Hutt's death the Lord Mayor, Alderman H. B. W. Cresswell, opened a fund to provide a memorial stone and plaque, and this was unveiled in the War Memorial Park in 1955. Afterwards a military procession, half a mile long, marched through the city centre.

Another VC who lived in his later years in Coventry was a Leamington man, Henry Tandey. He served in the Green Howards, landing at Zeebrugge in October 1914, and was wounded in the leg in 1916 and again wounded in 1917. He won the VC on 28th September 1918 "for desperate bravery and great initiative" during an attack when his platoon was stopped by machine-gun fire. He crawled forward under heavy fire, located the gun's position, and led a Lewis gun team into a house from which they knocked out the enemy gun, and his platoon continued the advance. A plank bridge had been broken, and under heavy fire he crawled forward and put the planks in position under a hail of bullets to enable a crossing to be made. Later with eight comrades he was surrounded by an overwhelming number of Germans and, although it seemed hopeless, led a bayonet charge through them, fighting so fiercely that thirty-seven of the enemy were driven into the hands of the company behind and were taken prisoner. He was wounded twice but refused to leave, leading parties into dugouts and capturing over twenty of the enemy. Mr. Tandey already held the Distinguished Conduct Medal for gallantry, and the Military Medal for gallantry. He worked for the Standard Motor Co. for thirty-eight years, and had been a member of the Triumph Co. when it was in Priory Street. His widow sold the VC and other medals for £27,000.

The late Mr. William Beesley was a third VC living in Coventry, but he was a native of Nuneaton, who gave him the freedom of the borough. Mr. Beesley, who lived at 24 Brooklyn Road, Coventry, was in the Rifle Brigade and was 22 when he won the award, for outstanding bravery in leading an attack during fighting in the French trenches, towards the end of the 1914–18 war.

Coventry had a link with another VC, of the 1939–45 war, in Petty Officer Alfred Edward Sephton, who served on HMS *Coventry*, the city's adopted ship, and whose home was once near Coventry. The award was made posthumously after he died from wounds received when the ship was under heavy fire. The citation said that his valiant and cheerful spirit, despite his wounds, gave heart to the wounded. His parents lived at Yardley, Birmingham. In 1971 his sister presented his VC to Coventry Cathedral at an HMS *Coventry* service of remembrance.

While many people in Coventry are unaware of it, there is a birthplace, at Canley, which Australian visitors seek out. It is the birthplace, now preserved by Coventry Corporation, of Sir Henry Parkes, who emigrated to Australia and became a leading statesman in the nineteenth century. He became Premier of New

South Wales, and because of his pioneering work in the movement to join the various states into a federation, had the title of
'Father of the Federation'. The town of Parkes was named after
him. From humble beginnings in a cottage at Canley, and a
struggle in his younger days, he became successful, and a friend
of such men as Gladstone. Gifts have been sent to Parkes, and
Coventry has a bond of friendship with the town. Although it is
so far away, when Alderman Callow, as Lord Mayor, called a
peace conference of leaders of friendship towns in Coventry,
because of the Berlin crisis and threat of war, Parkes sent a
representative to attend it.

Another Coventrian whose name is still honoured overseas, as
a result of emigration is John Davenport, who emigrated to
America and was a founder of New Haven Colony, and played
a part in the establishing of Yale. He was born in Coventry in
1597, and entered the Church. Because he became sympathetic
with Nonconformist views—Congregationalism—he was forced
to resign from the Church, and fled to Holland. He then decided
to find a new life in America, and reached there in 1637. Despite
the warning given by Laud, Archbishop of Canterbury, that "my
arm shall reach him there", he became pastor of the first church,
and shared with the governor in the work of establishing the
colony. He set the pattern of its school system, and Yale's
Davenport College bears his name. Over there, a tablet marks
where he lived, but in his native city he is quite unknown.

A name that often crops up in political and trade-union circles
is that of Tom Mann, who from very lowly beginnings became a
leading Socialist and trade-union leader. He was born at Longford, Coventry, in 1856, went to the 'Old Church' school and to
the Congregational School, Little Heath, and ended his formal
education at the tender age of 9. He began work then as a bird
scarer on a farm and thought how lucky he was because other
young boys were working long hours on looms in the 'cottage
factories'. Tom also worked as a miner at Victoria Colliery, at
Wyken, Coventry, but he was still a boy when the family moved
to Birmingham, and his future career, his involvement with the
trade-union movement and politics, are not directly part of the
Coventry story. His tie with the place of his birth is, however,
remembered—an old people's home at Longford is named the
Tom Mann Home, and Coventry Trades Council have the Tom
Mann Hall at Stoke Park. Tom Mann, one-time leader of the

Dockers Union, is honoured in the Socialist movement, and he is one of few natives of Coventry about whom biographies have been written.

In this century, Coventry has given civic recognition to some of its citizens and to some who were not, who have distinguished themselves or have given reason for expression of gratitude or appreciation. One way of doing this is by admission to the Roll of Honorary Freemen, and the other is a local 'honours list', the Coventry Award of Merit, instituted in 1964. Its aim is "to publicly acknowledge and honour personal behaviour reflecting the highest ideals of citizenship or outstanding performance in any worthy field of human endeavour which enhances the good name of Coventry, and inspires its citizens". This, like the honorary freedom, is very rarely bestowed.

The Roll of Honorary Freemen of Coventry in over fifty years has had only eleven names added to it. The first was that of Andrew Carnegie, who had given three branch libraries—at Earlsdon, Stoke and Foleshill—to Coventry. They were opened in 1913, and are still in use. He was made an honorary freeman in 1914, and it was not until ten years later that there was another similar honour, when Sir William Wyley, who had served on the council from 1876 to 1888, and who had been mayor, and an alderman for many years, was given this distinction. Another long-serving member, Alderman Alfred Drinkwater, was admitted in 1927. He was mayor from 1903 to 1905. Two prominent industrialists, Sir Alfred Herbert and Lord Nuffield, and Mr. Hugh Farren, J.P., were admitted in the 1930s. Mr. Frederick Smith, town clerk, was admitted in 1946, when he retired. Three long-serving aldermen and ex-mayors, A. R. Grindlay, G. E. Hodgkinson, and S. Stringer, were admitted in 1962, and the second Lord Iliffe, a benefactor in various ways to Coventry, was admitted in 1969.

Sixteen people have received the Coventry Award of Merit. The first five awards were presented in February, 1966, to Mr. Stanley Ashby, a Godiva Harriers official and former Olympic runner; Sir Donald Gibson, first Coventry City Architect and Planning Officer; Professor J. W. Linnett, professor of physical chemistry at Cambridge University; Miss M. R. Paton, M.B.E., superintendent of St. Faith's Shelter; Air Commodore Sir Frank Whittle, K.B.E., inventor of the jet engine.

Five more awards were presented in May, 1970, to Mr.

Derrick H. Robins, former president, Coventry City Football Club; Sir Basil Spence, O.M., O.B.E., architect and designer of Coventry Cathedral; Sir William Lyons, president, Jaguar Cars—British Leyland U.K.; Dr. H. Parry Williams, former consultant child specialist, Coventry Hospital Group; Mrs. A. L. Galpine, a former chairman of Coventry Magistrates and Coventry Juvenile Court.

In February, 1978, there were six more recipients of the award: Dr. Cuthbert Bardsley, Bishop of Coventry; Professor Joan Browne, C.B.E., former principal of Coventry College of Education; Mr. Walter Chinn, O.B.E., former Coventry Director of Education; Sir Stanley Harley, former chairman and managing director, Coventry Gauge and Tool Co. Ltd.; Mr. Jack Jones, M.B.E., former general secretary, Transport and General Workers' Union; Dr. Philip Larkin, Librarian, University of Hull, poet.

Few men, however, have their deeds commemorated by statues in Coventry, as is the case with Sir Thomas White. Yet he was not a Coventry man. He was born at Reading in 1492, but was for some reason a great benefactor of Coventry. The statue was erected in 1882 on Greyfriars Green, and there is an oil painting of him in St. Mary's Hall. From an apprenticeship to a London merchant, he became a wealthy merchant himself, and when the guilds were suppressed in the middle of the sixteenth century he made Coventry Corporation a gift of £1,400 so that they could buy back lands that had been confiscated by the Crown, and properties including St. Mary's Hall. The income from the lands was to be held in trust for charitable work, and the corporation covenanted to apply part of it in annual grants to twelve poor householders, and part for free loans to young men who had trained as apprentices, and who wished to set up their own businesses. The lands were extensive, and the annual income, now administered by trustees of Sir Thomas White's Charity, runs into tens of thousands of pounds. It is shared on a rota basis with other towns—Northampton, Leicester, Nottingham, and Warwick—and part of the income is paid to the Coventry School Foundation (Bablake and Henry VIII).

Other people whose names are recorded in Coventry's history for various reasons include two scholars who were connected with the city's Free Grammar School. Sir William Dugdale, the historian, was born at Shustoke, and came to the school in

Coventry for his education, from 1615 to 1620. He became Garter King-of-Arms, but his name lives on more for his work in compiling works like the *Antiquities of Warwickshire*, printed in 1656, which has a mine of information in it about the county and the city. Because he did not leave a similar reference work for posterity, Dr. Philemon Holland is not so familiar a name. In Dugdale's period at the school, Dr. Holland was an usher, and in 1628 became its master. An Essex man, educated at Cambridge, he was a distinguished scholar, and was known as the 'Translator General' because he translated many classics. Another recorder of history—about Coventry—was Thomas Sharp. He was a native of the city, born in 1770, and was a pupil, too, of the Free Grammar School. By trade a hatter, his bent was towards local history, and he wrote books and papers about it.

In our time the 'Thomas Sharps' have been the late Mr. J. B. Shelton and Mr. Abe Jephcott, who were imbued with great love of the history of the city, and were always keen on preservation of its antiquities. Mr. Shelton was not a native, but everybody in the central area knew him as a Coventry amateur historian. He wrote many papers about old Coventry, collected relics and presented them to the museum, and an annual memorial lecture is held in his name. Shelton Square is named after him. Mr. Jephcott was a native, and an old boy of St. Peter's School, Hillfields. A master builder, he had worked as a bricklayer and mason on ancient buildings in Coventry, and had great regard for them. He compiled a Godiva scroll, on leather, which was signed by successive mayors and Lord Mayors. He also compiled an Ellen Terry scroll, signed by many celebrities. He wrote copiously about old Coventry.

XI

THEN—AND NOW

BEFORE the war, Coventry was a closely-knit community around a town centre of narrow streets which seemed to become even smaller when the electric tramcars came along them, like queens of the road as they sailed down the centre of the highway. For a copper or two there was pleasure in a ride on a tram that had an open-top deck—unless it was raining. It was almost soundless motion, gliding along smooth track in the breeze or the sun.

For most of their length the lines were single track with double sections—the loops—for trams to pass. When we were in a hurry, those loops were tantalizing. How long to wait before a tram arrived from the opposite direction to enable you to proceed?

Coventry had a tramway service from 1882 until the fleet of fifty was knocked out and the tracks disrupted in the air raids. Bus services, which had begun as early as 1914, had been gradually replacing the trams, which now were abandoned. There were 10¼ miles of track still in use, compared with 12½ miles when Coventry Corporation bought the tram service in 1912 for £211,298, from the Coventry Electric Tramway Company.

The company's first service had been steam-operated, and ran between Bedworth and Coventry Station. In 1895 the company electrified it and added more lines. Services ran from Broadgate or from the station to several parts of the city. There was a service along Stoney Stanton Road to Bell Green terminus; along Paynes Lane and Binley Road to Uxbridge Avenue for the GEC; along Lower Ford Street and Far Gosford Street into Binley Road; along Queens Road, The Butts and Albany Road, to Earlsdon, to the terminus at St. Barbara's Church; along Spon Street and Allesley Old Road to the Maudslay Hotel.

There were depots at Priestley's Bridge, Stoney Stanton Road, and at Foleshill Road near Lythalls Lane, and there were sidings into Courtaulds works, Foleshill Road, and into the railway goods yard at Bell Green Road, near Navigation Bridge. The trams, some totally enclosed, some with open decks, sailed up and down these lines, paused with thrilling uncertainty in loops, sometimes ran off the tracks! Otherwise there were no violent swerves or jerky accelerations that some bus drivers resort to in order to shake up the passengers; just a steady progression into speed as more power was applied. Inside the car passengers sat sideways on, on wooden seats, and upstairs sat forward facing, the seats having reversing backs so that they could look to the front whichever way they were going. On the open-deck type the motorman had much the worst of it if the weather was bad. He had to stand, a waterproof cape pulled up to his nose, in the wet and cold. At the terminus he would detach the control handle and carry it to the other end of the car, and prepare for the return trip. His conductor took the overhead cable and walked round the car to reconnect the cable to the overhead wires for the run back.

The trams would make speed up to 25 or 30 miles an hour, but of course they could not have survived into the era where there is practically a car for every family. They took up too much of the centre of the road, and there was delay to traffic as passengers walked between the car and the pavement to board or alight. At peak times the narrow streets were congested. The trams would inch their way down Smithford Street, surrounded by packed crowds of week-end shoppers who had to cross the street in order to pass between the Market Square area on one side, and Woolworth's and the City Arcade on the other. Coventry people have forgotten those jostling crowds since they have had the traffic-free shopping precinct!

The trams were running at a loss, due to the annual repayment of outstanding debt charges, while the buses—there were over one-hundred in service before the war—were making an annual profit, so the writing was on the wall for the trams in every respect. They were part of the scene when more people owned bicycles than cars, and incidentally care was needed on a cycle when crossing those shining narrow tracks. If the tyres ran into the tracks it was time to prepare for an emergency landing!

Those were more leisured days, when the tram or the bus carried a letter box for use at night after the last postal collection from districts, and the boxes were cleared in the town. The trams were part of the scene when the 'town', as it was known, was not far from any of the suburbs. The Bell Green tram terminus at the junction with Hall Green Road marked the end of the built-up area of Coventry. From Hall Green Road outwards there was farmland, and the suburbs on other sides of the city were similarly well defined.

Going back a few more years, to the early thirties, children's adventures were walks that took them from home into the fields within the space of just a few minutes, to continue on by way of common, or canal towpath, or river bank. Early camping holidays were perhaps on farms nearby that today are covered by housing estates. The canal was popular with children, who went fishing for 'tiddlers', and to see the colourful working boats that passed up and down, taking coal to the wharf at Swan Lane or timber to the Bishop Street basin almost in the centre of town.

How clever the narrow-boat horses seemed! Unattended generally, they would plod along at unchanging pace, over bridges, under bridges, and children would press back into the hedge or scramble behind it to make way, not that the horse was very concerned for he was usually engaged in munching from the contents of the bag or gaily-painted can slung from his neck. Occasionally, excitement! A horse had fallen in! There would be a commotion before he was hauled out on to the towpath. It was a marvel that the working boats could approach and pass so tidily, without horses or lines getting into a tangle.

The canal, made 200 years ago, was an important transport system when roads were rough tracks and there were only horses and carts. It has been the only navigable waterway in Coventry, in the absence of a river of any size, and today is used more and more by pleasure boats, as well as being an amenity for anglers, artists, and towpath walkers. For many visitors to the city, the canal basin is the gateway, as they arrive by boat for the first time. So it has potential. When it is improved, as is planned, the basin will be an unusual waterways 'harbour' in the heart of the city, and will receive an increasing number of visitors seeing England by boat.

Childhood walks too were through the meadows, filled with buttercups, daisies, golden water blobs—marsh marigolds—harebells, wild dog roses in the hedgerows, sumptuous blackberries in autumn, and acorns and conkers, to the 'Miller's Brook' at Mill Lane, Courthouse Green. This was a favourite spot for picnics and paddling, where the water was so deliciously freezingly cold to the feet until they were acclimatized! Then a risky step over the waterfall, under the wooden footbridge. This was living! Now it is a built-up area, but in those days from Red Lane outwards there was open country and on Stoke Common the water-filled quarries had quite sizeable fish in them.

Children were lucky in their countryside surroundings. At Radford the built-up area ended short of Keresley Road, and there was countryside right out to Corley Rocks, a long hike away, ending with climbing adventures and picnic bags that would insist on swinging from necks, getting in the way of arms and legs in the scramble up, grasping at tree roots or branches. It was a day's outing, but on the way back, if the journey was by way of Radford spring, thirst could be eased. There has not been a spring for many years. It was piped away.

Wyken was not built up and the little hilltop church of St. Mary Magdalen was isolated. Walsgrave was a village in fields, far from the urban area that has now overtaken it. On the south side of the city, there was countryside at Canley, Westwood Heath, and Tile Hill, and there were the joys of bluebell time at Crackley Woods. To walk or cycle in that direction did not involve crossing the A45 Coventry by-pass, which was not in use until 1939—and then anyway it was a genuine by-pass, circling round Coventry, which now spreads far beyond it.

Coventry has not known a trade depression like that which ended in the early thirties, when children's pleasures had to be simple as there was little money to spend. But for a penny or halfpenny there were so many things to buy. Sticks of liquorice wood from the chemist, gob-stoppers, 'Old Joe's' toffee, bags of sherbet, tiger nuts. Shop windows were a delight at Christmas with new annuals, and one of these, or perhaps a mouth organ, was all we could want in our stocking. There was perhaps the first ride in a car; an occasional outing in a charabanc, all the more pleasurable if the hood was down; Sunday School outings to Stoneleigh Park—all those deer—or to Arbury Park.

It was the era of 'do-it-yourself' for sports and pastimes. Kites were home-made, so was the rod and line. Football and cricket were played with stones or jackets for goal-posts, and sticks, usually with coats folded round them, to give them bulk, for stumps. Children playing at camping-out, made tents from sacking. They were not waterproof, but it did not stop the adventurers, on occasions, from sleeping at night in them. Then there were those sudden changes of school games that were

Cheylesmore Manor House Gateway restoration
The abbey and moat in Coombe Countryside Park

signalled by some kind of bush telegraph. Everybody sat in playground or street, in little groups, playing at fivestones and trying to complete the sequence that ended with 'snatches'. Suddenly, nobody played fivestones any more. Cigarette card games like 'skim the farthest' and 'dropping on' were in; or there was the passion of the day for marbles—with 'knocking on' contests along gutters, and games of 'chock' when the marbles were sent into a hole in the ground. There were crazes for kites, and conker contests.

Streets were not dangerous with traffic. Only one or two families in a whole street would have cars. Tradesmen went round in horses and carts, the milkman used to measure into jugs from a churn, and popular transport was the bicycle. Street scenes, if a butcher had premises nearby, would include the sight of a few cows or sheep being driven along and causing some commotion as they ran in panic, in any direction, on the way from market to the butcher's yard to be slaughtered. It was before the public abattoir opened in Coventry and centralized the slaughtering, in 1932. All private slaughterhouses were then closed.

Funerals were special occasions. A death was followed by a street collection and all gave to it for the wreath, or for the widow. When it was nearly time for the funeral every blind and curtain was drawn to show respect. Children gathered to see the big black horses drawing the hearse and the carriages. It was a splendid sight, the horses tall and with plumes fixed over their heads, the drivers in black top hats. Children looked at the flowers when taken for walks to the London Road cemetery. It was a place of tree-lined drives and like a park. A beautiful spot, it was laid out by Mr. (later Sir) James Paxton, who designed Crystal Palace.

Solemn too, used to be Remembrance Day, 11th November, when children assembled in hall at school, the factory hooters sounded all over the city and the hush was almost unbearable as the two minutes' silence was observed. Nothing moved in school or outside, all traffic stopped; it was utterly still everywhere. Children put flowers round the roll of honour of the fallen, and sang "O Valiant Hearts".

On Empire Day they went to school in uniforms if they were members of organizations like scouts and guides, the Church Lads' Brigade or the Boys' Brigade. In some schools they sang "What Can We Do for England?" marched round the playground

Butcher Row, cleared away for the Trinity Street scheme

and saluted the Union Jack. They were thrilled when the R101 airship went overhead, watched by the whole school, teachers too. If school won a shield, they all marched behind the captain who held it, and sang as they went through the streets: "We played on the field and we won the shield . . ."

And what sensations there were on Good Friday morning, to awaken at some unearthly hour like 6 a.m. and hear a street sing-song gradually getting nearer and louder—"Hot Cross buns, one a ha'penny two a penny, Hot Cross buns!" Schoolboys would be doing the selling, from their mothers' washing baskets piled high with newly-baked, warm, and plainly crossed, buns, earning pocket money. Why did they come so early? Good Friday, with few exceptions, was a working day.

Easter Monday, the day of the annual Coventry Sunday Schools' rally at Pool Meadow, was another highlight, when—it seems in retrospect to have been sunny every Easter—boys turned out in Sunday best and girls in summer frocks, for the procession to the Meadow, hymns sung (after weeks of rehearsal) by thousands of young voices. Then a return procession, followed by dispersal of the various schools to their own districts, where each child received a bun and an orange. Numbers at local Sunday schools always rose remarkably just before Easter, only to decline, unaccountably, after it! Crowds lined the streets to see the processions pass, mothers dashing out when they saw their own offspring to give them sweets, an apple, or a banana, as though they were going to starve before they reached home again! At the front of each school contingent would be a great banner, showing its name, and embroidered with a figure from the Bible, perhaps Jesus with the Lamb. How the two banner-bearers struggled, when the wind gusted, each holding grimly to his weighty pole, while the children, tripping along holding the ropes that trailed from the banner, hardly assisted when they tugged too much one way or the other!

Then there was the annual Hospital Carnival Procession, when all the main streets along which it passed were bedecked with flags, bunting and streamers. Dense crowds, much anticipatory excitement! An annual procession is held today, organized by the Civic Recreation Department, but there is hardly a street decoration in sight! Then, the collection was a serious business because it was for the hospital, but the atmosphere was carnival and there was lots to laugh at, as well as to admire. A voluntary committee of the Hospital Saturday Fund ran it, and raised many thousands of pounds, until the war halted it. Before it was resumed there was the nationalization of the health service, in 1948. The need, to maintain the voluntary hospital, had gone.

The procession was brought back to life by the Festival of Britain, in 1951. To mark the festival, the corporation asked Mr. Leonard Turner, deputy principal of the technical college and a drama enthusiast, to organize a Godiva Pageant, and since 1954 the City Council have sponsored a procession and a gala at the War Memorial Park each summer, not of course including Lady Godiva each time, for her appearances are very rare. The street collection goes to a good cause, formerly the Lord Mayor's Christmas parcels fund for the old people, and any profit made at the gala is used for parks improvements, playing fields, or other amenities of the kind.

While the corporation maintain the tradition of the annual carnival procession, and provide a family day out with plenty of attraction at the park, one event in the Coventry calendar goes on, and on, and on, unchanged—the Great Whit Fair. Generations of Coventry children have been thrilled by it, generations of young couples have gone bargain-hunting to its crockery and linoleum sections in the business of setting up home. It is a familiar sight to see husbands staggering home under rolls of lino, or with a dining set in their arms! The venue used to be Pool Meadow, when it was a wide unpaved area on two sides of Priory Street, hemmed in by Ford Street on one side, and by the fire station and the River Sherbourne, not then culverted. Behind the river was the Triumph works, and the old central baths.

What an atmosphere the fair at the Meadow had! The crowds walked on grass if it had not been trodden out of sight, on straw if it had been very wet, and generally there was mud. It was like plunging into another world, with amusements such as the 'Big Horses' and the 'Dragons', and the 'King and Queen Boats', all in action against a background of garish fairground music from every one of them. Each of the rides had in the centre the musical 'works', pumping out music squeezebox fashion, with a display of pipes, drums, and little puppet figures. It was a medley of sounds, but very specially 'fairground'. Amusements now are more 'with it' for this age, with moon rockets and so on, but the big 'King and Queen Boats' were effective enough in their day, down on the ground almost, then high in the air, pockets emptying in the process! Youngsters could stay on the 'cat walk' for ages unless the crowd pressed them onward, and small children, on it for the first time, seemed likely to stay on indefinitely, when they were stranded at the end of one 'walk' and dare not take the quick step on to the next section! Stalls with brandy snaps and toffee apples, stalls selling paper balls stuffed with sawdust that were suspended on lengths of elastic, sideshows, the boxing booth; and then, separate from the amusements, the crock and lino fair, where the salesmen were barking their wares and bringing down the price in rapid stages before clinching the deal with a bang.

The Coventry Great Fair is famous among showmen and traders, and some still come to it after a lifetime, following in the family tradition. The venue is Hearsall Common, and there is a muster of well-appointed caravans for living quarters and expensive cars used by the traders. A trader can sell several thousands of pounds' worth of stock in a week at this fair, which explains why the same stalls appear every year. As befits a fair that operates under a royal charter dating back 700 years, it is closely linked with the civic life of Coventry. The Lord Mayor gives the showmen's representatives a civic lunch, then they drive to the fair, and he ceremoniously declares it open and usually has a ride on an amusement to set things going. Charges for rides are controlled by the council.

The showmen through their guild have made gifts to the city. They gave a cheque for £196 for lighting equipment for the cathedral's drama activities, and one for £70 for a fund for thalidomide babies. The corporation rent the site to them, and receive about £2,000 from the fair, so it brings not only pleasure, but profit. It never seems to outstay its welcome, although Hearsall Common is the venue for other fairs at holiday times during the year. The cars and buses bring loads of families—and cars are parked by the hundreds. The Great Fair is 'different', and it is the only one that is allowed to have crock and lino stalls.

Coventry has always been an expanding city, and there was plenty of house building in the thirties. Prices were usually between the £450 and £600 mark, with deposits as low as £25. Three-bedroomed houses at the Scotchill were selling at £499, and at Addison Road, off Keresley Road, for £500, repayments 12s. 2d. a week, no legal costs. At Cheylesmore, 'palace homes' were selling at £595, and the advertisements promised front and rear gardens laid out free of charge by an expert gardener.

Wages were proportionately low, probably between £2 and £5 a week. School-leavers could expect to start work at the age of 14 or 15 at 7s. 6d. or 10s. a week, and a birthday rise might be anything between 1s. and 2s. 6d.! Bingo, television, motoring and all that, had not arrived, and people relied for entertainment on the cinema—every district had one; dances, perhaps once a week at places like St. Margaret's hall, the GEC Ballroom, St. John's, or the Rialto; roller skating—there were several rinks including the Ritz at Albany Road, the Swift at Cheylesmore, and the Capitol at Longford. The library, night school and evening classes at the technical college were other interests and, at week-ends, there was sport, a visit to town, church, or cycle rides into the countryside.

Cinema-going changed from the silent films and the pianist who played the musical accompaniment, to the great luxury of the carpeted cinemas with the mighty Wurlitzers—the cinema organs—when, far from being the accompanist, the organist was a local celebrity, appropriately given star billing. He would begin to play before he could be seen, and gradually organ and player would rise from pit to stage level, the spotlights on them, to give intervals of music. Most of Coventry's cinemas, small and large, have closed—some because of war damage, but most because of the disappearance of the cinemagoers, lost to the home comforts of television, or the lure of prizes to be won at bingo. Car owner-ship, too, has enabled people to go farther afield, and greater affluence means the occasional meal at a country hotel.

At Foleshill, dry cleaners use the old 'Regal', which in earlier times was called the 'Grand'. When it closed in 1960 it had completed forty-nine years as a cinema, and was said to be the first place in Coventry to have a cinematograph licence. It gave our generation, a long time ago, Tom Mix, whose exploits would be repeated in a limited way on the journey home; Harold Lloyd, always about to plunge to his death over a skyscraper parapet but getting hung up somewhere on his descent; and Rin-Tin-Tin, the wonder dog.

The 'Grand' shared, with 'La Scala' at Far Gosford Street, the distinction of being first in Coventry to show talkies—on 11th March 1929. These were shorts. The 'Scala' showed J. H. Squire with his Celeste Octette, Bransby Williams as Grandfather Smallweed in a sketch from *Bleak House*, and Ernie Lotinga in a comedy sketch called "Nap". At the 'Grand' there was Teddy

Brown with his xylophone, Ethel Hook singing "Love's Old Sweet Song", the Blattner Orchestra, and two acrobatic dancers in "Toddling Along". The first full-length talkie was shown at the Scala on 8th April 1929. It was *Moulin Rouge*. *The Singing Fool* with Al Jolson came three weeks later, on 29th April, to the 'Alexandra'.

Many cinemas, to beat the post-war decline in attendances, made improvements and in doing so changed their names. The 'Scala' became the 'Odeon', but still had to close its doors in 1962, when bingo took over. The 'Alexandra' has kept going, and is now called 'Theatre One'. The 'Gaumont' is still going strong in Jordan Well, but now carries the name of 'Odeon'. The 'Empire' in Hertford Street, demolished for redevelopment, has been rebuilt as the ABC Cinema. The 'Standard', Tile Hill Lane, was modernized and became the 'Godiva'—but is no longer a cinema, nor, since 1981, is the 'Paris', formerly the 'Crown', at Far Gosford Street. Only three cinemas are left from the film-struck pre-war days when there were twenty-two.

If the 'Empire', 1906–1971, had the longest life for a cinema, the 'Rex', Corporation Street, must have had the shortest. It was opened just before the war and was hit by a bomb on 25th August 1940, before any of the big raids. This was the night before the film *Gone With the Wind* was due to be shown. Another raid victim that could not re-open was the 'Brookville', Holbrook Lane, later adapted for shopping. The 'Carlton', previously called the 'Cupid', at Stoney Stanton Road, closed and became a warehouse for a Coventry store. Another former cinema which became a warehouse was the 'Astoria', Albany Road, previously the 'Broadway'. It closed in 1959. The 'Prince of Wales', Stoney Stanton Road, closed three years earlier, and became St. Finbarr's Club for the Irish community. The 'Roxy', formerly the 'Redesdale', Foleshill Road, also became a club—first the 'Banba', then the Irish Hibernia Club. The 'Palladium', King William Street, closed in 1962, and became a cinema for use of the Indian and Pakistani community. The 'Ritz', formerly the 'Dovedale' and also once called the 'Rivoli'—at Windmill Road, closed in 1966, and became a club for Indian people.

The 'Plaza', at Spon End arches, was the first Coventry cinema to be built to show talkies. It was opened in October 1929, and featured the early sound film, *Broadway*. It closed in 1960, and for a time was used as a store and workshop for The Coventry

Theatre. The 'Globe' at Primrose Hill Street was closed as a cinema and became the Majestic Ballroom, but then came another change and it became the Orchid bingo hall. Another cinema used for bingo, is the 'Rialto', at Coundon. The 'Forum' at Walsgrave Road, despite having a large catchment area to draw on, also followed the trend, and after being closed became a shopping centre and had ten-pin bowling. The 'Savoy' at Radford Road, which, when it opened in 1938, was one of the largest suburban cinemas in the country, closed in 1962, for ten-pin bowling and later for bingo. The 'Lyric', Holbrook Lane, closed in 1968, and also became a bingo club.

All over the city the trend was the same. The 'Imperial' at Earlsdon Street, struggling against the tide, was renamed the 'Continental' and showed foreign films to attract a specialist following, but it, too, had to close its doors. Even before the war some cinemas were feeling the draught. The 'Tivoli', once called the 'Bijou', in Webster Street, Foleshill, closed and became a billiards hall, and later, a Co-op furnishing showroom. Those who are particularly interested in the subject will recall other bygone Coventry cinemas. The 'Sydenham Palace', Cox Street, showed movies at one time, and there were occasional films at the old skating rink, Ford Street.

The Opera House, although a cinema in its last years, was originally a theatre and is remembered for the excellence of Coventry Repertory Company from 1931 until October 1940, when the stage was wrecked by bombs. Opera House history went back to 1889, with *A Midsummer Night's Dream* staged by the first of many touring companies that performed there. 'Rep' opened on 6th April 1931 with *Aren't We All* by Frederick Lonsdale, and was a big success. The company performed a different play each week, last week's stars this week's bit players. Theatregoers marvelled that they could keep up the cracking pace, performing at night and rehearsing in the day for next week's play. Hwfa Pryse, Phyllis Calvert, Richard Williams, Gladys Spencer, Ann Titheradge, Hamilton Dyce, Julien Mitchell, Pauline Letts, Richard Hurndall, Peter Coleman, Charles Cameron, Anthony Hulme, Hugh Butt, Agatha Carroll, Cyril Wentzel, Raymond Francis, and many others at one time or another belonged to the company. Patrons could watch them for as little as 9d. in the balcony, or 1s. in the pit. Top price was 12s. 10d. for a box seating four.

There was an enthusiastic and faithful Repertory Circle with over one-thousand members. At least two special trains ran from Coventry to the West End so that the fans could see West End productions—apparently with the idea of comparing them—unfavourably of course—with the productions they had seen in Coventry.

When, in October 1940, the end came with the bombing, the director of productions, Mr. Geoffrey Staines, and some of the company, went to York Repertory Company, Mr. Staines promising confidently that rep would return after the war. But less than a year later people were going to the Opera House to see films—the first being *It All Came True*, starring Ann Sheridan and Humphrey Bogart. In 1961, the final blow: the theatre-turned-cinema was sold to Sketchley's Ltd., the dry-cleaning firm, and was demolished to make way for their premises.

Today there are shops at the spot in Hales Street where the Opera House stood, but fortunately rep has come back, in the form of the company of the Belgrade Civic Theatre, which in Corporation Street is not very far removed from the Hales Street site occupied by its illustrious predecessor. For nights out there was always the old 'Hippodrome', now The Coventry Theatre, also in Hales Street. In one building or another—for this theatre has had three of them—most of the stage personalities of their day have performed, from Nellie Wallace, Vesta Victoria, Gertie Gitana, Will Hay, Rob Wilton, onwards. The full list would be difficult to collate. There had been twice-nightly variety and revue for many years, followed, as fashions changed, by a wider range of entertainment including premières of Emile Littler productions, destined to become West End successes. There have been ballet, opera, straight plays, big band shows, pop stars.

It was The Coventry Theatre that staged the Coventry Festival of Music, in which the managing director, the late Mr. S. H. Newsome, and the late Alderman Mrs. Hyde, were chief organizers. It started in 1958, and was discontinued in 1964 due to lack of public support. Mr. Newsome brought to Coventry names like Beecham, Sargent, Kreisler, and some of the great orchestras. Gracie Fields, the Lunts, John Gielgud, Vivien Leigh, Sybil Thorndike, and Donald Wolfit, were among those appearing there. Other touring companies were the National Theatre Company, with Laurence Olivier, Celia Johnson and

Maggie Smith; the Royal Ballet with Dame Margot Fonteyn; the Covent Garden and Sadler's Wells Opera, and D'Oyly Carte. The theatre has also produced many of its own star-studded shows, its birthday shows and pantomimes, which enjoy long runs.

The first building was a corrugated iron structure, dating back to about 1890, on Pool Meadow. The second was built and opened at the beginning of 1907, and the present premises were opened in 1937. The three have been on adjacent sites, and the pleasant little Lady Herbert's Garden is on the site of the second theatre, well remembered for the wooden steps that served as seats, in the 'gods'. It closed on 30th October 1937, with a variety bill that included Tommy Handley. It was in this theatre that Charles Shadwell and the orchestra became well known, making numerous broadcasts. Mr. Bill Pethers took over the orchestra after Mr. Shadwell became director of the BBC Variety Orchestra.

The present theatre seats 2,000 people, cost £100,000, and was opened in November 1937, with Harry Roy's Band top of the bill. The name was changed to The Coventry Theatre in 1955, one reason being that it was drawing upon audiences from a wide area of the Midlands and it was thought useful to have Coventry in the title. Mr. Newsome had followed his father, Mr. S. T. Newsome, in 1930, in control of the theatre, and father and son together had a span of sixty years there. *South Pacific* was the production for the theatre's début under its new title.

The building escaped serious war damage. It was hit by a high-explosive bomb but it turned out to be a dud, and when the filling had been taken out the casing was used as a Red Cross collecting box! After a temporary break because water and power were cut off, the theatre reopened with a host of stars, including Evelyn Laye and Rawicz and Landauer, in a show in aid of the air-raid distress fund. Mr. Newsome said afterwards that his most rewarding experience in the theatre was that, at that tragic time, so many stars, "everyone", wanted to help Coventry. The theatre raised £50,000 for charities during the war.

Ten years later Mr. Newsome had another special show, marking the Festival of Britain celebrations. This was *The Winter's Tale*, and the cast included John Gielgud, Diana Wynyard, Lewis Casson, Flora Robson, George Howe, George Rose, and Paul Hardwick. Production was by Peter Brook.

The theatre had some unusual uses because of the war. In 1949, while the Methodist Central Hall was being repaired after war

damage, its services were held in the theatre. It was the only
place big enough for the hall's 1,000-strong congregation. Ten
years later, the same thing happened when the church hall was
being redecorated. The theatre was sold to the Grade Organization, one of the Bernard Delfont companies, in 1967, and later
Apollo Theatres took over and renamed it the Apollo.

Learning to dance meant for many young Coventrians the
teaching sessions given by Mr. Pattison at St. Margaret's hall,
where a whole roomful of young people would be lined up to
watch him demonstrate with his daughter Betty. The advent of
the tango was of great moment. Some of the biggest dances were
at the Drill Hall, Queen Victoria Road, where top bands, like
those of Joe Loss and Mantovani, played.

Coventry is a place of change and improvement, and this was
starting even before the war, when they pulled down Butcher
Row area to make Trinity Street. There were narrow cobbled
ways flanked by small shops and stalls selling fish, meat, pickles,
furniture and antiques, where at night there were gas lamps and
naphtha flares that made it colourful and mysterious, the old
timber-framed buildings leaning inwards, the access ways narrow
so that at the Broadgate end people could reach out and touch the
buildings on either side. It was Dickensian and tourists of today
would have loved it.

Trinity Street was opened in September 1937—quite an
eventful year, with Foleshill Baths also being brought into use;
Allesley Hall and grounds presented to the city by Lord Iliffe;
Gulson Road Welfare Centre and Clinic being opened; and the
first woman mayor, Miss Alice Arnold, being elected by the
first Labour council.

Another first, at least in modern times, was the admission of a
woman apprentice to be a Freeman of Coventry. Miss Lily
Stevenson, whose father was a chemist at Stoney Stanton Road,
had followed in his footsteps. The Freemen hotly opposed her
admission and had counsel to represent them. The mayor decided
that it was a question of sex equality, as far as he was concerned,
and Miss Stevenson was admitted! The Freemen then brought a
High Court action against the mayor, town clerk, and the new
woman Freeman, but the war intervened, and in 1944 the action
was discontinued.

There had been women apprentices as long ago as 1336. There
were women members of the Merchant Guild, who worked on

their own account as woolcombers, pinmakers, cutlers, thread-makers, hosiers, barbers, and drapers. In the fifteenth century there were fifteen women members of the Carpenters' company, and women belonged to various other craft guilds. There are various records of women being admitted as 'Freewomen'. So in 1937 it was a revival of ancient customs. Today, women are often admitted as Freemen. They are usually hairdressers and they have other similar occupations, but the men are still supreme in engineering.

Freemen of Coventry are part of the city's heritage. They are carrying on the tradition of the old craft guilds whose main purpose was to ensure that newcomers were thoroughly trained, that crafts did not become overloaded—there was a limit on how many apprentices a master could employ—and that they under-took to be good citizens and paid their dues. Not much change has been made. It is still necessary for a master to place his apprentice's indentures with the town clerk, and at the end of the period agreed, to attend with the apprentice at a court where the Lord Mayor swears in the new Freeman if he has satisfied all the conditions. They still take the oath of a Freeman, of obedience and loyalty to the Sovereign, mayor, and magistrates, to uphold the city's liberties and customs, and "be tributary to all contribu-tions, taxes, tollages, watch, summons, scot and lot, and all other charges ...". Their guild, which was started after the war, steps closely in the traditions, its officers having posts like searcher and chronicler, and they meet in a chamber in St. Mary's Hall which, as we have seen, was built by the craft guilds for their affairs. The only changes are that from seven years' apprentice-ship, the period has come down a few years, because seven years was considered unnecessarily long to become skilled in the craft. Also the boundary covered by the Freemanship has been extended because some Coventry factories have gone just beyond the limits of the city.

The old Trinity Guild was closely allied with the civic life of Coventry, its master becoming mayor, usually, and today the Lord Mayor is always president of the guild in his year of office, an honorary post, for the chief office is that of master. The guild is mainly a social organization, a club which Freemen join if they wish, and it is also a supporter of charities. Thousands of pounds have been raised at the guild's 'village fête' at the annual gala in the War Memorial Park, and more is raised by the guild's field day when they give profits to any charity nominated by the Lord Mayor. The Freeman himself has a certificate of admission which older Coventry industrialists say is as 'good as a passport' if he goes elsewhere and wants a reference for a job. So long as Coventry has its Freemen, it has a pool of well-trained technicians, and that augurs well for its industrial future. The Freemen's trustees administer considerable estates, and from the funds loans can be made to Freemen to help them set up in business. On retirement Freemen receive weekly payments. Many Freemen have their own businesses, and some, as managing directors of their firms, ensure that the tradition is handed on through the apprenticeship of their own young workers.

Another area of change in the thirties was Well Street, where eighty-five properties were demolished so that Corporation Street could be constructed. It was opened in 1931, the year that Lockhurst Lane railway bridge was opened, relieving traffic of delays at the level-crossing gates. Corporation Street, over forty years later, is still not fully developed. The gas and electricity showrooms were opened in 1934, and there were some commercial properties in the road, in use and under construction, when the war broke out. Some were war damaged, some, after the war, demolished in the redevelopment plan, and a portion of the street has never been developed. Wartime temporary shops are still in use at the Hill Street end of the road, but it is hoped that this will eventually be the site of a hotel. Between Corporation Street and the precinct lay West Orchard, where the Congregational church stood, as did the market hall with its clock tower.

This was an area of stone setts, from which we stepped into the market entrance. Several steps led up to the market hall, and they were like a pets' corner, with puppies and tortoises and so on installed in their boxes waiting for buyers. The market was a place where we could browse for hours, especially at the second-hand bookstall. Outside was an arcade walk where there were more traders, and then the market square, where some open-air selling was done. On Sunday nights the Salvation Army band played there, and later it was taken over by the soapbox specialists, one noted character being Albert Smith, who was a great humorist and was not at all serious when he sold us copies of his "ultimatum to the king"! The tower with its clock was still standing (towers seem to make a habit of it in Coventry) after the market hall was destroyed in the raids, but it had to be pulled down as it was unsafe. There is not the slightest trace of this area now, nor of Market Street that led into Smithford Street.

To imagine how things used to be it is necessary to fasten on to an old building or place and visualize the layout from that point. It is not too difficult in Broadgate, because there is still Holy Trinity Church as a landmark, and the solid pillared entrance of the National Provincial Bank (National Westminster today) at the other end. It is still flanked by Greyfriars Lane, and Lloyds Bank. High Street is no longer a busy traffic street. The road has been re-surfaced with coloured tiles, kerbs have gone, and it is almost a walkway, except for buses and special vehicles. The Craven Arms has been demolished, and Barclays Bank have built their new headquarters on the site.

Along High Street, from Broadgate, a turn left into Hay Lane leads to the 'Golden Cross' public house. The scene is familiar. But a turn right instead, shows only one or two buildings left to indicate that this wide thoroughfare is the Little Park Street that existed until some years after the war. The old houses, pubs, and and shops, have gone; a large block, the GPO telephone exchange is on the right, and the new police headquarters on the left. A new road, called New Union Street, has replaced the Union Street of old. The new street has long rows of shops and offices, and most of the estate agents of Coventry seem to occupy one side of it. Behind the estate agents, tucked discreetly away, is the restored and very handsome Cheylesmore Manor Gatehouse which is now the register office for births, deaths, and weddings, and across the road is the spire of Christ Church, also restored, both being reminders of historic Coventry amid all that is new.

Many of the changes in central streets have been a result of the construction of the inner ring road, because it has severed a number of what were busy traffic arteries funnelling nearly all the through traffic into the centre and out again! Queen Victoria Road is an example, once heavily used by through traffic, it had traffic lights at the Spon Street cross roads. Now, only an occasional car, because Holyhead Road has been severed, and at the city end there is a short cul-de-sac. Queen Victoria Road, at its upper end, where traffic queued to drive into Queen's Road, has no outlet, again because of the ring road! Bishop Street was a heavily-trafficked road, leading from town to Radford Road

and St. Nicholas Street, and to Foleshill Road, and here a police-
man was kept very busy on point duty. The ring road now crosses
the top of Bishop Street, and no traffic goes out.

Anyone far away, reading about the old city, will wonder
where on earth all the Radford and Foleshill traffic has gone to, and
there is an answer for that. The city end of Radford Road is high
and dry, another cul-de-sac, but in its place a new Radford radial
arm has been made, taking traffic from the old road and leading
it beneath the ring road, on a new approach to town. Foleshill
traffic also has a different approach along a radial arm that joins
the ring road at a roundabout. Several other roads have been
severed, and have lost their old importance, and the traffic flow
is removed from the centre that used to be clogged up.

One of the worst sectors for jams was where heavy traffic flowed
along Ford Street, White Street, and Jesson Street, all converging
on Hales Street and, hoping to cross the city via Corporation
Street or Trinity Street. It was a bottleneck of such dimensions
that four or five policemen were required at peak times, each
controlling a junction. Now we have no Ford Street, no Jesson
Street; and White Street, what remains of it, is part of the
approach to the ring road.

These changes are repeated all round the centre, and motorists
have adopted new routes, using one-way systems and slip roads,
and the ring road itself. Pedestrians are definitely safer. They go
under the ring road by subways, or over it by footbridges, and if
they want to take their lives in their hands they have to climb over
guard rails to get on to the ring road and cross it. (Some actually
do!) Once away from the central area, the roads of Coventry
take on their old identity, with here and there traffic management
arrangements, and more banning of parking, as traffic increases.
Foleshill Road and Stoney Stanton Road make their long, rather
dreary miles out to Longford and Bell Green respectively, and
after the clean lines and brightness of the centre it seems that here
are areas that have been neglected.

There has not been much change in these districts, in parts well-
shopped, in parts run-down, and almost shouting for help.
Foleshill, its residential property cheek-by-jowl with large
factories, is unable to decide whether it is for workshops or homes,
and planners must find it difficult to improve matters. Courtaulds,
and the sister company British Celanese, are firms that have
grown huge in the area, Dunlop have expanded tremendously,

Alfred Herbert Ltd. dominate Cross Road, and there are numerous other works, large and small. On the south side of Coventry, factory development is considerable, but is in defined areas, and the housing is generally fairly free of it.

Coventry, of course, had to change, and the war damage speeded it up. Fortunately, children can still enjoy the countryside, although they have to go a little farther to get to it, and through built-up areas in the process, and the means of getting there is probably the family car. They can't go so readily to the cinema in their area, but instead they have the cinema at home. They cannot roller-skate so readily, if at all, as the rinks have closed. But do they still have those games crazes, when the 'bush telegraph' signals all change?

XII

HIGHLIGHTS OF HISTORY

COVENTRY has had a colourful past. There was its first great cathedral, said to have been like that at Lichfield, but demolished at the Reformation; and its massive city wall, which took fifty years to build, dismantled by command of the King. Coventry was a pleasing town with beautiful churches and merchants' houses, where religious plays were performed by the craftsmen on mobile stages. Royalty and nobility were among the many who came to see them, or just to visit the town, for it was the fourth town in size, outside London, in England.

Historians agree that the first recorded date in Coventry's history is 1016, when the Danes rampaged through Mercia—which covered Warwickshire area—and destroyed the nunnery at what would then be a settlement near the River Sherbourne. They also agree that there was probably a settlement, in a cleared part of the Forest of Arden, a century or two before this.

Various origins are given for the city's name. From the many spellings of it, one chiefly referred to is Cofantreo, which meant Cofa Tree or Cofa's Tree. It is possible that the name had a link with the Sherbourne, as 'Couen' means 'shire-born'. The nunnery or convent that was destroyed may have had a bearing on it; it could have meant 'Covent town', *tre* being the Celtic word for settlement or village.

After the destruction of the nunnery Earl Leofric, Earl of Mercia, and his wife Godiva, founded a Benedictine monastery on the nunnery site, in 1043, and liberally endowed it with wealth and lands. Godiva lavished treasure on its church, sending for locksmiths to make crosses and images of gold and silver. The names of Leofric and Godiva have survived in an extraordinary way, for here we are nearly one thousand years later naming a hotel, businesses, and a service station, after Leofric; and a hotel, cinema, café, firms, even a fried fish shop, after Godiva. Streets too have been named after them.

Lady Godiva statue, Broadgate garden island

GODIVA

THEN SHE RODE BACK CLOTHED ON WITH
CHASTITY...SHE TOOK THE TAX AWAY AN
BUILT HERSELF AN EVERLASTING NAM

Tenny

Early Coventry grew round the priory, which attracted craftsmen, merchants, and employed labour. Sometimes it served as lodging for royalty who came to Coventry, and it was twice used for meetings of parliament, both of which gained notoriety. In 1404 the king ordered that no lawyers or ecclesiastics should be members of it, and it became known as the 'Unlearned Parliament'. In 1459, when all members of it were Lancastrians, who used it to pass decisions against the Yorkists, it earned the label of the 'Diabolical Parliament'. Coventry had its priory for nearly four hundred years, but it also had its other fine structures, in Holy Trinity, only yards away, St. Michael's parish church, and Greyfriars church, all with spires, plus St. John's Church with its tower. There was also Coventry Cross and St. Mary's Hall, so before the Dissolution the city made a very fine sight.

Half of them were destroyed or part-damaged at the Dissolution, and a century later, in 1662, the order came from Charles II to demolish the city wall. It had been built over a period of fifty years, starting in 1355, when there was a mayoral stone-laying ceremony, and the ratepayers of those days had groaned under the cost that they had to meet. The stone came from local quarries. The wall was between 2 and 3 miles long, 8 or 9 feet thick, and of varying height, and it had twelve gates and thirty-two towers.

A wall of those dimensions was not for show! It added to Coventry's status, and it made it a defended town. Monarchs were well aware of this, and of the value of having it on their side in times when there was ceaseless intrigue and plot against the throne, and no royal head was safe for long. Charles I, during the Civil War, was warned when he was in Warwickshire, in 1642, that Parliamentary troops were planning to occupy Coventry. Lord Northampton, who had influence in Coventry as he was recorder of the city, was sent in haste to contact his friends in it and to hold Coventry for the Royalist cause. But Coventry sided with Parliament against the unpopular king. They told him they would "respectfully welcome" the King, but would not allow his cavaliers, apart from his own retinue, to enter.

The answer, conveyed to Charles, infuriated him. He vowed to pull the wall apart, sent for pole-axes and battering rams, and had his gunners bombard it from high ground near Whitley Common. They breached the wall near its New Gate, (near the Whitefriars Museum) and the cavaliers charged. The citizens repelled them

The Godiva clock
Peeping Tom, *formerly in a window in Bull Yard*

and peppered them with musket shot. The cavaliers came again, and again were thrown back. After several attempts, and despite having artillery, the army had to fall back, defeated by the citizens of Coventry plus four hundred friends who had come from Birmingham to add their weight to the defence. The feeling against the King was such that Birmingham, Coventry, Warwick and Southam were all against him and were in touch with each other, helping with arms and information. After the attack had been thwarted, it was not long before Parliamentary troops reached the city. They occupied it for the remainder of the war.

The phrase 'sent to Coventry' is generally supposed to have originated at this time because Royalist prisoners who were sent to Coventry—and placed in St. John's Church for safekeeping —found when they were allowed out on parole that local people, who had strong Puritan sympathies, would not fraternize with them. It was, for cavaliers, an unpleasant place to be sent to, and this has remained the meaning of the saying. For the Parliamentary troops, however, it was a good place to be stationed, "with a stout wall, magnificent churches and stately streets, and several and pleasant sweet springs", according to a letter written by one of them at the time.

Twenty years later when Charles II was on the throne, he remembered the slight his father had received, and ordered the demolition. A city so strong and so independent in its outlook, could mean future trouble.

No doubt such a wall did make a great difference to the attitude of those inside it. At any rate, another delicate situation had arisen in the Wars of the Roses, which began in 1455. The court leet who ran the local government at that time made fast the defences in anticipation of trouble. They ruled that each of the ten wards should supply four men to keep and guard the gates, that leading citizens would provide headpieces and other equipment, including bows and arrows, and craftsmen were to provide the fighting power. Defence preparations included purchase of four brass guns, and the placing in readiness of iron chains which would be fastened across the streets. In a war between Yorkists and Lancastrians Coventry might have been expected to be neutral, but this was not the case. They favoured the House of Lancaster—perhaps influenced by the friendly terms enjoyed with three Henrys, the IV, V, and VI, who were even made members of the city's Trinity Guild. So in 1471 when the Yorkist Edward IV marched with an army to the fortified town of Coventry, surrounded by its wide ditch and its high wall, it was already held, for the Lancastrians, by Warwick the Kingmaker. There was no attack, Edward marched on to London; but he did not forget, and later returned to Coventry, deprived its mayor of the civic sword, as a sign of displeasure, and took away the city's liberties. To atone and win these back, the city had to pay him 300 marks.

The existence of the city wall was drastic in the lives of some people. In 1554 there was a rising against Queen Mary led by the Duke of Suffolk and Sir Thomas Wyatt. Suffolk had friends in the city of Coventry, a potential strongpoint, and hoped to take possession of it for the uprising. But when he got here, the gates were closed, and while the mayor and citizens were debating whether to allow him to enter, the Queen's forces were drawing near. When they reached Warwick, Suffolk decided to retreat. He owned Astley Park, near Coventry, so went there and hid in a hollow tree, but was betrayed. While warming himself at a cottager's fire, he was taken by the Queen's men who had been sent from Warwick. Suffolk was executed in the Tower, where shortly before, his daughter, Lady Jane Grey, had suffered a similar fate.

Mary Queen of Scots a few years later entered the city, but as a prisoner, by command of Elizabeth I. Coventry, as a town mainly of Protestant supporters, was a place where Mary could safely be lodged while there was trouble with Catholics in the north.

For centuries, England's throne brought colourful, exciting, and dangerous times, and as a famous city in the land, Coventry was constantly being involved in state issues. Gosford Green was the venue, in the closing years of the fourteenth century, of the famous 'non-duel' between Henry Bolingbroke, Duke of Hereford, and Thomas Mowbray, Duke of Norfolk, arising out of a charge of treason against Mowbray. This was a memorable scene and forms part of Shakespeare's *King Richard the Second*. Thousands of visitors converged on Gosford Green where the King had set up Royal lists. He had also taken the precaution of surrounding the area with an army, in case trouble broke out between opposing sides, for the two dukes were supported by their lords and gentlemen. Hereford entered the lists on a white charger caparisoned in embroidered green and velvet, while Norfolk's mount was in embroidered crimson velvet.

After the reading out of the proclamation, according to *Staffordshire and Warwickshire Past and Present*, the duellists' spears were checked by the Lord Marshall, for length, then, watched by the King and all the peers of the realm, visors were closed and spears placed in rests. Hereford moved forward and Norfolk was about to do so when the King "cast down his warder and his heralds cried 'Ho Ho'". The duel had been stopped, at the eleventh hour. Spears were taken away, and the dukes returned to chairs where they waited for the decision of the King and his counsellors. When the King's secretary read the sentence, it was that Hereford should depart the realm and not return before ten years, while Norfolk, because he had sown sedition in the land by his words, was banished never to return. He was to die, an exile, in Venice. But Hereford, who went to France, did not stay away for ten years. Within two years, the King, Richard II, had been deposed, and Hereford had succeeded him, as King Henry IV.

Of course, the Gosford Green we know, where there is a plaque commemorating the duel scene, is only a small area of the original green on which the affair was staged. It must have been a noted spot in those days because the historians tell us that in 1466, in another of the plots that surrounded accession to the throne, the Earl of Rivers and his son were beheaded there, on the order of the great Earl of Warwick.

Within the town, while their peers were plotting and fighting for power, the merchants and the craftsmen built up a prosperous trading community, and from a very early date won rights and privileges, to trade and hold courts, when few towns had them. In the twelfth century, Ranulf, Earl of Chester, whose line had come into possession of the area of Coventry that was known as the 'Earl's Half'—the priory had the other—granted his tenants the right to elect their own justice, and hold their own court, instead of being under the jurisdiction of his steward. They also gained a charter giving trading rights, and merchants arriving in the town could trade free of rent or other charges for two years if they wished to settle in Coventry. A charter from Henry III granted the right to hold an annual eight-day fair. These privileges helped to bring migrants to Coventry and to develop it into a thriving place. Later, in the fourteenth century, merchants were allowed to form guilds and finally won the right to elect a mayor and corporation. This was followed by a charter uniting the earl's and prior's halves.

Wool was the town's first trade. There was also trade in metal, leather, and later it became an important cloth centre. The cloth trade was a thriving one in Coventry for many years and gave the city wealth. It had a wide sale at home and abroad and Coventry's dyers made a blue dye that was famous for its lasting qualities. It gave rise to the saying, "True as Coventry blue", and this superior colour was said to be due to the purity of the water of the Sherbourne used for dyeing. The dyers were mainly at Spon End by the river, and there is a public house there called the 'Old Dyer's Arms'. The French firm who made the Cathedral tapestry after the Second World War preferred to dye the wool themselves, in the River Creuse. The Coventry blue was well-known enough to be mentioned in the works of Ben Jonson, who, in 1621, had a character say: "I have lost my skein of Coventry Blue"; and in another play of 1626 he uses the words: ". . . though his hue be not Coventry Blue". Michael Drayton in "Dowsabell", refers to "His breech of Coventry Blewe".

Guilds for merchants and craftsmen became part of the life of Coventry after 1340. The Merchant Guild of St. Mary was founded, followed two years later by the Guild of St. John, whose guild church was St. John's, and by St. Katherine's Guild which had headquarters at the Hospital of St. John. Trinity Guild, founded in 1364, combined the three. Their function had been to safeguard rights already gained, and they did philanthropic work, but when Trinity Guild was formed it was also quite powerful and close to the municipal scene. One privilege of guild members was that they could trade free of toll or custom, while others had to pay. Being free to trade gave Freemen, descendants of the guildsmen, their name, and was the origin of the Freedom. The importance of Coventry as a trading centre caused merchants of other towns to join the Trinity Guild, and it enrolled visiting royalty, and nobility.

From the fourteenth century to the end of the sixteenth, the craft guilds were famous for their Coventry Mystery Plays, religious plays thought to have originated with the Greyfriars. They were performed before great crowds drawn to the city on Corpus Christi day and special occasions, and in those times must have been outstanding events.

There were ten plays or pageants, and all were performed in turn in each of the city's ten wards: Gosford Street, Jordan Well, Much Park Street, Bayley Lane, Earl Street, Broadgate, Smithford

Street, Spon Street, Cross Cheaping, and Bishop Street. They were on mobile stages on wheels, each vehicle having 'two storeys', the lower one for a dressing-room for actors and their gear, screened from the public by painted cloths, the upper storey being the stage. When the performances were over the stages and properties were stored in pageant houses. The drapers, who were owners of a pageant in 1392, had as their subject Doomsday. They included in their cast two demons, four angels, and two "worms of conscience". The "shearmen and taylors" had the play about the birth of Jesus and offering of the Magi, with the flight into Egypt and murder of the innocents, and their songs included the carol "Lully lulla". The play of the smiths company was the trial, condemnation and crucifixion of Christ, and their 'machinery' included the Cross, two pairs of gallows, scaffold, four scourges and a pillar, while their costumes included four gowns and four hoods "for the tormentors", "God's coat of white leather", and "a staff for the demon". For music they required trumpet, bagpipe, "minstrells", and "wayts" for "piping". God's coat of white leather was made of several skins, and there were also a girdle, and a gilt wig or peruke, and a seat for him. The devil had an appropriate mask, and a black, hairy, leather covering. Pilate wore a green silk gown and hat and gloves, while for Herod there was a helmet of iron decorated with gold and silver foil and coloured foil, and a painted gown. The tormentors wore black coats. Property included "hell mouth", and there were thunder effects, earthquakes, and storms. Details recorded about the smiths company noted that the players and drivers had ale, but Pilate had wine.

When the pageants went to their next station the carts were moved by men, and were seen by 'multitudes' of people, according to Sharp. A great sight on Corpus Christi Day was the procession, with members of the craft companies in their liveries, torchbearers, and journeymen, the mayor and civic dignitaries, processional crucifix, candlesticks, gilt chalice, banners, crosses, minstrels, and various other processionists and trappings. Coventry was a great place in those days for processions and plays, as on the Eve of St. John, and on St. Peter's Eve. There was also the procession of the Watch on Midsummer Night.

In 1416 Henry V and his nobles saw the Coventry plays; in 1456 Queen Margaret with her lords and ladies came from Kenilworth for the performances; in 1484 Richard III; and in

1486, Henry VII was present and came again in 1492 with the Queen. In 1565 Queen Elizabeth saw the Drapers Pageant perform, "and the Tanners Pageant stood at St. John's Church, the Weavers stood at Much Park Street". Sometimes there were special pageants for royal visits, as when Henry VIII and his queen visited the city in 1510. Only two of the texts of plays are preserved, one about the presentation of Jesus in the temple, the other the birth of Jesus and the plot of King Herod. In post-war years a revival of them in Coventry aroused a lot of interest among drama enthusiasts. The two were combined into one, and performed in the cathedral ruins by the Cathedral Players during June 1951 to mark the Festival of Britain (among many other Coventry activities), in 1962 for the Cathedral Festival, and in 1964 to mark Shakespeare's 400th anniversary. Belgrade Theatre actors now perform them annually in the ruins.

The plays were performed regularly until 1580, apart from in 1575, the year of a plague. From 1580 there was another gap until 1584 because, according to Sharp, "the temper of the times was hostile to such exhibitions of sacred subjects, especially among the clergy and the higher orders of Society who had embraced the Protestant religion, and men in power". In 1584 the smiths company brought out a new pageant, "Destruction of Jerusalem", which appeared not to give offence and all the companies co-operated to perform it. In 1591 the plays came to an end with joint productions of this pageant, and another called the "Conquest of the Danes".

Coventry has had big crowds too for modern Lady Godiva processions. In 1936, for example, forty special trains conveyed people to the city to see it. Streets were packed, and windows were hired out along the route. It was estimated that 200,000 people lined the route, and that at one time 100,000 people were at the War Memorial Park for the fair and other attractions. It seems that most people have heard of Lady Godiva, and in Coventry you cannot forget her. The bronze statue of Lady Godiva on her horse stands in the centre of Broadgate; there is a statue of her in St. Mary's Hall; there are paintings in the art gallery; there are postcards and souvenirs. Peeping Tom effigies used to lean from windows in the centre, but most have gone from public view. Tom also makes his sole public appearance peeping out from the puppet clock.

Whether or not Lady Godiva actually rode naked through the

market nobody can say, but the legend has survived for about eight hundred years. It is a matter about which historians have had lots of discussion over the years, and it is interesting to recount what they have had to say. F. Bliss Burbidge, who wrote *Old Coventry and Lady Godiva*, goes into it very fully. He dismisses Peeping Tom out of hand, because early accounts of Lady Godiva's ride had one thing in common—none of them mentioned Tom; he appeared centuries later as an embellishment of the story. Probably the earliest account of the ride is given, says Mr. Burbidge, in *Flowers of History* by Roger of Wendover, written between 1188 and 1237 when he was history writer to the Abbey of St. Albans. His version says:

> The Countess Godiva, a true lover of the Mother of God, longed to free the town of Coventry (Conventrensam) from heavy bondage and servitude, and often with urgent prayers begged her husband, that out of regard for Jesus Christ and His Mother, he would free the town from that service and from all other heavy burdens.
>
> The Earl constantly refused and sharply rebuked her for asking what was so much to his damage and forbade her evermore to speak to him again on the matter. Godiva however with womanly pertinacity never ceased to worry her husband on that matter until at last he answered and said, "Mount your horse naked, and ride through the market of the town from the beginning to the end when the people are assembled, and when you return, you shall have what you ask." To which Godiva, replying said, "And if I am willing to do this will you grant me leave?" "I will," he said. Then the Countess, cherished of God, attended by two soldiers, as is said before, mounted her horse naked, letting down the hair and tresses of her head so that her whole body was veiled except for her very beautiful legs, and no one saw her as she traversed the market place. The journey completed, she returned to her husband rejoicing and he, filled with admiration, freed the town of Coventry, and its people, from servitude and confirmed it by his charter.

This account was from the Latin, as is a second version by Matthew of Westminster which is in almost the same words, but a variation occurs in a third account given by Ranulphus Higden, a monk of St. Werburga's at Chester, who says of Leofric, "at the earnest request of his wife he made his town of Coventry free from all toll save that on horses. To secure which his Countess Godiva rode on horseback through the middle of the town naked on a certain morning early, but hidden by her hair." There are several other accounts, using their various spellings of Godiva

—Godgiva and Godiua—and of Coventry—Conventreia, Coventryam, Couentria.

A slight alteration in the story was given by Richard Grafton, MP for Coventry in 1562–3, who has Leofric saying he would grant her request if she would "ride naked thorow the Towne" (not mentioning that the town must be full of people) and says that Godiva

> called, in secret manner by such as she put speciall trust in, all those that were magistrates and rulers of the sayde citie of Couentrie and uttered unto them what goodwill she bare unto the sayde citie and how she had moved the earl her husband to make the same free . . . she required of them that for the reverence of womanhood, that at that day and tyme that she should ryde (which was made certaine unto them) that streight commandment should be given throughout all the citie that evrie person should shut in their houses and windows and none soe hardy to looke out into the streets, nor remaine in the streets, upon a great paine. Soe that when the tyme came of her outryding none saw her . . .

This version adds that "shortly after her returne when she had arrayed herselfe in most comely and seemly manner, then she showed herselfe openly to the people of the Citie of Couentrie, to the great joy and marvellous rejoysing of all the citizens and inhabitants of the same who by her had received so great a benefit".

Mr. Burbidge notes that no date has been given anywhere for the ride, and that several reputable chroniclers of the eleventh and twelfth centuries write of Leofric and Godiva with respect, and one speaks of Godiva's great beauty, but they make no mention of the ride. This could mean that it did not, in fact, happen; but on the other hand the ride would have been a local matter, the story might have been regarded as unsuitable for monastic contemplation, and monkish writers usually preferred to record anecdotes calculated to enhance the reputation of their own particular foundation. However, Mr. Burbidge regards it as important that Godiva's ride was not recorded in the chronicles of monasteries where she was very well known. An Evesham chronicle, for instance refers to the gifts of Leoffricus et Godgiva, their creation of a church, Holy Trinity, at Evesham, and "Godiva's burial there"—but says nothing about the ride. He feels that the silence of these chronicles makes it certain that the story of Godiva's ride is apochryphal, but that the story nevertheless contains an original germ of truth, found in folklore, and connected with some type of fertility custom.

Coventry was an agricultural community, and the fertility of crops and herds was of great importance or the people starved. There had been tree worship by the Saxons, and May Day dancing round the maypole is a survival of worship of the spring goddess of fertility (the May Queen) and the sacred tree (maypole). Our Saxon forefathers, says Mr. Burbidge, carried in procession through the community the sacred tree or a bough, accompanied by a maiden decked in flowers and leaves. Sometimes there was a man, or a male animal. The procession represented the spirit of fertility. Coventry, embedded in the Forest of Arden, was the sort of place where such old practices might linger "and I have little doubt that the supposed transit of Godiva is yet another instance of them. Those who have examined the remains of the Godiva window in Holy Trinity Church will remember the little figure of the lady riding a horse and carrying a white flowery branch". He adds: "Whether Cofa was the name of the original Godiva-goddess we can only speculate. Probably the strong devotion of the natives to the local divinity survived all the teaching of the monks with the result that she was eventually appropriated to the benefit of the monastery and claimed as none other than Godiva, their pious patron."

Peeping Tom appears first in writing in the seventeenth century, when it was stated that Godiva's horse neighed, "whereat one desirous to see the Strange Case lett downe a window, and looked out, for which fact, or for that the horse did neigh, as the cause thereof, though all the Towne were franchised, yet horses were not toll free to this day". The earliest historian to mention Tom was Paul de Rapin, in the seventeenth century. In his history of England he says: there was one who could not forbear giving a look, but it cost him his life". Tom was evidently invented just prior to the Restoration, says Mr. Burbidge, and in fact the effigy of Tom for many years was dressed in a style of the reign of Charles II. By the eighteenth century Tom was well established, and is mentioned by various authors. Daniel Defoe speaks of "the poor fellow that peep'd out of the window to see her . . ." and other references made to Tom are of "a certain taylour", and "one prying slave".

Mr. Burbidge also quotes from a local history of Lady Godiva by a Mr. Tomkinson, in 1876, in which he says that after the

Roman Catholic religion was prohibited, the pageants for which the city was famous were continued with alterations and as a mockery, and that "a naked woman was introduced to ridicule the Sacred Host, immediately after her came a Merry Andrew to divert the populace with profane jests; he was drawn in a kind of house on wheels and from frequently looking out of the window acquired the name of Peeping Tom; but one of these adventurers dying on leaving the house, no one afterwards could be found with sufficient hardihood to follow his example— hence Peeping Tom has ceased to be part of the procession."

In Joan C. Lancaster's book *Godiva of Coventry*, H. R. Ellis Davidson contributes a chapter on the folk tradition of the story, and says that the part of the tale that seems unlikely in an eleventh-century context is the nature of Leofric's demand that his wife should ride naked through the market place in the presence of the people. This suggests the possibility of a verbal misunder-standing. "If for instance Godiva was said in an early account to have stripped herself of her possessions in order to give to the church, or to help the people, this metaphorical statement may have been taken literally by the twelfth-century historians. Alternatively the suggestion has been made that it was the horse, and not the lady, which was 'naked', because Godiva rode it on one occasion denuded of all the usual trappings and marks of her rank, as an act of penance and humility which was long re-membered." Discussing the suggestion that has been made that the tradition of a woman riding naked through the town was based on the memory of pagan rites, practised to promote fertility, in which nakedness played an essential part, this writer says there are elements in the traditions about Godiva that suggest she became identified in the popular mind with supernatural heroines of folktales, but this is far from claiming that the story was based on an active pagan cult of the eleventh century. He suggests that the story was linked with Godiva and first recorded about 150 years after her death, because there was a genuine local tradition about her known to the Coventry people in the twelfth century, based on memory of her piety and her share in atoning for her husband's sins in taking land from monastic foundations of Worcester and Evesham, and on removal of a tax while she was ruling over them. The story about this was, he suggests, later elaborated. The story is "basically founded on fact, although the facts were not precisely related by Roger of Wendover and other early chroniclers".

The truth of the matter will never be known, but in a remarkable way the legend has lived on through the centuries. The one definite conclusion the experts seem to have drawn is that Peeping Tom can be eliminated. He 'got into the act' too late.

Before the war there were three Toms on view, and one of them had a vantage point in Bishop Street until a few years ago, on shop property that has since been demolished to be replaced by a new store. The senior Tom is the effigy in the glass case in the Hotel Leofric, safely preserved. He was on public display for about 250 years, first in the house of Alderman Owen in Greyfriars Lane, then in a house adjoining the pre-blitz King's Head Hotel, Smithford Street, and when Hertford Street was made in 1812 he was promoted to a turret of the hotel and for more than one-hundred years looked down on Broadgate traffic. He was removed from the turret a few years before the Second World War and kept in a glass case in the hotel. When the hotel was bombed and destroyed by fire he was rescued by a Coventry headmaster then in the Auxiliary Fire Service, and was given an 'auxiliary fireman's lift' from the building. He was dumped outside a bank nearby and afterwards spent the duration in the bank vaults and later at the offices of Band Hatton and Co., solicitors. He is privately owned and is loaned to the Hotel Leofric.

This Tom was sent to a London museum for treatment before he took up residence at the hotel, for over the years he had received many added coats of paint. He is now a full-size figure in plain oak, wearing helmet and armour, but not as he was over three centuries ago when he had a plume on his helmet, and complete arms. Someone cut away the plume so that he could be given other headgear for processions. He would wear a wig, cravat or neckcloth, and a cocked hat. He probably lost his forearms so that he could lean from a window. The figure is thought to have been taken from one of Coventry's religious houses, and that he was perhaps St. George, the patron saint of the city. When he had arms he may have carried a sword and shield. It is also thought he may have been St. Michael.

A Tom who is on view looks down from a niche in Hertford Street precinct upon the shoppers below. He languished for years in a museum store, minus his head which came off when he was being moved about, but now he looks as good as new. When the figure leaned from a window of the Railway Hotel at Bull

Yard before the war it was held in position with heavy iron clamps. This Tom was so well known that few people used the public house's proper name, referring to it as the 'Peeping Tom'. It closed in 1938 and the premises were used as a retail shop, Tom lingering on upstairs until he had to be removed when the building was demolished.

A Peeping Tom bust is kept in the shoe shop of Charles Ager, in Corporation Street. It is a plaster cast with a heavy core, and once looked out from David Cooke's tobacconist's shop in Smithford Street. After the shop was demolished in the twenties the bust was given to Mr. C. J. Hodson and he put it in the vestibule of his shop, Charles Ager, in Smithford Street. It is still with the firm in their present shop. A Peeping Tom in beeswax has been in the possession of one Coventry family for over one-hundred years, and shares their dining-room. It was not always so privileged, for when the children were small they did not like the look of him and he was banished for a few years to a cupboard. In 1936 the family lent this Tom to the city's Godiva Pageant. A fifth Tom is the bust from Bishop Street, which was placed on top of a wall at shop premises. Tom had this spot because he was originally stationed there when he was made in 1934, to go into the gable window of what was then a confectionery shop. His owner finally put Tom in his garden! This Tom is made of stone and is the work of the Ormerod Brothers, who were local sculptors. He was given tousled hair and beard and rough woollen gown such as common people would wear in Saxon times. Tom can also be found in a carving under the clock tower at the Council House, and in Stevengraphs at the Herbert Museum.

Lady Godiva, however, is seen by the public every day, as befits a heroine. The Lady Godiva statue in the city centre was a gift to Coventry by the late Mr. W. H. Bassett-Green, a native of Coventry and business man in the area, who among other gifts presented to the nation a Spitfire aircraft after the bombing of Coventry, and named it 'Godiva'. Landseer's painting "Godiva's Prayer", was a gift to Coventry by Mr. Bassett-Green. It was exhibited at the Royal Academy in 1866. The statue was executed by Sir William Reid Dick, whose works include the King George V Memorial in London, the Roosevelt Memorial, the Lion on the Menin Gate, and the statue of Livingstone at Victoria Falls. Work on the Lady Godiva statue started before the war, and continued during most of the bombing.

The model for the horse was lent by the mounted police. The statue, in bronze, weighs 2 tons, and the stone plinth weighs 30 tons. It was unveiled by Mrs. Lewis W. Douglas, wife of the American Ambassador, in October 1949.

The legend of Lady Godiva, true or false, has generally been held in great respect by older Coventrians. Mr. Bassett-Green, at a luncheon after the unveiling ceremony, was quite specific that she rode. He said: "True, we have a statue of Lady Godiva here [in St. Mary's Hall] but how many Coventrians ever see it? I venture to assert that many are unaware of its existence. When offering this statue to the city my only stipulation was that it be erected in the public eye and *preferably in a street through which she rode* ..." Lady Godiva also figures in the speech made on that occasion by Mrs. Douglas, who said: "It is difficult for me as an American to speak of Coventry without becoming emotional. You were a symbol to the world of courage, loyalty and faith. You set a pattern to the rest of the world and the world is grateful to you for that example. It is important in these hurried days to pause for a minute, as we did this morning, and remember the past.

"If we trace the history of Coventry from the early days when the city was the home of the romantic Lady Godiva, through its industrial development when Coventry became a great centre of commerce, and then come to the recent grim ordeal which you have borne, it is evident that through the ages Coventry has shown the courage and determination that has always been the core of England's strength. *It was Lady Godiva's refusal to accept defeat* and her faith in her fellow citizens that won her fame. It was your refusal to accept defeat and your determination to get on with the job you were doing that brought you the admiration and respect of the world ..." And so on. Even if it is only a legend, Godiva's ride has certainly been a marvellous 'peg' line for any visitor burdened with the duty of making an after-dinner speech!

The statue in Broadgate, easy of access and much photographed, has not escaped the attentions of practical jokers. There was the sailor's hat perched rakishly on her head not long after a football match between two naval shore teams—and it happened also to be St. David's Day. And there was an intrepid university undergraduate from Cambridge, who during a car rally and treasure hunt had to be photographed sitting on a horse. Nobody said the

horse had to be a real one, so he climbed the statue and sat behind
Lady Godiva! New Year revellers put a white bra on Godiva, and
she was seen on another occasion holding a broom in her hand.

The puppet clock Lady Godiva has had an even more eventful
career in Broadgate, for sightseers were never sure if Lady
Godive would ride, and Tom would peep down on her, when
the mechanism behaved temperamentally, and Lady Godiva
could not be sure if she would get indoors safely or would have to
stay out on her balcony. The idea for the clock was suggested by
Donald Gibson, city architect, as an additional attraction in the
new city centre. The figures were carved in white pine by the
sculptor Trevor Tennant. On their first appearance they caused
a storm. Coventry people of the older school claimed that they
were an insult to the legend, and "out of keeping" with the
dignity of Godiva, but the criticism soon died down and the
puppet clock is a big attraction to visitors and to children when-
ever they are taken to town. The horse and rider, 4 feet long and
3 feet high, weigh 110 pounds, and Tom is 3 feet 6 inches from
head to waist and weighs 80 pounds.

As a concession to guests of the Hotel Leofric, because the
chimes of the clock woke them up at night, they are now silenced
until morning. The clock has also had its effect on traffic. Imagine
a long-distance coach slowly circling Broadgate garden island
four times, so that its passengers could see Lady Godiva make her
journey! They were lucky it was not one of those days when the
doors opened and closed about a dozen times trying to entice
Godiva out, without any appearance by her. On the other hand
Godiva has been known to ride round the balcony continuously
for twenty minutes—trying to make up perhaps for lost time. Ex-
Lord Mayor Tom Meffen stood once with a party of visitors
waiting for the hourly ride and when the clock struck and the
doors opened, out flew two pigeons! An indignant letter writer to
the *Evening Telegraph* took the occasion of one of these mishaps
to urge, as recently as 1960, that the "so called amusing showpiece" should be removed and scrapped. "It is not only crude and
cheap in appearance but also most distasteful. This would leave
the beautiful bronze statue of Lady Godiva in the centre of
Broadgate as a perpetual reminder to the present citizens of
Coventry of the kindly and courageous deed of a very gracious
and great benefactress." His hope was nearly fulfilled a year later
when, after becoming jammed in the sliding door, Godiva and

horse fell over the parapet to the road below. Some of the watching crowd picked up the pieces. Godiva lost an arm and her wire eyelashes were flattened, but her steed lost all four legs and an ear. There were doubts about whether they could be repaired, and again came the newspaper letters, such as this one from a well known local resident: "Must Godiva ride again! Burn the rubbish and forget it! Eight years of ridicule forced upon us is more than enough to bear. This comic 'strip' cartoon is offensive to most Coventrians. Without it the dignity of Broadgate may be partially restored." But repairs were made and for the past few years the puppet figures have performed on the hour with scarcely any failure, much photographed by visitors, and apparently accepted by the local critics, if one can assume this from their silence.

The tradition of the goodness of Lady Godiva, irrespective of the ride she may or may not have made, lives on very strongly in Coventry. In 1967, for example, there was a cathedral service marking the nine-hundredth anniversary of her death. Members of the cathedral's drama group represented Leofric and Godiva, and the city archivist, flanked by four candle bearers, carried to the chancel steps a thirteenth-century statute book from the Bodleian Library, Oxford, which records the dates of the deaths of Leofric on 28th September 1057, and of Godiva on 10th September 1067 —a year after the Norman Conquest. These entries were read out in Latin and English. After the service, which, it was said, "had the aim of recapturing the quality of compassion that made her famous", there were processions to Priory Row for the unveiling by the Lord Mayor of a plaque commemorating Godiva's death and burial. With Leofric she is said to have been buried in the porch of the priory church and not at Evesham (p 185).

Leofric and Godiva had one son, Aelfgar, who became Earl of Mercia after Leofric's death, but there is a less known legend that their second son was no other than Hereward the Wake, who continued the struggle against the Normans. Among those who set out to join him in the Isle of Ely were two grandsons of Leofric and Godiva, Edwin and Morcar. Miss Lancaster, dealing with the legend in her book, says that Edwin did not reach Ely, being treacherously slain by his followers, but Morcar did. She points out that whereas a chronicler describes Edwin and Morcar as persons of rank—they were earls—Hereward was described as a magnificent warrior, with the inference that he was not noble.

Hereward was described as son of Leofric of Bourne, and Miss Lancaster feels that the source of the error about Hereward was confusion between Leofric, Earl of Mercia, and the Leofric of Bourne. She mentions however as coincidences that Morcar according to the Doomsday Book held land at Bourne in Lincolnshire, that a Hereward held land in Warwickshire—at Weddington, Marston Jabbett and Barnacle—and in Worcestershire, and that the wife of Leofric of Bourne, whose name was Aedina or Aediva, had a very similar name to Godiva. "Was Hereward a son of Leofric and Godiva? Probably not, and in any case such a relationship, though not historically impossible, could not be proved," she concludes.

Leofric and Godiva made their names live on in Coventry and also gave inspiration to writers of plays, operas and stories. There was an opera based on the legend by Pietro Mascagni and performed in Milan in 1910, and a comic opera called *Peeping Tom of Coventry* was produced at the Haymarket as long ago as 1784. There was pantomime at Sanger's National Amphitheatre in 1875-6, and a burlesque at the Strand Theatre, London, in 1851. *The Lady of Mercia* was performed by the Coventry Players at the Empire Theatre, Coventry, in 1928. Hans Frank's play *Godiva* was performed at Munich, Germany, in 1919. Several plays have been written since the Second World War, including Clemence Dane's *Scandal at Coventry*, performed on BBC radio in 1958; and on French radio Claude Des Presles's prizewinning play *La Dame de Coventry*. Among other written works, there was the marathon romance *The Lady Godiva, or Peeping Tom of Coventry*, of 1849, which was published in thirty-one instalments in *Lloyd's Weekly London Newspaper*.

The custom of holding Lady Godiva processions started in 1678, and on that occasion, to proclaim the Great Fair, a youth impersonated her, riding ahead of the mayor. At one time they were looked on with disfavour, and efforts were made to stop them. The bishop, in 1848, wrote to the mayor denouncing "the parading through the streets of a woman dressed in tight fitting clothes so as to appear naked and followed by a mob of the lowest rabble in Coventry"! Apparently for a long time the ladies who impersonated Lady Godiva did not have their names made public, and it has only been in recent times that the Godiva pageant has been dignified, and that the rider on the white horse has been a celebrity and a civic guest.

In the anxiety to make it respectable, some of the ladies used to overdo it! In one procession only the rider's arms and neck were visible, and in 1919 Miss Gladys Mann wore the *full-dress robes of a Saxon countess*. Even her horse wore trousers! She was the first and only Coventry girl to act the role, and it may have been felt that it was better for her to be dressed. The view about not choosing a Coventry girl had been that it would be onerous for her, since she would have to live in the city afterwards, and would probably be 'pointed out'. Godiva processions were held about every three to seven years, and sometimes were arranged for special occasions. The 1902 procession, when Miss Vera Guedes, a London Hippodrome equestrienne, was Lady Godiva, was the year of the coronation of Edward VII; and when Miss Viola Hamilton, actress, rode in the 1911 procession, it was King George V's coronation. The last pre-war Godiva procession was that in 1936, when the crowd was so huge. Miss Frances Burchell, of Birmingham, took the part, riding Robin, a white horse loaned by Birmingham City Police.

In modern times a very high standard has been maintained at the few Lady Godiva processions that have been held. In keeping with the theme that Lady Godiva was an unselfish person who helped the citizens, the 1936 procession included representatives of such brave and selfless women as Nurse Cavell, Florence Nightingale, Grace Darling, and Elizabeth Fry. These special pageants have been serious affairs. Lady Godiva would pass along the route to an admiring murmur, and applause for someone sustaining a difficult role. Coventry people are pleased if the ride is made with dignity, poise, and sympathy. The atmosphere could not possibly exist in the few places where Lady Godiva has had imitators!

The 1951 Festival of Britain was marked by Coventry's first post-war Godiva Pageant, organized for the corporation by Mr. Leonard Turner. It was an occasion of splendid pageantry, with sixty tableaux in two sections, historical and industrial. Mr. Turner wanted authenticity and he obtained 1,500 period costumes from London costumiers, for tableaux representing occasions such as the visit to Coventry, in 1500, of Henry VII. There were kings and queens, beefeaters and pikemen, bowmen and pages, in a procession 5 miles long. A London actress, Miss Ann Wrigg, aged 28, portrayed Lady Godiva with dignity and charm despite some moments of anxiety because her horse, a white hunter named Willoughby Warrior, normally quiet, was very restless and hard to control. Later the theory was put forward that the reason for this was the proximity of elephants. Only one elephant, for the coat-of-arms elephant and castle representation, should have been in the big parade, but there had to be two because Sauce and Salt, who came from a local circus, were inseparable. They always performed together so they had to walk together! Huge crowds watched the procession, which was described in the Press as "half gay, half solemn". The latter mood was no doubt set by the very impressiveness of the historical tableaux; there was also a 'Spirit of Coventry, 1940' tableau, and a giant phoenix symbol of Coventry rising from the ashes.

Cathedral Festival Year, 1962, was another special occasion and featured only the second Godiva Pageant that Coventry has had since the war. Historical episodes were re-enacted on each of four days at the park, including Lady Godiva's ride. Performances were in mime with an enormous cast, and episodes were described in a commentary. Finally, there was the procession through the streets, watched by great crowds lining the route. But Lady Godiva of Coventry, impersonated by Mrs. Joyce Parker, of Leamington, was seen this time by millions. For the first time, the legend, which as we have seen, may or may not be true, reached the television screens from the script penned by a monk nearly eight-hundred years earlier.

XIII

TEN YEARS ON

COVENTRY has changed very little in the ten years that have passed since the first edition of this book was published. By 1972, of course, much of the reconstruction had been completed, so a slowing of tempo was to be expected. But the reform of local government in 1974 appears to have robbed Coventry City Council of drive, as well as of some of its responsibilities, and combined with this has been the tightening of government control over public spending. Before 1974 the old city council would have been protesting and sending deputations to Whitehall and generally pressurizing for special treatment to keep the ball rolling. It doesn't happen now.

There are still plenty of reminders of the war. Among them, at the Hill Street corner of Corporation Street, at the corner of Queen Victoria Road, and in High Street itself just a few yards from the Council House, wartime 'temporary' shops are in use. It seems odd that High Street has been given a semi-precinct improvement treatment by re-surfacing the road with coloured tiles, removing the kerbing, and banning general traffic from it, yet the wartime 'prefab' shops have been allowed to remain. Another change in High Street is the demolition of the old Craven Arms public house, and Barclay's Bank have built new premises on the site. Various schemes have been put forward for Hill Street corner, these including an hotel and a cinema. The most recent is a proposal for a church. Commercial development —stores and offices—has been proposed by developers for the Queen Victoria Road and Greyfriars Road sites, the former entailing demolition of the vacant Drill Hall, but local protests are being made by people who want to retain the Drill Hall for community uses.

Still awaited are the proposed new Law Courts, to be built on land used for car parking in Little Park Street, but there may soon be a start, we are told. For years magistrates' courts have been in cramped accommodation, and there have been overflow courts in Drapers Hall, while more recently even the old Wheatley Street School has been pressed into service. Crime has increased, court lists have lengthened, and solicitors, defendants, witnesses, and police still have to scramble about in small crowded corridors to sort out, interview, and prepare for hearings. The hold-up in the Law Courts has put back the completion of the city's new library. The first block, the Reference Library, was built in Bayley Lane several years ago, and the completion was to have been reached by acquiring the Drapers Hall. It was acquired, but has never been out of use because it has been needed for the overflow courts. And as a result the lending library, in what remains of the nineteenth-century Gulson Library which was damaged in the war, has remained in use into the eighties. By an internal reorganization it is hoped to rehouse the lending library in Bayley Lane, but it can only be a temporary expedient at the expense of other sections. On the credit side, the council have, with Chamber of Commerce assistance, opened the Museum of British Road Transport in Cook Street.

Another plus is the biggest council project completed in the centre in the past decade, the sports hall in Fairfax Street, which joins up with the baths to form an indoor sports complex. It was planned and started before 1974, and is now a welcome and much used leisure facility. On the other side of Fairfax Street, the new Pool Meadow bus station never did materialize, and is forgotten. The bus lanes and shelters have been improved and the bus crews have a new headquarters building, but otherwise, no change. However, Coventry people coming back on a visit do find Broadgate different. The council have banned general traffic, demolished temporary shops, and made the garden island accessible to the public. Its beauty has been marred, though, with paved walks cutting through it, but these are a convenient step towards the planned link-up with the cathedral ruins, and possibly a piazza layout, with suitable shops, between Broadgate and County Hall. The whole concept is for a pedestrian route from St. John's Church, through the precinct, over Broadgate, through archways in County Hall, to the ruins.

An addition to tourist attractions, between Holy Trinity Church and the ruins, is the unusual ornamental Coventry Cross, completed in 1976—a £40,000 gift of the Coventry Boy

Foundation. It is the third cross. The first was set up about 1422. It was replaced in 1541 by another given by a Lord Mayor of London, Sir William Holles, who was born in Coventry. This fell into disrepair and was demolished in 1771. The Coventry Boy Foundation, 200 years later, sentimentally decided to build another, exactly like that given in 1541, which stood in Cross Cheaping. It is 57 ft high, is made of pink Hollington stone, and has on it forty-two figures of kings and saints, monks, naked boys and beasts, each from 2½ ft to 4½ ft in height. It entailed two years of research by architect Rolf Hellberg, who was enthusiastic about the unusual project and gave his professional services free of charge, and for the Chelsea sculptor Phillip Bentham who made the figures it was also a two-year job, and a most unusual commission. The cross is a replica medieval structure with four steps at base, flying buttresses and pinnacles, and on top, a lantern light surmounted by a gold crown and flag. It is on the site of the Festival cafe, which will eventually close when the area is redeveloped in connection with the layout of Broadgate and removal of the Gulson Library.

Local radio arrived in the city in 1980 when Mercia Sound, who have their station in Hertford Place, came on the air, to broadcast nineteen hours a day, six days a week, and slightly less on Sundays. When a commercial station was first mooted four groups hoped to win the franchise—Three Spires Radio, Radio Coventry and Radio Warwickshire Ltd., Midland Community Radio Ltd., and Coventry Broadcasting Ltd. It was given to Midland Community Radio whose chairman is John Butterworth, vice-chancellor of the University of Warwick. Their aim: "to create a radio station which will be truly representative of the people who live in the community". Community-minded, Mercia Sound includes in its output two programmes a week in Hindustani for the Asian community. And in 1981 there was more broadcasting news for Coventry, when the BBC announced that they would have a radio station in the city, to cover Coventry and Warwickshire, within three years. It would be, they said, complementary to Mercia Sound. Independents were basically music-based; BBC would be language-based, with news and information.

Elsewhere in the book I have tried to show that Coventry is community-minded, and I have mentioned the tremendous response when Walsgrave Hospital wanted a scanner. We've seen another example since, after an Asian doctor was fatally stabbed in the street by a white youth. Racialism is not a trait in Coventry, and people made this apparent when they responded to a local newspaper appeal for donations to aid the Cyrenians Shelter, at which Dr. Amal Dharry had been a voluntary worker. The newspaper suggested a target of £1,000, but within a short time £7,000 had been donated, with more to come. It was a way in which the man-in-the-street could show that Coventry did not support racialism. There have been some outbreaks of violence by groups of young people; these were thought to be racialist, but a senior police officer has said that they usually involved mixed groups of blacks and whites together, who were frustrated because of unemployment. Migration, incidentally, may well have slowed down or stopped, judging by the trend in population. (In 1980 there were approximately 30,000 immigrants, predominantly Sikhs, in Coventry. In the Coventry Church of England Diocese some schools had up to 90 per cent Asian and West Indian children at primary level. In one sixth form of 120, only two students were white.)

Coventry grew at a fantastic rate after the Second World War. Between 1951 and 1961, there was an increase of 50,000, equal to the size of a small town. In the next ten years, 1961–71, there was another gain, this time of a more modest 18,000. But according to the provisional figures from the 1981 Census, between 1971 and 1981 the population *fell* by as much as 20,000. The provisional 1981 Census total, which will be adjusted when final figures are announced, is 314,124. Migration into the city would naturally fall off if an unemployment problem arose— which it has—and Coventry men made redundant at an early age are likely to go elsewhere for work, some of them emigrating. Another factor is that housing being more readily available at a lower price in smaller neighbouring towns, young Coventry families have been moving outside the boundary. Quite apart from these pressurized moves, there has been a trend outwards from big cities into the countryside for preference, as a way of life, and as Coventry's population has gone down, so Warwick-shire county figures have gone up, underlining this trend. It appears that Coventry reached its peak in mid-1977, when the Registrar General's estimated total was 340,500. Since that year, there has been an annual decline.

To a small extent, a part of the drift of population may have been triggered off by redundancy pay, which in some cases for shop-floor workers with lengthy service has been in the five-figure bracket. To be suddenly flush with money which they could never have saved up for themselves has given couples a new outlook. To sell the house, and move to the seaside, is an appealing prospect for the late middle-aged who have little hope of future employment. For younger people, to sell the house and with the redundancy money in hand invest in a retail shop to safeguard the future, in whatever part of the UK it happens to be, is a reasonable alternative to unemployment. Those who stay put in Coventry, too, have a new scope with their pay-off money. The mortgage, that millstone round the neck, can be paid off. The old car, costing more for repairs, can be sold and replaced by a new one. The eighties trade recession is so different from the depression of the thirties! In those days the 'sack' usually meant that the family's sole breadwinner was on the dole. Redundancy money was unheard of. There was real hardship, as families were generally larger than they are now. But today when many husbands and wives work, the redundancy of one of the partners is often cushioned by the fact that the other partner is earning a wage packet.

So although Coventry is passing through a recession, it is not very apparent. Traffic queues of home-going workers are not so long as they were; pavements empty more quickly of those on foot; but the city centre looks more lively than before, when family shopping jaunts were limited to weekends. The precincts are more like the 'top of the town' of pre-war days, for meeting up with friends. It would be a good idea if, to cheer it up some more, the city council encouraged entertainment of the kind we already see in a limited way—more bands and dancers, more exhibitions (and more seats!). For young people, at a loose end without a job, the council might give a lead, despite lack of finance. Why not open the parks' pitches for sport, cheaply or without charge; present cups for football, cricket, netball, or tennis; or allow free or cheap swimming, with coaching and some recognition for proficiency. The City of Coventry Golf Course at Brandon Lane, a sports development of which the council can be proud, might have special cheap rate days, and some coaching, to interest unemployed people. The Butts Stadium, too, might offer its facilities to them.

Ideas like these would have been sparked off by the city council in former days when it felt responsible for the welfare of the community and had the freedom of movement to experiment. But the post-1974 councils have lived under the shadow of Big Brother, the West Midlands County Council, which took over much of the local powers and, so it seems to an observer, took away at the same time local initiative and civic pride. Somebody else is running things, although our reputation was good and we were known as go-ahead. We have lost our independence and our individuality. Locally-run departments had chiefs who were civic personalities, and they were accountable to the local authority and the ratepayers. Today, hardly any man-in-the-street could name the head of Coventry's police, whereas when we had our own force, with a Chief Constable, his name was widely known and he presented annual reports, made statements, was a guest of honour at dinners, and gave out the Speech Day prizes. Coventry is now a division of the West Midlands police, and is headed by someone of superintendent rank, who is not infrequently changed. Nor could the average man name the chief of the fire brigade, for similar reasons.

A glance at the map shows how Coventry became a strange bedfellow of distant places like Wolverhampton and Walsall in the West Midlands area. Someone took a pencil and drew a sausage shape from Birmingham deep into the heart of Warwickshire, where Coventry sits. It was removed administratively from its natural place, leaving Warwickshire with a horseshoe of territory lying round the city. Perhaps one day we'll regain our civic pride and our progressive outlook, which I miss. Perhaps we will find ourselves after all, Warwickshire folk, and the county and city will be united. I hope so. Then, if we can attract new industry to make use of our wealth of skilled workers, we can again show a swinging image.

INDEX

A

Adcocks, Stan, 100
Air raids, 24, 25, 31-4
Airports, 19
Allen, Les, 102
Allesley, 77, 84, 145, 170
Alvis, 131, 133
Angling, 102
Ansty Aerodrome, 26
Apollo Theatre, 170
Apprentices, 71
Argosy aircraft, 134
Armstrong Siddeley, 133
Armstrong Whitworth, 133, 134
Arnhem, 107, 108
Arnold, Miss Alice, 117
Ashby family, 100, 154
Award of Merit, 154

B

Bablake, 81, 82, 146
Bailey, Bryan, 47
Barclay's Bank, 196
Bardsley, Dr Cuthbert, 155
Bardsley House, 74
Barratt, Charles, 119, 149
Bassett-Green, W. H., 189, 190
Bayley Lane, 80, 86, 93
Bayliss, Len, 96
BBC Radio, 198
Beaverbrook, Lord, 30
Bede Road, 143
Beesley, William VC, 152
Belgrade, 110
Belgrade Square, 47, 48
Belgrade Theatre, 46, 47, 90, 112
Bell Green, 53
Berlin, 63
Berry, Dennis, 110
Bevin, Ernest, 30
Beyer, Ralph, 69
Binley Road, 84, 99
Birmingham Road, 84

Bishops of Coventry, 31, 62, 63, 72
Bishop Street, 173, 174
Black, John, 148
Black Prince, 84
Blue Coat School, 78
BMC-BL, 129, 131, 133, 147
Bogey, origin of, 101
Bologna, 111
Bond's Hospital, 81, 82
Boots the Chemist, 42
Bourton, Clarrie, 96
Brandt, Willi, 63
Brandon Bees, 21
Brazil, Angela, 143
Briggs, George, 29, 106
British Celanese, 174
British Home Stores, 42, 74
Broadgate, 19, 21, 37-40, 50, 77, 86,
   197
Brooke, H. L., 35
Brown, Margaret, 35
Browne, Prof. Joan, 155
Bull's Head, 84
Bull Yard, 43
Burton, Elaine, 120
Burton, Joyce, 35
Bus crews, 88
Bus fare concessions, 90, 117
Butts Stadium, 98, 99, 102
Butcher Row, 113, 170
Butterworth, J. B., 59, 198

C

C & A Store, 42
Caen, 107
Callow, William, 112
Camera Principis, 84
Campbell, A. F., 36
Canal, 27, 159
Canine Fund, 92
Canley Road, 26
Cannon Hill Road, 26
Cappers' Guild, 76

Car ownership, 45
Carbodies Ltd, 135
Carnegie, Andrew, 154
Carnival processions, 162, 163, 193–5
Cartwright, Tom, 95
Carver, Jesse, 96
Cash, J and J Ltd, 48, 135
Cathedral, 21, 27, 30, 32, 50, 51,
  62–76, 77, 105, 110
Cathedral Square, 50
Census, 199
Charterhouse, 85, 107
Chauntries, 80
Cheylesmore Manor, 84
Children's homes, 59
Chinn, W. L., 119, 155
Christmas Lights, 46
Christ Church, 34, 51, 85
Chrysler, 130
Churchill, Winston, 36
Churches, 34, 81, 178
Cinemas, 165, 166, 167
City Arcade, 26, 43
City Council, 33, 65, 115–18
City Wall, 177–9
Civil Defence, 25, 117–18
Civil War, 177–8
Clarke Cluley & Co., 125
Clarke, Geoffrey, 70
Cleobury Mortimer, 56
Clifford Bridge Road, 60
Clitheroe, Canon G. W., 34
Coat-of-Arms, 84
College of Art, 45, 57
College of Education, 57
Collier, G., 35
Comprehensive Schools, 54–6
Cook Street Gate, 80
Coombe, Abbey, 22, 93
Co-op, 74
Conservation Areas, 77
Cope Street, 57
Cordery, S. J., 106
Cork, 111
Corn, Raymond, 36
Corporation Street, 81, 172
Council House, 28, 30, 74, 113, 114
County Hall, 80, 119
Courtaulds Ltd, 136, 150, 174
Coventrians RFC, 99
Coventry and N.W. Club, 99
Coventry blue, 181
Coventry Boy Foundation, 92
Coventry Boy Statue, 83, 93
Coventry Broadcasting, 198

Coventry By-Pass, 160
Coventry City FC, 21, 26, 95, 96
Coventry Climax, 91
Coventry (Connecticut), 110
Coventry Corporation, 78, 119, 122,
  155
Coventry Cross, 93, 197
Coventry Cycling Club, 103
Coventry Eagle, 126
Coventry FC, 95, 97
Coventry Folk Workshop, 107
Coventry Gauge & Tool, 138
Coventry General Charities, 92
Coventry Golf Club, 100–101
Coventry Movement Co., 127
Coventry—origin of, 176
Coventry (Rhode Island), 110
Cov. Sewing Machine Co., 123
Coventry Standard, 44
Coventry Theatre, the, 73, 80, 168–70
Cox, H. E., 113
Cox Street, 58, 137
Cresswell, H. B. W., 117, 151
Cross of Nails, 63, 105
Crossman, R. H. S., 120

D
Daimler (car), 58, 128, 129, 132
Dark, Frankland, 71
Davenport, John, 153
Dewis, T. H., 112
De Vere Hotel, 50, 51
Dick, Alick, 147
Dissolution, 177
Douglas, Mrs. Lewis W., 190
Drapers Hall, 49
Dresden, 43, 63, 110
Drill Hall, 196
Drinkwater, Alfred, 154
Duckham, David, 97
Duel (at Gosford Green), 179–80
Dugdale, Sir William, 155, 156
Dunaujvaros, 111
Dunlop, 127, 174

E
Earlsdon RFC, 99
Easter procession, 162
Eccles, David, 65, 66
Edelman, Maurice, 120
Eliot, George, 142, 143
Empire Day, 161
Epstein, Jacob, 67, 74, 93
European Prize, 112
Evening Telegraph, 144–6

F
Fairbrother, Jack, 96
Fairfax Street, 50, 78
Farren, Hugh, 154
Fearn, Albert, 35
Fennell, John, 108
Ferguson, Harry, 148
Flinn, O. M., 29
Foleshill, 20, 89, 142, 143
Foleshill Baths, 31, 50
Foleshill RDC, 120
Food Office, 43
Ford's Hospital, 26, 82
Ford, William, 82
Forseth, Einar, 69
Francis Barnett, 128
Freemen, 121, 170–2, 181
Frith, Billy, 96

G
Galatzi, 111
Galpine, Alice, 155
Gardner, Fred, 99
Garner, Jack, 36
GEC, 36, 126, 137
Gibberd, Frederick, 149, 150
Gibbet Hill Road, 58, 59
Gibson, Donald, 38, 42, 149, 154
Godiva Harriers, 21, 99, 103
Godiva, Lady, 21, 24, 48, 83, 176,
    183–94
Godiva Puppet Clock, 21
Golden Cross, the, 80, 173
Good Friday, 162
Gosford Green, 179
Gosford Street, 58, 134, 135
Graf Spee, 25
Grammar School, 86, 107, 149, 156
Granby, 111
Grapes Inn, 34
Graz, 109
Great Fair, 82, 117, 163, 164, 180
Greenwood, Arthur, 30
Gregg, H. N., 35
Gregory, Terence, 43
Greyfriars Green, 19, 77, 82
Griffiths, Gilbert, 35
Grindlay, A. R., 29, 154
Guilds, 181
Gulson, John, 49
Gulson Road, 85

H
Hales, John, 85, 86
Halliwell, W. E., 29

Hanson, John, 150
Harley, Harry, 138, 148
Harley, Stanley, 73, 138, 148
Harriman, George, 147
Hawker Siddeley, 134
Harris, Mary Dormer, 84
Hattrells, 41
Hearsall Golf Club, 100
Heatley, Basil, 100
Hellberg and Harris, 40
Hender, J. D., 119
Henley College, 57, 58
Herbert, Alfred, 33, 38, 48, 80, 137,
    138, 154
Herbert, Alfred, Ltd., 137
Herbert Art Gallery, 48
Herbert, Son and Sawday, 48
Hereward College, 57, 58
Hereward the Wake, 192–3
Hertford Street, 19, 39, 40, 43, 82, 145
Hill, Aubrey, 99
Hill, Jimmy, 95, 96
Hill, Mervyn, 102
Hill, S. C., 35
Hill Street, 81, 82
Hill Top, 74, 77, 78
Hillfields, 19, 26, 53, 89, 143
Hillman, 124, 130
Hillman House, 42
Hocking, Philip, 120, 121
Hodgkinson, G. E., 29, 115, 154
Holy Trinity, 34, 51, 64, 77, 107, 173
Horne, Sister, 35
Hospitals, 31, 34, 60
Hotchkiss, 134
Hotel Leofric, 40, 191
Houses, war damaged, 28
Housing, 52–4
Howard, Provost R. T., 27, 63, 64,
    71, 73, 106
Humber, 126, 130
Hutt, Arthur, VC, 151
Hutton, John, 68, 69
Hyde, Pearl, 35, 91, 117

I
Iliffe & Sturmey, 144, 145
Iliffe family, 48, 71, 144, 145, 154
Industrial growth, 18
Inner ring road, 51, 52
Ironmonger Row, 40

J
Jaguar Cars, 129, 131, 132
Jardine Crescent, 53, 90

Jephcott, Abe, 156
John, T. G., 133
Jones, Jack, 155
Jordan Well, 48, 58
Judd, Phil, 97

K
Kearton, Lord, 150
Kecskemet, 111
Kelly, C. J., 35
Kenilworth Castle, 23, 62
Kenilworth, Lord, 71, 133, 134, 147
Kenilworth Road, 22, 58, 77, 83
Kennedy House, 74
Kensington Road, 30
Keresley Church, 93
Kiel, 63, 69, 106–8
Kilby, Brian, 100
King's Head Hotel, 34, 41
Kingston, 111

L
Lady Herbert's Garden, 77, 80, 138, 169
Laing, John and Sons, 66
Lambury, Lord, 146
Lanchester, W. F., 58, 129, 131
Lanchester Cars, 129
Lanchester Polytechnic, 50, 51, 58, 131
Lane, Billy, 102
Larkin, Dr Philip, 155
Law Courts, 196
Lawson, H. J., 128, 129
Lea Francis Cars, 58, 126, 131
Lee, Lawrence, 70
Lee, Thomas, 35
Leigh Mills, 57, 127
Leofric, Earl, 176, 193
Levelling Stone, 37
Library, 49, 51
Lidice, 109, 112
Lifford family, 147
Ling, Arthur, 42
Linnett, Prof. J. W., 154
Little Park Street, 17, 173
Locarno, 43
Lockhurst Lane Bridge, 172
London Road Cemetery, 25, 32, 161
Lord Mayoralty, 116, 117
Lyons, William, 133, 155

M
Malcolm, W. H., 106
Mander Hadley, 143
Mann, Tom, 153

Market Hall and clock, 19, 172
Market, retail, 43, 44
Market Street, 19, 173
Market Way, 42
Marks and Spencer, 42, 74
Marshall, A. H., 119
Martyrs Memorial, 44, 83
Massed Grave, 32
Massey Ferguson, 90
Matthews, Dennis, 151
Matthews, Reg, 97
Meffen, Tom, 89, 90, 191
Mercia House, 42
Mercia Sound, 198
Meriden, 18, 102
Merry-go-round, 45
Middlemarch Road, 143
Midland Community Radio, 198
Midland Theatre Co., 47
Moffitt, Ralph, 100
Montgomery, Viscount, 22
Morris Works, 134, 135
Morrison, Herbert, 25, 29
Moseley, J. A., 29, 30
Moss, Brandon, 35
Mottram, Tony, 103
Much Park Street, 58, 131
Municipal Art School, 56
Museum of Transport, 197
Mystery Plays, 181–3

N
Nat'l Emergency Committee, 29
Netherlands gift, 37, 38
New Coventry, 111
New, Keith, 70
New Street, 58
New Union Street, 173
Northcliffe, Lord, 144
Nowell, Norman, 35
Nuffield, Lord, 154

O
Old people's homes, 59
Opera House, 26, 47, 167, 168
Ostrova, 109
Owen Owen (store), 26, 40

P
Palace Yard, 34
Palmer, Lane, 40
Parbury, John, 94
Parkes, Henry, 152, 153
Parkes (Australia), 111, 153
Parking, 45

Parliaments, 177
Paton, Margaret, 154
Pattison, Mr and Betty, 170
Peace conference, 111, 112
Pearl Hyde Boat, 91
Peeping Tom, 34, 41, 186–9
Perkins, Marjorie, 35
Pinton Freres, 66
Piper, John, 68, 69
Pool Meadow, 50, 162, 163
Poole, J. W. Canon, 74
Population, 18, 88, 89
Prague, 109
Precinct, shopping, 39–46
Preece, Ivor, 97
Priory Row, 77, 78
Priory Street, 51, 58, 67
Processions, 193–5
Puppet Clock, 191, 192

Q
Quadrant, the, 82, 143
Quarter Sessions, 79, 119
Queen's Hotel, 34
Queen's Road Church, 144
Queen Victoria Road, 80, 173
Quinn, Betty, 35

R
Radcliffe, Lord, 59
Radio Coventry, 198
Railway Station, 60–61
Raynor, George, 96
Reith, Lord, 30, 32
Remembrance Day, 161
Repertory Company, 167, 168
Rex Cinema, 26
Reyntien, Patrick, 68
Richards, G. S. N., 118
Richmond, Alan, 149
Riley Co., 135
Ritchie, Walter, 45
Roberts, G. E., 29
Robins, Derrick, 95, 155
Rolls Royce, 134
Rootes Brothers, 29, 59, 130, 131
Rootes Group, 131
Ross, Canon, 71, 73
Rotherhams, 136
Rover Co., 43, 125, 129, 130
Royal Show, 23
Royal Engineers, 70
Royalty, Visits, 29, 36, 43, 46, 62, 72, 79, 113, 179

Rudge Whitworth, 126

S
Sarajevo, 110
Saunders, Rev. Lawrence, 83
School of Music, 94, 107, 149
Schools, 34, 54–7
Scott, Sir Giles G., 64
Sculpture, 45
Sent to Coventry, 23, 90, 178
Sephton, Alfred, VC, 152
Shanks, Erle, 96
Sharp, Thomas, 156
Shelton, J. B., 17, 156
Shelton Square, 43, 44, 93, 156
Sherbourne, river, 27, 50, 86
Sheridan, Eileen, 103
Sheridan, G. W., 116
Siddeley Deasy, 133
Silkin, Lord, 40
Singer Co., 125, 131
Singer, George, 96, 131
Smithford Street, 19, 41, 173
Smithford Way, 42
Smoke control, 45
Spence, Sir Basil, 51, 62, 65–7, 70, 71, 75, 155
Spencer, Wilfred, 106
Spon End, 20, 86
Spon Street, 41, 53, 77, 80, 81
Squires, Charlie, 102
St. Etienne, 108, 109
St. Mary's Hall, 34, 77, 78, 80, 114, 115
Stack, Michael, 102
Stalingrad, 104–7, 112
Standard Motors, 26, 88, 131, 148
Starley family, 123, 124
Starley memorial, 83, 124
Statham, Jack, 45
Stevengraphs, 48, 136, 137
Stivichall Hamlet, 83
Stoke Green and park, 77, 83
Stoke Heath, 32
Stoke Philanthropic, 90
Stone House, 84
Stoneleigh Abbey, 22, 23, 83, 160
Storer, Harry, 96
Strickland, Capt. W. F., 120
Stringer, Sidney, 115, 154
Sunbeam Talbot, 131
Sutherland, Graham, 48, 67, 146
Swanswell Gate, 80
Swimming Baths, 21, 49, 50, 58, 170
Sykes, Stephen, 70

T
Talbot, 131
Tandey, Henry, VC, 151, 152
Taylor, W. G., RNVR, 35
Technical College, 47, 56, 57, 113
Terry, Ellen, 141, 142, 156
Textile firms, 127
Three Spires Radio, 198
Tiffany's, 43
Tile Hill, 53
Tile Hill College, 57, 58
Tile Hill Nature Reserve, 22
Townend Brothers, 126
Traherne, Margaret, 69
Tramway service, 34, 157, 158
Trinity Guild RFC, 99
Trinity Street, 170
Triple Triangle Club, 90
Triumph Works, 36, 58, 126, 128, 131, 132
Trotter, Reg, 84
Turner, Rowley, 123
Turpins (boxers), 102

U
University of Warwick, 57, 58, 59

V
Victoria Buildings, 44
Visser, Dr. W. A., 69
Volgograd, 104–6

W
Walker, F. V., 35
War Memorial Park, 22, 73, 151
Ward, Joan, 83
Warren, Harry, 96
Warsaw, 107, 111, 112
Warwick Castle, 23
Warwick Road, 22, 43, 83
Warwick Row, 82
Warwickshire Cty Ccl, 58

Warwicks CCC, 95
Watchmaking trade, 127
WAVA Hall, 90
Wearmouth, John, 40
Well St Cong'l Church, 34
Wellington Gardens, 33
Westerby, Joan, 35
West Orchard, 19, 172
West Orchard Congregational Church, 34, 85, 172
Weston, Harry, 92, 110, 139
Wheatley Brothers, 97
Wheatley, Thomas, 82
White & Poppe, 132
White, Sir Thomas, 83, 155
White Charity, Sir Thomas, 155
Whitefriars Monastery, 78, 85
Whitelaw, Billie, 151
Whitley bomber, 25, 134
Whitley Common, 36
Whittle, Frank, 148, 154
Wickman, Axel Charles, 138
Wickman Ltd., 139
Williams, Gwilym, 106
Williams, Dr. H. C. N., 73
Williams, Johnny, 102
Williams, Dr. Parry, 155
Wilkinson, Sir George, 33
Willenhall Wood, 53
Willoughby de Broke, Lord, 72
Wilson, William, 120, 121
Wimpey, George, 53
Wimpy Bar, 77
Windsor, 111
Woodhead, Bill, 91
Working men's clubs, 89
WVS (WRVS), 28, 35, 72, 90, 92
Wyatt, R. E. S., 99
Wyley, William, Sir, 80, 85, 154

Y
Yoxall, W. H., 35
Yugoslavia, 47